The Great Life

Essays on Doctrine and Holiness

Edited by
Michael J. Aquilina and Kenneth M. Ogorek

With a Foreword by Donald W. Wuerl,
Bishop of Pittsburgh

EMMAUS
ROAD
PUBLISHING

A division of Catholics United for the Faith
Steubenville, Ohio

Emmaus Road Publishing
827 North Fourth Street
Steubenville, Ohio 43952

Library of Congress Control Number: 2005938651
ISBN: 2005935490

Cover design by
Michael Andaloro

Editorial assistance by
Christopher Bailey and C. T. Maier

THE GREAT LIFE
Essays on Doctrine and Holiness

Table of Contents

Foreword

BISHOP DONALD W. WUERL

It is a privilege to offer these words of introduction to the Festschrift honoring Father Ronald Lawler, O.F.M. Cap. This is particularly so because I had the great joy not only of working with Father Ronald on many projects over nearly forty years but also of having him as a spiritual director and guide for a substantial part of that time.

Two of the most endearing qualities of Father Ronald were the sharpness of his mind and the gentleness of his heart. He combined the best of intellect and will and did so clothed in all the humility and detachment of a son of Saint Francis. Everyone who knew Father Ronald knew that he was a gentle and skilled teacher. He understood his priesthood as an extension of Christ's voice proclaiming the Lord's way through life.

The Church in her liturgy and pastoral office speaks of the threefold task of the priest: to teach, to lead, and to sanctify. While he understood and embraced all of the aspects of priesthood, Father Ronald shone his brightest as he exercised the *munus docendi* (office of teaching). In recognition of that quality of his life and ministry I want to reflect on the role of the priest as teacher of the Faith.

At different times, one aspect of this threefold ministry has received more emphasis than the others. Not long ago priesthood was depicted almost entirely in terms of sacramental ministry and, specifically, the celebration of the Eucharist. The priest as steward of the sacred mysteries (cf. 1 Cor. 4:1) was recognizable at the altar,

---

Most Reverend Donald W. Wuerl, S.T.D., is bishop of Pittsburgh, PA.

in anointing the sick, in the confessional, or in preparing people for the sacraments, especially Matrimony.

In the early years of the Church in our own country, the leadership role of the priest was particularly important. He was the recognized leader and spokesman for the faithful—many of whom had only recently come to this land. While clearly the "steward of the mysteries" of Christ, the priest was also the leader of God's people as their builder, guide, organizer, and counselor.

The leadership and sanctifying roles of the priest certainly continue, even though they may find expression in an expanded context. Nonetheless, today, there is a need to focus on the priest's prophetic ministry—the task of proclaiming the call to faith in God, to life in His name, and to the kingdom to come.

The need for catechetical renewal in our country highlights the imperative of a more explicit teaching of the Faith. We refer to the "lost generation," "religious illiteracy," and "catechetical deficiencies" as a way of expressing the diminished level of intellectual awareness of and personal loyalty to the revealed teaching of Christ and its application that we refer to as the "received Tradition."

The faithful who sit in the pews around us at Sunday Mass have not all had the advantage of continuous religious instruction as they grew and developed intellectually and spiritually. Today, the majority of the generation passing on the Faith to their own children did not themselves learn of it from the consecrated women and men who were once so prominent in Catholic schools. They may have had only sporadic, superficial instruction in the Faith leaving them with little foundation for addressing the issues of life, including life's purpose for themselves and their children.

At the same time, we see a disintegration of those community and social structures that once supported religious faith and encouraged family life. The heavy emphasis on the individual and his or her rights has greatly eroded the concept of the common good and its ability to call people to something beyond them. When the individual is the starting point, there is a diminished awareness of the intrinsic value of others and even a temptation to see others as objects or means to an end. In this setting, their value is determined only by what they can "do for me."

We experience this in our society and in the law, for example, when one person's right to life falls victim to another person's right to privacy. This conflict impacts strongly on the capacity of some to accept a teaching that is revealed by God and not decided by democratic vote, or to follow an absolute moral imperative despite its inconvenience or unpopularity.

When we hear the claim that a number of Catholics do not accept the Church's teaching, whether on abortion, euthanasia, capital punishment, marriage, sexuality, racism, societal care for the poor, or some other moral issue, we need continually to remind ourselves that there is a clearly articulated body of Catholic teaching. At the same time, we need to recall that the Faith is not forced on anyone. It must be freely embraced and generously lived. This can only happen if there is someone to proclaim fully, clearly, and convincingly God's word and the teaching of Christ. A part of bringing Jesus into our lives includes acceptance of the teaching of Christ's Church as the voice of Christ Himself. "He who hears you," Jesus said to His apostles, "hears me" (Lk. 10:16).

In his preaching and teaching, the priest needs to be the countercultural voice, as Father Ronald was, that offers sound and sure answers to life's questions. These responses derive from the Church's Tradition—the millennia of reflection on the human condition under the guidance of the Holy Spirit. While these responses may not always be popular, they are true. They lead us to God. Like John the Baptist who pointed and proclaimed "Behold the Lamb of God" (Jn. 1:29), so the priest needs to point to Christ, His way, His teaching, His Gospel in a world that all-too-readily does not see Him in the midst of all the other alternatives.

Today we often encounter young parents who, when called to be the first teachers of their children in the ways of the Faith, experience their own first serious personal catechesis as they share in the catechetical programs for their children. While this is far from the ideal, let us not lament but accept this as a second chance for both them and us.

The "new evangelization" unfolds on two levels simultaneously: the introduction of the Faith to very young children and the instruction of their parents. For both catechists and those already catechized, this can be a particularly enriching moment as these young adults approach the Faith with a great deal more openness and out of their own felt need to know more.

The priest is prophet and pastor. He stands in the midst of the faith community as the good shepherd whose voice is recognized as that of Christ. For this reason, his proclamation of the truth from the pulpit is balanced by his compassionate care of the flock when they come for counseling and sacramental confession. These two dimensions of priestly service are components of effective ministry.

The priest, as shepherd and prophet, can neither guide in the ways of the truth nor heal what has been broken by isolating or separating these two aspects of the same rich, Christ-like ministry. From the pulpit the priest must proclaim the truth—the complete and unvarnished truth—that is the way to salvation. As confessor, counselor, and spiritual guide, the priest as shepherd must meet the members of his flock where they are to support and walk with them on their pilgrimage to the Father.

In his post-synodal apostolic exhortation *The Church in America*, Pope John Paul II reminded us that our encounter with Christ begins with conversion. The priest stands in the midst of the faith community as one who introduces the believer to Christ, helps the believer to deepen a relationship with the Lord, and continually proclaims the way that we who walk with Jesus are to follow. It is not an exaggeration when the Church says that as the priest proclaims the teaching of the Church, he speaks with the voice of Christ. This is what priestly, prophetic ministry is about today.

I had the great satisfaction of working with Father Ronald on a range of catechetical and theological activities, most especially the production of *The Teaching of Christ: A Catholic Catechism for Adults*, *The Catholic Catechism*, and *The Gift of Faith*.

The fifth edition of *The Teaching of Christ* is dedicated to the memory of Father Ronald. It recalls his role as teacher and catechist. Over thirty years ago at a dinner hosted by Cardinal John Wright, then prefect of the Congregation for the Clergy, the Vatican office responsible also for catechesis, Father Ronald, the recently deceased Frank Schneider, and I began the conversation that led eventually, together with Father Ronald's brother, Thomas Comerford Lawler, to the publication of *The Teaching of Christ.*

It is not an exaggeration to say that Father Ronald's dedication to this project kept all of us engaged in this work. He always demonstrated a penetrating grasp of the Church's faith as it has been expounded in her great Tradition. It was that teaching he was so insistent be carefully preserved, invitingly presented, and faithfully transmitted.

In reflecting on Father Lawler I linger on the memories associated with the production of *The Teaching of Christ* because they speak, at least to me, of some of his wonderful and enduring qualities. The 1970s, which is the period of time in which this catechism was written and published (January 1976), were turbulent times for the Church. There was a sense of disconnectedness, from the tradition and heritage of the Church, that pervaded so much of the world of catechesis and catechetics. When the decision was made to produce *The Teaching of Christ* invitations went out to a number of lay women and men, religious, and clergy to collaborate and to produce a text that would be faithful to the teaching of the Church and at the same time written in an inviting manner.

For consistency, the decision was made that Father Ronald, his brother Tom, and I would do the final editing and rewrite any portions that needed to be redone. Many a warm August day we spent in a basement room graciously provided by the friars at Capuchin College in Washington, D. C. working on what finally emerged as the text that Cardinal Wright in his prefatory note to the first edition described as "indispensable." Here he opines in his comments that "a better text book for schools could scarcely be imagined at the moment and its universality, orthodoxy, clarity and style should make it ideal for study groups in catechetics or religious education generally."

In May 1976 Father Ronald, Tom, and I had the exceptional honor, thanks to the intervention of Cardinal Wright, of presenting a specially bound edition of *The Teaching of Christ* to Pope Paul VI. His words will echo in my heart as they certainly did in Father Ronald's as he pointed out to us that what we were doing was meeting the most significant need of the Church at that moment.

In latter years, Father Ronald and I would often joke that, when we go before the judgment seat of God, we would both like to have in our hands a copy of *The Teaching of Christ* as evidence that we gave it our best shot. He has reached that moment before me, but I still cherish the hope.

The 1970s, as I have mentioned, were a time of turmoil not just for catechetics but also in the whole world of Catholic academia. Father Ronald and Monsignor George A. Kelly, director of the Institute for Advanced Studies in Catholic Doctrine at Saint John's University, New York, were among the most determined to respond in some systematic way to the unraveling of Catholic teaching in Catholic institutions of higher education. They, together with many others, were appalled at the ease with which Catholic journals, theological and otherwise, had not only devoted enormous amounts of space to theologically diminished articles but also refused to balance their new agenda with scholarship rooted in the great Tradition. We had gone, as one Catholic intellectual noted, from "mandarin" theology or a form of gnosis to collage thinking in less time than it took for a subscription to some theological journals to expire.

The same situation existed in Catholic universities and colleges across the country. Under the banner of "academic freedom," personal opinion began to supplant authentic Catholic teaching.

One of the major cornerstones of the Catholic "identity" is the communal character of faith. The Church is not simply a collection of individuals who think and act the same way. The Church, as the Body of Christ, precedes the present gathering of individuals. The Church's Magisterium is a central part of the communal character of the Faith and something that is of the very constitution of the Church to provide it direction, stability, self-awareness, and unity.

Christ's promise to remain with his Church until the end of time takes on a special significance when we address the matter of the continual, authentic teaching of the truth of revelation. All in the Church are called to spread the Word and receive gifts appropriate to their calling and baptismal character. It is necessary for the community, as it grows and its members exercise their own gifts, to maintain unity and the tie with the Church of the Apostles. As the gifts are given to build up the one Church and as they derive from the one same Spirit, so they interrelate and must be coordinated. Individual gifts also need to be verified. The final judgment on the authenticity of any particular gift—or any particular teaching—rests with the bishops, who are charged to foster the unity of the Church. There can be no unity with multiple, contradictory teachings.

Today academic freedom has also come to include not only freedom of investigation and of expression, but also freedom to teach and to advocate a way of action. As presented by some, the concept of academic freedom carries with it the idea of unlimited, unfettered freedom to express any thought, with its inherent consequences, and the concomitant right to propose theories as the basis for personal action.

It is this last point—the proposal of various teachings as the basis for alternate pastoral practice and an alternate Christian moral code—that raises particular difficulties for the Church and especially for Catholic universities.

It was against this background that Father Ronald, together with a number of others, envisioned what became the Fellowship of Catholic Scholars. I recall with warm memories the long discussions with Father Ronald, Monsignor Kelly, and His Eminence William Cardinal Baum, then Archbishop of Washington, D.C., on the nature of this initiative and how it could best serve the Church.

Just recently I had the joy of celebrating Mass and offering some remarks to the twenty-seventh annual convention of the Fellowship of Catholic Scholars at a September 2004 meeting in Pittsburgh. It seemed both a fitting time and place to salute Father Ronald for his steadfastness in upholding the Catholic faith and Tradition and his foresight in bringing together likeminded Catholic scholars in a fellowship that has become an institutional support for the hierarchy today.

As Father Ronald was a scholar, he was also a pastor of souls. In matters of the heart, when he turned his attention to pastoral ministry, Father Ronald was a caring, compassionate, and loving priest. As a pastor of souls he approached issues with such serene gentleness that what came across was the intensity of his faith that he lived in a manner that invited others to follow in his footsteps.

For a good number of years Father Ronald served in the secretariat for education for the Diocese of Pittsburgh in a variety of capacities but particularly in the area of adult faith formation. Recently I spoke with some of the people involved in the marriage preparation programs of the diocese, and they all recalled with great regard and affection the thoroughness of Father Ronald's presentations and the encouraging manner that he gave them. *The Catholic Vision of Love*, a program of the Diocese of Pittsburgh, as well as the adult faith formation process and materials, all bear the handprint of Father Ronald, always faithful, ever wise, and singularly caring.

As the length of his days grew shorter, and he was very much aware that the end was near, the calm with which he faced death and his witness to faith in a life to come was his last gift to all of us who knew him, turned to him for spiritual counsel and advice, and loved him in the Lord.

When I asked if I could come to Saint Augustine Friary to administer the Sacrament of the Anointing of the Sick for him, he responded that he would like to receive the Sacrament in the Chapel with as many of his beloved friars as would wish to be present. It was a beautiful testimony to the meaning of the Sacrament, the power of faith, and the fullest grasp of Saint Francis' prayer, "Lord, make me an instrument of your peace."

Father Ronald Lawler was every inch a priest after the heart of Christ and he was every ounce a friar in the image of Saint Francis. Thinking of him necessarily brings to mind the images of the great Good Shepherd and the Poverello.

Preface:
Father Ronald Lawler, O.F.M. Cap.
1926-2003

MICHAEL AQUILINA

Through more than six decades of catechetical work, he held just about every teaching position a Catholic can hold, from pastor to seminary president, from Oxford don to CCD instructor, from chancery administrator to author of a best-selling catechism. What was said of his Master could easily be applied to Father Ronald Lawler's life of teaching: *bene omnia fecit.* "He has done all things well" (Mk. 7:37).

The secret to his success was surely as much his good cheer as his brilliant mind. He wore hope and joy as if they were part of his rumpled Capuchin habit. As he turned seventy-seven, his hair was still boyish-blonde and his smile still mischievous. And to the end he was still teaching.

Providence groomed Father Lawler well for his catechetical work. Born on July 29, 1926, he was baptized David Arthur Lawler at Saints Peter and Paul Church in Cumberland, Maryland. Capuchin Franciscans ran the parish and they helped young David discern his vocation early and rather precisely. He was just 13 when he asked to enter the Capuchins' minor seminary. His mother was delighted to learn of her son's openness to the priesthood but she urged him to consider the Society of Jesus instead. He dutifully packed his bags and made his visit to the Jesuits. On returning home, he told his mother how impressed he was but that he felt certain God wanted him to be a Capuchin.

Michael Aquilina is vice president of the Saint Paul Center for Biblical Theology.

His notebooks from minor seminary—Saint Fidelis in Herman, Pennsylvania—show him to be a precocious student of literature (especially poetry), Latin, the sciences, and religion. At his junior-college commencement, he delivered, in Latin, the address, "Newman as Writer." A few weeks later he was invested with the Capuchin habit and took the name Ronald. Brother Ronald made his temporary profession on July 14, 1946, with perpetual vows three years later. He proceeded to theological studies at Saint Fidelis College in Victoria, Kansas, and later Capuchin College in Washington, D.C. It was at Saint Fidelis in Victoria that his philosophy professor, Father Edwin Dorzweiler, described him as "a giant among pygmies."

Ronald was ordained to the priesthood August 28, 1951, and began his teaching career at his *almae matres*, the Capuchin seminaries (both named Saint Fidelis) in Victoria and Herman.

In the mid-1950s he pursued graduate studies in philosophy at Harvard and at Saint Louis University. Already he was beginning to distinguish himself as a thinker. He was a Franciscan and a scholastic; yet he was a disciple not of Saint Bonaventure or Blessed Duns Scotus, but of the Dominican Saint Thomas Aquinas, and Father Ronald was eager to apply the Angelic Doctor's wisdom to the problems of the day. He had been drawn in this direction by no less a man than Jacques Maritain, the leading light of Scholasticism of the mid-twentieth-century, who urged him to remain always fully Franciscan and fully Thomistic.

He received a master's degree from Saint Louis in 1957, and completed his doctoral work under the direction of Vernon Bourke in 1959. In his dissertation he examined *The Moral Judgment in Contemporary Analytic Philosophy.*

Again, he returned to Saint Fidelis in Herman, where he was dean of studies 1960-64, and then president of the college 1964-69. Among his young students were the future archbishops Seán O'Malley of Boston and Charles Chaput of Denver. He loved teaching them. He loved teaching anyone. "Teaching," he once told a reporter, "is a wonderful, wonderful life."

He conveyed the deepest mysteries of faith with great clarity and warmth—though he conducted his classes in fluent Latin, as was then the custom in seminaries. Archbishop Chaput testifies that "Father Ronald, almost single-handedly, imparted an immense amount of foundational knowledge to all of his students." Archbishop O'Malley agrees: "The good influence that Father Ronald had on so many Capuchins and diocesan priests cannot be exaggerated."

Through those years—and throughout the rest of his life—he wrote prodigiously and prolifically. His personal files show a steady stream of academic papers and spiritual conferences. As the sixties drew to a close, Bruce Publishing brought out his first book, *Philosophical Analysis and Ethics.*

The bishop of Pittsburgh, John J. Wright, admired Father Ronald's work and named him to the diocesan theological commission in 1967. Bishop Wright encouraged the friar to be ambitious for Saint Fidelis seminary, even to invite White House cabinet members to serve on its board.

Nineteen sixty-eight marked a turning point—a moment of decision—for many Catholics, but especially for those in academic philosophy, theology, and administration. Father Ronald Lawler served in all of those fields.

On and around American college campuses, the youth counter-culture was celebrating the new "sexual liberation," as it was called. And, smack in the middle of that summer—on Father Ronald Lawler's forty-second birthday—Pope Paul VI promulgated his encyclical letter *Humanae Vitae* (On Human Life).

Pope Paul VI had a different idea of what constituted sexual liberation. The encyclical reaffirmed the Church's traditional teaching on married love, fidelity, and openness to life. But American Catholicism had its own emerging counterculture, and many theologians reacted with disbelief and public dissent.

Father Ronald, for his part, found the encyclical profoundly moving and beautiful. Within days, he and all the priests of his deanery signed a public statement of support for *Humanae Vitae.* Bishop Wright, who was away at Notre Dame, sent a telegram and then a handwritten letter of thanks to Father Ronald, for a gesture that might "offset some of the inevitable scandal which will be given by the less thoughtful and less loyal declarations of others."

The scandal surely came and, with it, further dissent. Religious orders awoke to find themselves divided into seemingly irreconcilable camps. The Capuchins did. And, in the ensuing melee, Father Ronald was, as he put it many years later, "unceremoniously fired."

It would be an upward fall. But that would become apparent only after many years. At the time, Father Ronald bore it as the cross.

From Saint Fidelis, the friar jumped out of the frying pan and into the fire at the Catholic University of America, then the site of the most public acts of dissent from the papal Magisterium. But, in the philosophy department, Father Ronald was kept far from the flames.

Teaching was his great consolation, and he delighted especially in teaching the truth of Catholic sexual ethics—the philosophical underpinnings of *Humanae Vitae*. One student fondly remembers his first class with Father Ronald: "He told us that if we were interested in sharpening our minds that we should take calculus, because philosophy was more than mental exercise. . . . The goal of philosophy was truth."

His intensive study of the British analytical philosophers had taught him to respect great thinkers with whom he disagreed. And he passed this art of sympathetic reading on to his students: "He introduced David Hume as a brilliant mind, who just happened to get everything wrong," one student recalled.

Father Ronald taught at Catholic University 1970-71 and 1974-75, and returned there intermittently through 1982. In the early seventies he taught occasional courses also at Oxford University (Greyfriars), and he eventually went on to teach at the Pontifical College Josephinum, the University of Saint Thomas (Houston), Saint John's University (New York), Holy Apostles Seminary (Connecticut), and Franciscan University (Ohio).

Meanwhile, Father Ronald's great patron John Wright received the call to Rome, to serve as prefect of the Sacred Congregation for the Clergy—at the time, one of the most powerful positions in the curia. Among Cardinal Wright's duties was the oversight of catechesis, which had been in disarray since the mid-1960s. Catechists assumed that Trent was now outdated, but that left a vacuum. The infamous *Dutch Catechism* seemed to apply an episcopal seal to the vacuum, though, and later catechisms made matters worse.

In 1973, Cardinal Wright invited a number of friends, including Father Ronald, to dinner in Rome. They gathered at La Carbonara restaurant in the Campo di Fiori, and there, over pasta, they brooded over the situation of catechetics. Suddenly, the cardinal announced emphatically that the Church *needed* a catechism.

Father Ronald and Father Donald Wuerl, who was then the cardinal's secretary, could read between the lines. "And when Cardinal Wright asked for something," Father Ronald later recalled, "the only proper answer was yes."

In the discussion that followed, Fathers Lawler and Wuerl emerged as leaders of the project: a book that would eventually emerge as *The Teaching of Christ: A Catholic Catechism for Adults.* Another man was nominated, *in absentia*, as an editor: Father Ronald's brother, Thomas Comerford Lawler, who was an executive in the U.S. Central Intelligence Agency. Thomas Lawler was also a noted patristics scholar, a protege of Johannes Quasten, a translator of Saint Augustine, and a longtime editor of the prestigious Ancient Christian Writers series.

The Lawlers and Father Wuerl outlined the catechism, set standards, and drew up a list of great Catholic minds who might contribute chapters. Invitations went out to British legal philosopher John Finnis, Dominican spiritual theologian Jordan Aumann, Father Lorenzo Albacete, Germain Grisez, Archbishop John Whealon of Hartford, Father John Hugo, Father Frederick Jelly, O.P., and others.

Great minds, however, do not always think alike. Even less do they write in similar styles. It was up to the editors to impose a unifying voice and format upon the work. One of the first things they did was to strike out anything that was speculative or merely "interesting." They intended to present only the teaching of the Church.

They also placed a premium on clarity and simplicity. Father Ronald later recalled: "Archbishop Whealon used to say, over and over again, 'Mrs. Magillicuddy would not understand that.' And, if Mrs. Magillicuddy wouldn't understand, we had to change it."

Though *The Teaching of Christ* was written in turbulent times, its voice is steady, serene, and authoritative. The lasting impression is of doctrine as solid, reliable, and unchanging as the granite face of a mountain. Father Ronald told a newspaper reporter: "When we wrote the catechism, it was Cardinal Wright's mind that we should not be fighting anybody and that we should not do things in an idiosyncratic way."

Our Sunday Visitor published the first edition of *The Teaching of Christ*. At the time of his death, Father Ronald and his colleagues were preparing a fifth edition, updated to reflect the Church's most recent magisterial documents.

Down through the years, the catechism also appeared in an abridged version, two question-and-answer versions, and at least thirteen foreign-language translations. The book has provided the foundation for a long-running television series (also called "The Teaching of Christ"), hosted by now-Bishop Donald Wuerl, and several series of catechetical audio and video tapes.

Since the editors waived all rights and royalties on the foreign editions, there is no way of knowing how many copies—how many millions of copies—have been distributed throughout the world. Only God knows the good that *The Teaching of Christ* has accomplished. For the editors, it was enough that Pope Paul VI summoned them to Rome to receive his personal thanks.

The 1980s and 1990s were, for Father Ronald, decades of great accomplishments. In 1980, in a letter from Cardinal Agostino Casaroli, Vatican Secretary of State, Pope John Paul II commended him: "His Holiness is deeply grateful for your loyal support of the Magisterium and your sustained efforts on behalf of the word of God." In 1982 Pope John Paul appointed Father Ronald to the elite Pontifical Roman Theological Academy. For many years, he was the only academy member from the United States. He was inducted the same day as two giants of modern theology, Henri de Lubac and Hans Urs von Balthasar.

He held a number of important administrative positions. From 1974 to 1977, he taught and served as dean of theology at the

Pontifical College Josephinum, near Columbus, Ohio. At Saint John's in Queens, New York, he was director of the Institute for Advanced Studies in Catholic Doctrine, 1982-88. From there, he moved to Cromwell, Connecticut, to take the presidency of Holy Apostles Seminary, a magnet seminary known for its orthodoxy. During a brief leave from Holy Apostles, he worked as director of education at the Pope John Center for Biological Research (now the National Catholic Bioethics Center) in Braintree, Massachusetts. And in 1996 he returned to Pittsburgh as director of the diocesan office for adult and family catechesis, a position he held until his death. Under his aegis were all the programs for training in natural family planning.

He was, as well, co-founder and first president of the Fellowship of Catholic Scholars, an academic organization that continues to thrive after more than a quarter-century.

Yet he was never able to rest content with a full-time job or two. He wrote, it seems, without ceasing, producing hundreds of articles and homilies, and a number of important books. In addition to the volumes already mentioned, he was editor and co-author of *Philosophy in Priestly Formation* (Catholic University of America, 1978) and co-editor of *Excellence in Seminary Education* (Gannon University Press, 1988). He was author of *The Christian Personalism of John Paul II* (Franciscan Herald Press, 1981), one of the first popular studies of the thought of Karol Wojtyla. He was co-author of *Perspectives in Bioethics* (Pope John Center, 1983). With William May and Joseph Boyle, he wrote *Catholic Sexual Ethics*, the definitive introductory text in its field.

It was *The Christian Personalism of John Paul II* that first caught the attention of the Poor Clares. Having read the book, the nuns petitioned the Holy See to appoint Father Ronald "spiritual assistant," a position he would always describe as "very important in my life." He regularly visited thirteen Poor Clare monasteries in the United States and Holland, giving spiritual conferences and theology classes to the nuns, whom he described as living "a heroic life, a very, very generous, holy life." The sisters buoyed him with their prayers, especially as his health began to fail, and they seemed always to work practical miracles in the lives of his friends, for whom Father Ronald always asked the Poor Clares' intercession.

He loved the lay apostolate as much as he loved his Poor Clares. He believed, with all his might, in the universal call to holiness. Catholic journalist Bob Lockwood has observed: "The word 'great' was always on his lips. He reminded people that they could be great. . . . By great, of course, he meant holy. Will Rogers might have never met a man he didn't like; Father Lawler never met a person who couldn't be holy."

He delighted in the company of many families, whose kids he named his "honorary grandchildren." He accompanied busloads of families on the March for Life each year. His friends recall that he could move from a conversation with a three-year-old to a graduate seminar in theology in a matter of an hour. In both, his message would be the same, and the language not all that different. As he approached the golden jubilee of his ordination, he wrote: "The cause dearest to my heart is helping people maintain or recover the light of faith and the joy of being richly Catholic."

With small words and great notions, Father Ronald was a winsome catechist and apologist and, as he grew older, he refined his techniques. He often said that, when discussing philosophical matters, he preferred to use "words of no more than three syllables." This method served him well. Somehow, in the 1980s, he found himself face to face with a hostile Phil Donahue on what was then America's most popular television talk show. It was the usual network-TV anti-Catholic setup job. Phil was unrelenting in his attack on the Church's supposed insensitivity, especially in matters sexual. An uncommon guest, however, Father Ronald refused to be ruffled and responded with common sense. During a commercial break, the host's handlers said that viewers were calling in, and they overwhelmingly favored "the priest." Phil backed off for the time remaining, but he never invited "the priest" back again.

In his last years, from Pittsburgh, Father Ronald taught occasional courses at the nearby Franciscan University of Steubenville, and he organized a prestigious lecture series for the diocese. In its first years the series spotlighted Robert George, Maggie Gallagher, Robert Royal, Laura Garcia, Father Benedict Groeschel, Janet Smith, Scott Hahn, John Haas, and Gerard Bradley.

Early in 2002, Father Ronald was diagnosed with inoperable lung cancer. The biopsies alone were a painful procedure, involving the cracking of several ribs. Yet, within weeks of the surgery, Father Ronald was traveling to Rome with two large families, to visit the pope and attend a meeting of the Pontifical Roman Theological Academy.

The doctors did not expect Father Ronald to live long enough to attend the Fellowship of Catholic Scholars' convention in autumn of 2003. But Father Ronald asked the Poor Clares to pray for the intention, and he confidently planned to make the trip with friends and his brother Tom. In the weeks before the convention, he grew more ill, but pressed on with his plans.

And he made it. Remarkably, through the days of the convention, he experienced a remission from many of the symptoms of his disease and the side-effects of his medication. His appetite returned, and he ate three hearty meals a day. He slept seven hours a night and two in the afternoon—whereas, until then, he had been averaging around forty minutes per night.

Members of the fellowship knew that Father Ronald was dying. But his smiles made them bold. Many approached him and frankly asked his prayers when he got to "the other side."

Back in Pittsburgh after the convention, he fell several times in his room, and later he fell in the hospital. With each fall, he grew weaker.

But, to the end, he remained alert—and always a priest. It was a new doctor, a young man from Latin America, who had to tell Father Ronald that death was likely just days away. The doctor and the friar spoke to one another of Jesus Christ; both smiled broadly, and both men wept.

In his life, Father Ronald Lawler had mastered the abstract ethics of the British analytical philosophers, and had taught graduate courses in mystical theology. But, in his last weeks, he examined his conscience daily with a maxim his mother had taught him in kindergarten:

Kindness is to do and say
the kindest thing in the kindest way.

So he did, and so he said. His honorary grandchildren judged him well by this standard. Father Ronald died a peaceful and holy death November 5, 2003. At his funeral Mass, two little ones could be heard disputing over whether Father Ronald would be the patron saint of licorice or of chocolate.

His confessor pointed out that there's no reason one man couldn't do both.

Bibliography

"Father Ronald Lawler Tribute Page," www.mikeaquilina.com/lawler.

"Ronald David Lawler, O.F.M Cap.," Rev. Brendan Malloy, O.F.M. Cap., in the Necrology of the Saint Augustine Province of the Capuchins.

"Catechism Co-authored by Wuerl Remains Popular after 25 Years," Ann Rodgers-Melnick, *Pittsburgh Post-Gazette*, January 22, 2001.

"A Meat'n Potatoes Catechism," Mike Aquilina, *Our Sunday Visitor*, July 30, 1995.

"Obituary: The Rev. Ronald Lawler: Priest, Author, Spiritual Adviser," Ann Rodgers-Melnick, *Pittsburgh Post-Gazette*, November 8, 2003.

"A Life Dedicated Completely to the Teachings of Christ," Mike Aquilina, *Our Sunday Visitor*, November 30, 2003.

"Living the Great Life," Robert P. Lockwood, *Our Sunday Visitor*, November 30, 2003.

"Turn Down Pride and You'll Find Mercy," Scott Hahn, *Breaking the Bread*, January 2004.

"Capuchin Priest Held in High Esteem by Catholic Scholastic Community," Patricia Bartos, *Pittsburgh Catholic*, October 3, 2003.

The Ronald Lawler Collection, John Paul II Library Archives, Franciscan University of Steubenville, Ohio.

Introduction

KENNETH OGOREK

"Have I told you today that you're a great man?" These words were often on the lips of Father Ronald Lawler, O.F.M. Cap.

Father Lawler understood that to be great is simply to be holy, and to be holy is to be truly healthy: mentally, spiritually, emotionally, and, God-willing, physically. To be healthy includes an appreciation—a healthy appreciation—of the value of doctrine.

In applying himself to the work of teaching Catholic doctrine, Father Lawler encountered dozens of brilliant women and men—scholars and leaders in their respective fields—many of whom got to know him well and, knowing him, loved him.

Many of these great Catholic minds and hearts desired to honor Father Lawler's memory by offering their thoughts on the teaching of the Faith. This book presents these essays, not only to honor Father Lawler, but more importantly to continue his work of presenting the Faith in its fullness and beauty.

In the preface Michael Aquilina began by introducing Father Lawler to readers not familiar with his great life. Three Catholic (arch)diocesan ordinaries—Donald Wuerl, Charles Chaput, and Seán O'Malley—offer glimpses of Father Lawler's influence, while also commenting on the actual process of teaching the Faith. Father Thomas Weinandy then comments specifically on the nature of doctrine.

The sacraments form a focus for the next three essays. Katrina Zeno offers a thought-provoking look at Confirmation, specifically the catechesis leading up to it. Russell Shaw touches on both

Kenneth Ogorek is director for catechesis in the Department for Religious Education, Diocese of Pittsburgh.

Matrimony and Holy Orders in addressing the concept of personal vocation. Scott Hahn reflects on priesthood, in particular on the value of ongoing doctrinal formation for all clergy.

Public life and policies pertaining to matters such as education are the topics of the next three essays. How does and how should the Catholic faith impact our lives together as a society? Janet and Brian Benestad share their thoughts on this question in their essay. Robert George then addresses the area of the Faith as it relates to political candidacy, while Gerard Bradley discusses the practice of home-schooling.

Marriage and family life are areas particularly hard-hit by several recent cultural trends. William May shares his thoughts on catechizing in the area of chastity and sexual morality. Evelyn and John Billings reflect on the complementary relationship between Church teaching on contraception and the well-established science behind Natural Family Planning.

Fathers Augustine DiNoia and Kris Stubna next consider recent developments in the field of catechesis—developments brought about in part as a response to the challenges of our culture, which is both secularized and often hostile to Christianity. Patrick Riley relates some details concerning Father Lawler's best-known book, before William Saunders shares some personal reflections on Father Lawler as a man who immersed himself both in doctrine and in holiness. We hear from Father Lawler in his essay "Has Christ Only One Church?" Then Robert Lockwood brings this celebration of a great priest and the work he held dear to conclusion.

"You're doing great work for the Republic." Father Lawler's euphemism for God's Kingdom was the Republic. Like a republic, the Kingdom of God consists of many women and men making individual contributions to the common good by leading lives of holiness—by living great lives. This book would not have been possible without the financial participation of many who came to call Father Lawler friend. Father Lawler's dearest desire was for all women and men to walk with our Lord as their saving Friend, living the great life of faith as members of His one Body, our Church. May these essays inspire many on their walk of faith, especially those whom God calls to careers in a discipline to which we are all called in Baptism: namely, catechesis.

The Church as Mother and Teacher

ARCHBISHOP CHARLES CHAPUT, O.F.M. CAP.

C.S. Lewis' novel, *The Great Divorce*, is about a bus ride from hell to heaven. People get on the bus in hell, and they get off at the gateway to heaven. And once they arrive, they can freely choose to walk right into paradise, but there's one catch. They have to leave behind the sin that separated them from God in the first place.

I remember one particular soul in the story, because his sin perches on his shoulder like a pet animal, biting him and digging its nails into his skin. But when God's angels ask permission to kill it so the man can enter heaven, he almost can't let it go—because after all, it's familiar, because it's *his*, and because it promises never to misbehave again.

Now, eventually he does give permission, the angels do kill it, and the man is set free to enter heaven. But most of the souls on the bus—either out of pride or fear or cynicism or indifference—get back on the bus. They go back to hell because they don't like heaven. They don't *want* it. And the reason they don't want it is simple. Heaven hurts. It's too real. The blades of grass are so intensely real that the souls from the bus cut their feet.

For Lewis, God is our creator, the source and meaning of everything real. In other words, God is real. Everything divorced from Him isn't. God lives in the sunlight. We live in the shadow lands, and for eyes unaccustomed to the sun, the light can be painful.

Souls who turn away from God turn into the dark. They block God's light with the shadow of their own selfishness. Hell is the state of freely choosing that darkness forever. It's the state of choosing ourselves and our sins instead of choosing God, choosing the unreal

Most Rev. Charles Chaput, O.F.M. Cap., is archbishop of Denver.

instead of the real. And for souls addicted to the unreal, reality
hurts—which is why Lewis tells us that "heaven is an acquired taste."

   One of the features of modern life, unfortunately, is that we try to
change reality to suit our tastes and behaviors, instead of changing
our tastes and behaviors to suit reality. Bishops get a lot of mail, and
most of it's important for one reason or another. But once in awhile a
letter or an email comes in that's very strange and very useful at the
same time. Some months ago I got an email informing me that I'd been
turned into a vampire. Now, I like to keep up on current events—
especially when they involve my own health—so I went to the web
address where this information was posted. It was an Internet site
for people involved in *Vampire: The Masquerade*, which is a role-
playing game like *Dungeons and Dragons*.

   Somebody turned me into one of the vampire characters, and I
think I'm supposed to be offended, but actually I'm very grateful
because they handed me a way to illustrate how we more and more
prefer the unreal to the real.

   Over the last thirty years, role-playing games have turned into a
very big American subculture, and not just for teen-agers but for
adults too. Many parents already know this. The point of a game like
Vampire is that people get together, both in person and over the
Internet, to weave a story that becomes an alternate reality. Each of
the persons weaving the story becomes a character, and he or she
really "inhabits" that character—in every way—inside that alternate
reality. Then the characters bond themselves into vampire clans who
socialize together, make alliances, go to war with one another, and
so on. It's not just a game. It's a self-contained world that the partic-
ipants create and control. And for many of the players, it's a parallel reality—a place to go to get away from the messiness of real life.

   Computer games provide the same kind of escape. In fact, *Vampire*
started as a board game, but now it can also be played as a computer
game on the Internet against real people anywhere in the world. More
than 92 percent of American children between the ages of two and
seventeen play video or computer games. Computer gaming—and
especially Internet multiplayer gaming—is now the fastest-growing
segment of the American entertainment industry. Statistically, the
most active gamers are young adult males and middle-aged women.
The average age of an interactive game player is twenty-eight years old

and climbing. Nearly 64 million Americans played online computer games last year, and 43 percent of those were women.

And here's another curious detail. One of the most popular computer games right now is *The Sims*, which is a "god game," where the player takes on the role of a deity who creates and develops a planet or a society. In *The Sims*, the player creates, manages, nurtures, or destroys a cyber-family. The game sold 1 million copies at $50 apiece in its first ten weeks.

What's the point of this information?

Author Sherry Turkle wrote some years ago that "computer screens are the new location for our fantasies, both erotic and intellectual." She said that "We're using life on computer screens to become comfortable with new ways of thinking about evolution, relationships, sexuality, politics and identity." Neil Postman put it more bluntly when he warned that we're "amusing ourselves to death" with "technological narcotics." But either way, the world we all inhabit is becoming a world *hooked on unreality*, not just in computer games or on TV, but in almost every area of our lives.

Therapists tell us that sin doesn't exist. Scientists tell us that God doesn't exist. Linguists tell us that meaningful questions don't exist, so don't try to ask any. And what we're too often left with is a vacuum of meaning in our lives that we try to fill with the unreality of possessions and distractions.

So the key question in every life becomes: How do we come to desire what's *real*? How do we acquire the taste for heaven? The answer is: We learn it. And if we need to learn, someone has to teach us. Every life is an arc of growing. As we grow we observe more, and we want to understand more. We develop the hunger to learn. How and what we learn determines whom and what we become. That's why parents and pastors, teachers and catechists, are so powerful. They shape our learning, and in doing that, they influence our choices throughout our lives.

Of course, while teachers are very important, not all teachers are equal. Some care about us more than others. Some have more skill than others. And some teachers teach the wrong things. As adults, one of the most important choices we make is which teachers we listen to—and which we teach our *children* to listen to.

When we call ourselves "Catholic," what does that mean? Theologically, it means that we've been saved from sin in Baptism and incorporated into new life in the community of Catholic faith. It means that we accept Jesus Christ as our savior, and we commit ourselves to follow Him as His disciples. But what we *say*, what we *mean*, and then what we *do* aren't always the same things. The space between our intentions and our actions is where daily life is lived. And in that battle zone, day in and day out, we have two very different teachers struggling for the podium in our hearts. The two teachers are the Church and the world. Each has a map for our lives, but the maps lead in very different directions.

For forty years, Catholics have heard a steady chorus of how we need to be open to the world, learn from the world, honor the good things in the world, and be more humble in our approach to the world. All of this is true. God created the world, and He loves it, and He sent His only Son to redeem it.

But at the same time, God wills that the world should be converted and sanctified, *not worshiped.* In his Gospel, Saint John describes the "world" as everything that is aligned against God. Jesus shed His blood on the cross because that was the price of redeeming the world—from its sins and our sins. The cross was real. Christ's suffering was real. And if the world isn't a holier place today than yesterday, it's because we Catholics have chosen the *unreality* of the world and its distractions over the *reality* of the cross.

We've assimilated. We've been too comfortable and accommodating. We've listened to the world too politely when it lies about abortion, or contraception, or divorce, or the death penalty, or our obligations to the poor, or the rights of undocumented workers, or the real meaning of pluralism, or our international responsibilities—and we haven't shouted out the truth.

The world is a powerful and attractive teacher, but while it can often give us what we want, it can't give us what we need. We need God. We're hungry for things that are real because God—the source of everything real—made us to share in His life. And this is exactly the meaning of Matthew 4:1-4. Jesus says, "Man shall not live by bread alone, but by every word that proceeds from the mouth of God." And when Satan literally offers Christ the world and all its power if He'll just make a deal, Jesus answers, "You shall worship the Lord your God, and Him only shall you serve."

Since the Jubilee Year, I've been thinking a lot about how we live our faith as Christians, compared to people in other religions. I've been struck by the posture of Muslims at prayer. The word "Islam" means *submission*, and Muslims embody that word in the way they pray. Islam didn't invent the idea of submission. It was borrowed from Judaism and early Christianity. But Muslims make it the heart of their faith. We can relearn something about our own faith from the posture of Muslims at prayer—some important things about our own proper relationship with God.

How do we serve God? We serve Him by following His will with our whole body, mind, and soul, and the one reliable teacher and guide we have to knowing His will is the Church. And I don't mean the Church as we'd like her to be, but the Church Jesus intended her to be—His bride and our mother. Jesus said, "You are Peter, and on this rock I will build my Church, and the powers of death shall not prevail against it" (Mt. 16:18). He said, "I will give you the keys of the kingdom of heaven, and whatever you bind on earth shall be bound in heaven, and whatever you loose on earth shall be loosed in heaven" (Mt. 16:19).

Jesus sent His disciples out in His name, with His authority, to continue His work in the world as the Church—and only *through* the Church could we be talking about Jesus Christ today. The fidelity of Catholics to the Church, generation after generation, even when her leaders have sometimes been weak or sinful—*that fidelity* is what carries the message of the Gospel through time. Without the Church, Jesus Christ cannot be known. So obedience to the Church and faithfulness to her teaching is not some sort of servitude; it's a choice to participate in the act of giving life to the world. Without the Church, we have only the world, and the world is not enough to feed the hunger in our hearts.

I've always been puzzled by two things in my adult life as a Catholic. I've been puzzled, first, by people who claim that Vatican II somehow changed the identity or the mission of the Church. In fact the council says that the Church is "the universal sacrament of salvation" (*Lumen Gentium* 48). The council says that "Christ is the light

of humanity . . . and that light of Christ [shines] out visibly from the
Church" (LG 1). The council says there can be no distinction drawn
between the institutional Church and the "real" Church—they are
one and the same (LG 8). The council says that "the whole Church is
missionary and the work of evangelization [is] the fundamental task
of the people of God" (*Ad Gentes Divinitus* 35). The council says that
outside Jesus Christ, "there is no other name under heaven given
among men by which they can be saved" (*Gaudium et Spes* 10).

I've been puzzled, second, by people who misunderstand the
ministry of Blessed Pope John XXIII. John had a short pontificate
and died before the council ended, so it's easy for some biographers
to create the impression that, if he had only lived a little longer, he
would have changed so much more about the Church. That's a fan-
tasy. Nothing in his life or his writing supports such an idea, and
frankly that kind of misrepresentation dishonors the memory of a
very saintly man. In fact, John XXIII saw the Catholic Church as
the soul of the world—and he said so in the opening lines of his great
1961 encyclical, *Mater et Magistra:*

> Mother and teacher of all nations—such is the Catholic
> Church in the mind of her founder, Jesus Christ; [her voca-
> tion is] to hold the world in an embrace of love, that men in
> every age should find in her their own completeness in a
> higher order of living, and their ultimate salvation. She is the
> 'pillar and the ground of truth.' To her was entrusted by her
> holy founder the twofold task of giving life to her children
> and of teaching them and guiding them—both as individuals
> and as nations—with maternal care (MM 1).

When we try to soften the content of the council, or rewrite the
meaning of John XXIII's life, or sweeten the mission of the Church
in the world, what we're really doing is building an alibi for our own
lack of courage. For each of us as a believer, there's no way around
Christ's mandate to engage *and convert* the world. Jesus said, "Go
therefore and make disciples of all nations" (Mt. 28:19). And what
that also means is that there's no way around the cross, because the
cross is the salvation of the world, and as disciples, we're meant to
take part in the cross.

The great Jewish Catholic writer Leon Bloy once said, "Man has places in his heart which do not yet exist, and into them enters suffering, in order that they may have existence." Cardinal Augustine Meyer once wrote, "Nothing great is ever achieved without suffering." And Pope John Paul II once said, "The redemption was accomplished through the suffering of Christ [and] every man has his own share in the redemption. Each one [of us] is also called to share in that suffering through which the redemption was accomplished."

Does this mean that Christians should enjoy pain? No, of course not. But suffering pointed to a higher purpose *becomes something greater than itself.* Olympic athletes win their medals by "suffering" the discipline of their sport, which stretches them toward greatness. Some kind of suffering—the loss of a loved one, or an illness, or a broken relationship—forces its way into every life. We can't avoid it, but we *can* choose how we use it. Our suffering will either *shape us,* the way a burden bends the back of a mule, or *we* will *shape it* into a prayer for other people and something beautiful for God.

What are the lessons for each of us? Four things.

First, we need to stop thinking of the Church as some kind of religious corporation, and start treating the Church as our mother and teacher. The Church is not an *it.* The Church is a *she.* We can love our mother; we can't love an institution. And while the Church has institutional forms, she is always much more than the offices that serve her mission. When we talk about the Church as if she were just another impersonal bureaucracy disconnected from the problems of daily life, what we're really doing is creating an excuse to ignore her when she teaches.

Lumen Gentium 68 reminds us that Mary, "the mother of Jesus . . . is the image and beginning of the Church as [she] is to be perfected in the world to come. Likewise [the Church] shines forth on earth until the day of the Lord shall come (cf. 2 Pt. 3:10), a sign of certain hope and comfort to the pilgrim people of God." That's the image we need to nourish in our hearts to keep us focused on the *reality* of the Church that gives life to her institutional forms.

Second, if we say we're Catholic, we need to act like it. Very often we treat the Church the same way we treat our flesh-and-blood mothers. We want the mommy part, but we don't want the teacher part. We want her around to feed us, encourage us, and comfort us when things are going badly. But we don't want her guidance, especially when it interferes with our plans. That's dishonest.

Third, if we teach and preach in the name of the Church, we need to do it fully, zealously, and with all the persuasive skill God gives us. All of us sooner or later get tempted to edit what the Church teaches so we can please our audience. But if we refuse to teach the things we disagree with, or we teach them with a "wink and a nod" to let others know that we don't really believe what the Church says—that's also dishonest. It's a kind of pride that puts our personal judgments above the judgments of the Church and her Spouse, who is Jesus Himself.

Fourth and finally, we need to live in a way that honors each other, and honors the mission of the Church—because in us and through our actions, the outside world will judge the Gospel we claim to believe. Nothing can wound the Church more deeply than the sins and the indifference of her own people, especially people in ministry.

I will close with two images.

The Gospel of John 19:26-27, says that on Golgotha "when Jesus saw His mother, and the disciple whom He loved standing near, He said to his mother, 'Woman, behold, your son!' Then He said to the disciple, 'Behold, your mother!' And from that hour the disciple took her into his own home." Each of us today is that disciple whom Jesus loved and loves. And from the cross He is asking us to take the Church into our hearts as John took Mary into his home, to defend her and care for her and advance her mission in the world.

The second image comes from Robert Frost and the last few lines from one my favorite poems.

Two roads diverged in a wood, and I—
I took the one less traveled by,
And that has made all the difference.

Jesus says, "I am the way, the truth and the life." Following Him may be "the road less traveled," but it's the one road that leads us to reality and joy and the light of God's love.

For me, the guide on that road has always been the Church. The greatest blessing I can offer you today, or any day, is my prayer that she will become the same for you.

Passing On the Faith

ARCHBISHOP SEÁN O'MALLEY, O.F.M. CAP.

Hear O Israel: The Lord our God is one Lord; and you shall love the Lord your God with all your heart, and with all your soul, and with all your might. And these words which I command you today shall be upon your heart; and you shall teach them diligently to your children, and shall talk of them when you sit in your house, and when you walk by the way, and when you lie down, and when you rise. And you shall bind them as a sign upon your hand, and they shall be as frontlets between your eyes. And you shall write them on the doorposts of your house and on your gates (Deut. 6:4-9).

If we really believe, passing on the faith is not an option. It is an imperative. In Deuteronomy 6 we are given the commandment to pass on the faith to new generations. God charged Israel with the great commandment and wants us to keep those words in our hearts. Get them inside of you and then get them inside of your children, God is telling us. Talk about them wherever you are. When you are at home. As you walk down the street. Talk about them from the time you get up in the morning to when you fall into bed at night. Tie them on your hands and foreheads as a reminder. Write them on the doorpost and the bathroom mirrors in your home and on your city gates or the dashboards of your cars. In other words, know and live out the great commandment and pass it on to your children and to your children's children. It kind of kills the theory of a private faith, doesn't it? If we are faithful and our faith in God

Most Rev. Seán O'Malley, O.F.M. Cap. is archbishop of Boston.

means something to us, we will strive to follow His word and live out what it says. Then our faith is anything but private. We pass it on. We talk about it. We tell the story of our faith to our children and to the people God has put in our path.

Passing on faith is not merely a human enterprise. It is God's work. Even when we fall down on the job, God never sleeps.

In *The Power and the Glory* the English author Graham Greene tells the story of a whiskey priest, the only priest who did not flee the persecution of the Church in the Province of Tabasco, Mexico. He is hunted down like a dog and finally caught because they tricked him into coming to attend the needs of a dying man. In prison the army lieutenant taunts him because he had not been a particularly good or virtuous priest, and brags that his government would do much more for the people than the Church could do.

The priest said, "I am certainly not a saint, I am not even brave. That's the difference. It's no good your working for your ends to better society unless you are a good man and have good men in your party. And we know that there won't always be good men in your party. Then you'll have all the old starvation, and exploitation. But it doesn't matter so much that I am a whiskey priest, and a coward and all the rest. I can put God into a man's mouth just the same—and I can give him God's pardon. It wouldn't make any difference to that if every priest in the Church was like me."

The point that the priest is trying to make is that passing on the faith is God's enterprise. Sometimes priests and bishops and religious and parents may seem to fail miserably, but then it does not depend entirely on us. Having said that, I know that we all have to do a better job, but that happens only when we become more pliable clay in the potter's hands.

The great evangelizer is Christ, the Word made Flesh, the missionary of the Father, the anointed of the Spirit who founds the Church, as an extension of Himself. Because the Incarnation has taken place and is a present reality, our Redeemer lives and He continues to call us to discipleship, to friendship, to holiness.

As Pope John Paul II reminded us, two thousand years of history have passed without diminishing the freshness of that which *today* resounds in the Gospels when the angels proclaim, "For *today* is born to you . . ." or when Jesus inaugurates His public life in the synagogue in Nazareth and declares, "*Today* this scripture has been fulfilled in your hearing." Two thousand years have passed, but sinners can still rejoice at the consoling words of Jesus on the cross to the repentant sinner: "*Today* you shall be with me in paradise."

Today this same Jesus gathers us in His Church, instructs us with His Gospel, and nurtures us with His sacraments. Having come to share our life, He invites us to share His mission: "Go therefore and make disciples of all nations, baptizing them in the name of the Father and of the Son and of the Holy Spirit" (Mt. 28:19).

Three years ago I was sent by the Holy See to prepare a report on the two seminaries in Cuba. I was pleased to find sixty seminarians in theology and some twenty in philosophy. I was amazed to hear their stories. Ninety percent of the young men were converts who became Catholics during and after their university studies and after years of indoctrination in Marxism, reinforced by family, by peers, by the mass media, by the educational system. They knew very few Catholics and everything they were told about the Church was bad. Yet somehow the grace of God touched their hearts and led them into the Church and into the seminary at the cost of enormous personal sacrifices. It made me think of Jesus' words that God can change these stones into sons of Abraham.

I have always loved Saint Luke's Gospel and his Acts of the Apostles, which he wrote as a continuation of the Gospel. In Luke's Gospel we see the action of the Spirit: overshadowing Mary at the Annunciation, leading Jesus into the wilderness, anointing Jesus at His Baptism, and accompanying Him in His ministry. In Acts Luke gives the history of the Church, in which he shows how the body of Christ relives the great events in the life of Christ and how the Spirit is guiding and accompanying the Church. I have always been struck by the fact that, although Saint Luke has composed the Gospel and Acts so carefully, he ends the Acts of the Apostles quite abruptly. I think he is telling us that the Acts continue in our lives as members of the Church: the story goes on, the Spirit is still guiding and accompanying us, the Good News is still being proclaimed, we are still united in following the teaching of the Apostles, in fellowship, in the breaking of the bread, and in prayer.

The Church's impulse to evangelize, to pass on the faith, to fulfill the great commission to make disciples of all nations begins at Pentecost. Indeed Pentecost is a sort of paradigm for the Church. It was a moment of crisis, of fear, and of confusion. The Church came together to pray. Our tradition claims they gathered at the place of the first Eucharist, in the company of Mary and of Peter and the Apostles. And they prayed intensely. Their prayer opened their hearts to the Spirit that filled their hearts, enlightened, emboldened, and energized them to go out and share what they had received—and thousands were baptized by the man who people first thought was a drunk.

Today passing on the faith must take place in a Pentecost experience. It begins with intense prayer—together, in the company of Mary and with the ministry of Peter and the Apostolic College. Passing on the faith requires a courageous proclamation of the Good News of Jesus Christ, a call to conversion and an invitation to discipleship and a challenge to be on fire with a mission that we received from the Risen Lord.

The outreach of Pentecost is to all the pilgrims and strangers in Jerusalem. It is not about ethnocentricity or cultural Catholicism or Western civilization. The outreach of Pentecost is Catholic; it is directed to everybody; and although we may speak different languages, the power of love overcomes every barrier and frontier.

Pentecost is about being the body of Christ, God's people, part of a community. It is not enough to be "spiritual," as people say today. Pentecost is not about a religion of the warm fuzzies. It is about answering a call to a way of life and to be part of something bigger than ourselves. At Pentecost the Church began to pass on the faith, to make disciples of all nations.

We need to teach people, especially children and young people, how to pray. If we do not go to our chamber and shut the door and pray to our Father in secret, we shall never form part of a worshipping community.

The Apostles said to Jesus, "Lord, teach us how to pray, as John taught his disciples" (Lk. 11:1). We need to be men and women of prayer, and we need to be teachers of prayer. It is impossible to pass on the faith without forming people in the life of prayer. Faith without prayer is a contradiction. It is information. It is doctrine. It is history. It is not faith. Prayer and worship are the paths of discipleship.

Kierkegaard puts it very well when he says that Christ came to call followers, not to cultivate admirers. Christ came into the world with the purpose of saving, not just instructing it. At the same time—as is implied in His saving work—He came to be the pattern, to leave footprints for the person who would join Him, who would become a follower. A follower strives to be what he or she admires. The simple admirer keeps himself detached; he fails to see that what is admired has a claim on him. These admirers are not bad people; they simply want to follow Christ at a safe distance. They fail to see that Christ's life is a demand. John presents Nicodemus as the classic admirer of Christ: fascinated by Jesus, but not ready to risk all and become a disciple (see Jn. 3:1-21).

From the first Christian community described in the Acts of the Apostles, the Church presents itself in history as connected with the living Christ. Christ's followers did not disband after His death because the risen Christ made Himself present in their midst. Through the lives and testimony of those first disciples, so many martyrs, the Church communicates to us that God did not come down to earth for just one instant to be some kind of point in history, elusive to those born afterwards. God has come into our world to stay in the world: Christ is Emmanuel, "God with us."

From this vantage evangelization is the mission of the Church, which is itself an extension of Jesus Christ who is the *Magister*, the Teacher. He wants to communicate to us life in abundance. The mission of the Church is about making disciples, helping people respond to the call to holiness by being part of a faith-filled, worshipping community struggling to be faithful to the Gospel. Discipleship is about living with Christ, in a faith community striving to model our lives on His teaching and example and then to pass on the faith.

This is not something new in the history of the Church. We have been doing this for two thousand years. One of the first attempts is documented in a stunning book that comes to us from the first century. It is called the *Didache*, which means "training." It is the first training manual for initiating people into the life of the Church. It was memorized by the mentors or teachers who used it as a lesson plan, a catechism, a liturgical worship aid, and a primer for faithful discipleship. The *Didache* described the step-by-step transformation by which converts were to be prepared for a full active participation in the life of the Church. As Milavec says in his commentary on this remarkable document: "Any community that cannot artfully and effectively pass on its cherished way of life as a program for divine wisdom and graced existence cannot long endure. Any way of life that cannot be clearly specified, exhibited, and differentiated from the alternative modes operative within the surrounding culture is doomed to growing insignificance and gradual assimilation."

The *Didache* shows us that, for the Church, teaching the faith is always a process of mentoring. Then, as now, we are not transmitting our own theories or notions, but speaking and (we hope) witnessing the Word of God; the word of life is not to be received as mere information. The mentor was expected to illustrate, inquire, question, listen, and challenge his candidate in such ways that not only the words but the deeper meanings of the Way of Life were being suitably assimilated at every step. The *Didache* also tries to prepare its novices for rejection by their friends, by their relatives, and even by the dominant culture, which is hostile to the Gospel teachings.

Another early writing that has always fascinated me is the *Letter to Diognetus*, where the author is describing to his friend what Christians are like. He says that they live in the same neighborhoods, speak the same language, dress like everybody else; but they do not kill their babies and they respect the marriage bond. Very quaint indeed. It is a little scary to think that Diognetus' letter could have been written last week.

In today's world Catholic education must be *Didache*, training in a way of life which is increasingly alien in the secular world, where our concern about unborn children or the sacredness of marriage makes us appear quaint and even nettlesome. We need mentors: parents, grandparents, Godparents, teachers, youth ministers, neighbors, who are ready to pass on the faith.

In our own country, American Catholics have worked arduously in our attempts to pass on the faith and to educate our young people to be good citizens of this country, the world, and our eternal homeland. In the midst of present difficulties, we tend to look back to a supposed golden age and often overlook the great challenges of the past.

When Boston was established as a diocese two centuries ago, the Pope was a virtual prisoner of Napoleon. Consequently Bishop Chevres' consecration was postponed for two years because the documents were unobtainable. The Know-nothings burnt down the Ursuline Convent and Catholic School, and one of the first rectors of Boston College was tarred and feathered. In Boston, "them was the good old days."

The United States is a country of immigrants, and we are an Immigrant Church. Immigrants came fleeing religious persecution, political oppression, hunger, and misery. As the immigrants in McCourt's play about the Irish say: "We came to America because they told us the streets were paved in gold. When we got here, we discovered that the streets were not paved at all and we had to pave 'em."

The Catholic schools did so much to help the children of immigrants get a fine education. There was a great synergism between what was being taught in school and what Catholic parents were trying to impart at home. The spiritual formation and Catholic identity in the schools were promoted by the presence of an army of religious. To them we owe the greatest debt of gratitude for the existence of our Catholic schools and universities. Without the many sacrifices by generations of religious, especially sisters, there would be no Catholic schools.

In 1950, the year I started at Catholic school, there were 84,000 nuns, 8,000 priests, and 3,500 brothers teaching in Catholic schools—almost 100,000 total. In our parish school we had about 50 or 60 students in each grade; some grades had double grades, and we had morning sessions for half the students and afternoon sessions for the other half. All the kids in the parish went to the school, and it was free. That particular school is still thriving, and it is still free. Free because of the nuns in the past and still free because of the constant support of parishioners.

Today only about one-third of United States parishes have Catholic schools. These are doing an outstanding job educating our young, often from immigrant and minority groups. Our Catholic lay teachers have stepped into the breach and do us all proud. The majority of our young Catholics are in public schools, and many of them attend the parish religious education programs. By some estimates there are 350,000 teachers, mostly volunteers, teaching in those programs under very challenging circumstances. Our Catholic schoolteachers and catechists are our unsung heroes in the ongoing saga of the *Didache* in the third millennium. We need to help them be mentors and try to recapture the synergism between school, home, and parish.

The huge area where we are most deficient and which hampers our attempts to pass on the faith is that of *adult faith formation*. I believe we have much to learn from the apostolic movements, which have often had great success at communicating a deep spirituality to their members in the context of a close-knit community. The movements have often been able to energize their people to be evangelizers. I always shudder when I recall the words of Paul VI in *Evangelii Nuntiandi*: "The evangelized person is an evangelizer." Our challenge in the new evangelization is to transform secularized Christians into apostles and inviters.

Our adult faith formation needs to reach out to three groups. First of all to our active parishioners, who are our volunteers, and lay ministers and committed Catholics. We need to help them have a deeper understanding of the faith and enjoy the richness of the Scriptures, the *Catechism*, the social encyclicals, the spiritual masters, and medical ethics.

We also need outreach to the unchurched by having a good RCIA program and teams that are ever finding new ways to invite people to consider joining the Church. Scriptural apologetics and early Christian writers are important resources for our attempts to help new Catholics and prospective Catholics to discover the Church's treasures of faith.

The last group, the inactive Catholics, is the most difficult; and here much reflection, prayer, and planning need to take place on how to reach out to them. There are at least 17 million in the United States who for reasons great and small have stormed off, dozed off, or simply fallen through the cracks. We have a responsibility to them. Christmas, Easter, weddings, and funerals are moments when inactive Catholics find themselves in Church. We must learn to make the most of these moments to welcome people home and put on the Church's best face. There need to be discussions at the level of parish councils and priest council, as well as other groups in the Church, concerning an appropriate way to reach out to inactive Catholics. We need to assume some responsibility for these brothers and sisters who have stormed off or just drifted away.

Our belief must be in a God who so loved the world that He sent us His only Son, Jesus Christ, to establish a people, a Church entrusted with His mission to make disciples of all nations and to build a civilization of love.

As a young priest, I was present at the Puebla Conference. It was Pope John Paul II's first trip after being elected Pope. As the Pope's plane landed in Mexico City all the church bells in the country rang out with joy. The successor of Saint Peter was here in our midst. The crowd extended along the highway from Mexico City to Puebla. People had come the day before and slept on the highway. It reminded me of the Acts of the Apostles, where Luke describes how the people put the sick by the side of the road so that Peter's shadow would touch them.

The crowd made up of millions of Mexicans extended over the 60-mile highway connecting Mexico City and Puebla. The government had tried to discourage people from going. The word was "watch the Pope on television." Nobody paid any attention to that plea, but afterwards the government officials reported that there were no troublesome incidents due to the crowds as they had feared. Indeed the crime rate fell to an all-time low while the Pope was in the country. The government speculated that even the burglars and pickpockets went for the Pope's blessing.

The Holy Father upon arriving in Puebla got out of the open car, walked across the soccer field to the makeshift altar and celebrated the opening Mass of the Puebla Conference. I shall never forget his homily. He challenged us to be teachers and to teach the truth about Christ, about the Church, about the human person.

The same message is as crucial to us today. The content of our teaching must embrace all these truths. The truth about Christ: the

Son of the Father, true God and true man, our crucified redeemer, our Risen Lord who has promised to be with us always and who establishes His Church on the rock of Peter.

The truth about the Church: founded by Jesus on the Apostles, guided by the Holy Spirit, gathering God's people around the altar, calling people to discipleship, conversion and ministry; a Church teaching with authority, witnessing to the presence of the Risen Lord, serving Christ especially in the poor and downtrodden.

The truth about the human person: that each one is an irreplaceable mystery made in God's image and likeness called to an eternal destiny. The Church's teachings on human rights, Gospel of Life, sexual morality, and social justice are all corollaries of this great truth about our origins and our destiny.

The Church's medical ethics, service to the poor, sick, and infirm, the works of mercy and social services, and the promotion of a more just society are all interconnected and crucial in our task of passing on the faith and building a civilization of love.

Our American culture celebrates individual freedom and autonomy, often to the detriment of the common good. The hero of Ayn Rand's *The Fountainhead*, the brilliant, successful architect Howard Rourke, declares: "I come here to say that I am a man who does not exist for others." This is certainly in stark contrast to our concept of discipleship and being a man for others.

The celebration of the individual hero is a standard feature in such popular American genres as the Western film and the detective story. Lone cowboy heroes such as Shane or the Lone Ranger or Hopalong Cassidy came to the rescue of communities of helpless citizens unable to save themselves from evil criminals, and whether the detective is Sam Spade working out of a seedy San Francisco office or Jessica Fletcher sleuthing in the more wholesome atmosphere of Cabot Cove, the same formula is at play. Success and triumph of good over evil are products of individual efforts. The role of social factors in contributing to individual success remains in the background. The American ideal of the rugged individual has given rise to the isolation and alienation that Putnam documents in *Bowling Alone*, his sociological study of the growing individualism enshrined in our culture.

For all its positive aspects American individualism when it is unbridled and exaggerated becomes a liability. An early observer of our American ways, Alexis de Toqueville, said, "Each man is forever thrown back on himself alone and there is danger that he may be shut up in the solitude of his own heart." Can people shut up in the solitude of their own hearts form a democratic society? Passing on the faith is an important contribution to our country. The culture that is born of our faith is a culture of interdependence, of solidarity, of sacrifice for the common good. "There is no greater love than to lay down one's life for a friend." Our task in the face of our modern American notion of exaggerated freedom and individualism is to build a new civilization of love; the alternative is that there will be no civilization at all.

In the past, the Church was persecuted and embattled for the assertions we make about God, Christ, the Trinity, the mystery of grace, interpretation of Scripture, or sacraments. Today the Church is attacked for what we teach about the human person.

The Parable of Lazarus and the Rich Man is lived out every day in our world. As a young priest I was staying in a refugee camp during the civil war in El Salvador. The camp was full of children whose bellies were bloated by malnutrition. One day I asked a sister working in the camp why they did not slaughter some of the cattle from a herd in a neighboring field to feed the families in the refugee camp. She explained to me that that would not be possible because those cattle were slated to be used for dog food for the United States. Too often human life is devalued by our contemporary culture—the most basic right to life is subordinated to the exaggerated entitlements of the autonomous self.

We believe that the human person should be the subject, but too often the human person is the object. The Church's teaching today on the human person made in God's image, redeemed in Christ's blood, and called to a vocation of holiness must be the centerpiece of our social Gospel.

Today our catechesis must joyfully and boldly proclaim these same truths about Christ, about the Church, about the human person. These truths are the content of our faith and are the truths that will set us free. Authentic freedom is based on truth and that freedom allows us to love. True freedom points us on the path to holiness and on the path to a civilization of love.

When Pope John Paul II was in Madrid addressing one million young people, he told them: "Respond to the blind violence and inhuman hatred with the fascinating power of love." We all know that evil has its fascination and attraction, but too often we lose sight of the fact that love and goodness also have the power to attract and that virtue is winsome.

Passing on the faith means helping people to have a real relationship with Christ that will equip them to lead a good life, a moral life, a just life. *Thus part of our job as teachers of the faith is to help our people become virtuous.* Plato thought that virtue was knowledge. But Chaim Ginott, the concentration camp survivor, reminds us that doctors, nurses, scientists, soldiers were part of holocaust machinery, showing that knowledge is not virtue and often science and technology have been put at the service of evil.

Peter Kreeft has said that in our contemporary society we have reduced all virtues to one: being nice. Kreeft laments that for the first time in history moral relativism and subjectivism are not an aberration of rebels but the reigning orthodoxy of the intellectual establishment. So often university academics and those in the media reject any belief in a universal and objective morality. And in our public schools values clarification based on a moral ping-pong of preferences and discussion serves us "values" that are often more about feelings and calculations rather than about truths and principles.

Stanley Hauerwas has said that learning to be moral is like learning to speak a language. You do not teach someone how to speak by first teaching that person the rules of grammar. The way most of us learn to speak a language is by listening to others speak and then imitating them. You learn to speak by being initiated into a community of language, by observing your elders, by mimicking those who speak well. Accordingly, Hauerwas describes how the Church's task is to expose us to significant examples of Christian living. He describes how a group of confirmation-program teachers discussed what was the goal of their program. Was it to help young people learn about the Church, about Jesus? Then someone said, "What we really want out of Confirmation is about a dozen youth who in their adult life come to resemble John Black." John Black was one of the faith-filled and holy members of their congregation.

We need to equip our young people to be disciples. They need to know the truths of our faith, but they need to know how to live those truths. The way most of us become real Christians is by looking over someone else's shoulder, emulating some admired older member of our family or parish, saying yes and taking up a way of life that was made real and accessible through the witness of someone else. Young Christians need mentors, just as the *Didache* called for mentors to accompany the neophytes of the early Church.

We live in a world obsessed by celebrities. Celebrities have replaced heroes and heroines for our young people. Often these celebrities, for all their good looks, talents in singing, acting or sports, lead lives that are superficial, self-absorbed, and chaotic.

The Church has always held up for us the lives of our saints. Pope John Paul II canonized so many to impress on us the universal call to holiness. The saints model for us the struggle to overcome human weakness and sinfulness and embrace God's will in our lives.

It is healthy for young people today to hear about our saints and contemporary heroes like Dorothy Day, who after having an abortion and another child out of wedlock became one of the most outstanding persons in the history of the Church in our country.

Our young people want to see the ideals of the Gospel lived in our lives. One of the worse results of the sexual-abuse scandal in the Church can be a cynicism about the call to holiness in the Church. We run the risk of being overwhelmed by the bad example of priests and bishops and need to remind people that there have always been saints and sinners in the Church. The Church's task is to call everyone to conversion. We have our successes and our failures. The saints are the success stories our young people need to know. It helps them to see that we, their teachers, are struggling on the same path to holiness.

We must also break the bad habit of presenting the Church in such a way that people are deceived into thinking that they can be Christians and remain strangers. The privatization of religion in today's climate of new-age individualism is poisonous to the Gospel message of community, of connectedness in the Body of Christ.

As a seminarian, I read an interview with Flannery O'Connor about growing up Catholic in the South. The famous author related how as a child she had a playmate, a little Baptist girl who was the closest of friends. She invited her friend to Mass one day. The little girl got permission from her mom and went with Flannery to church. Flannery couldn't wait to hear her friend's reaction. "Well, what do you think?" Flannery asked. Her little girlfriend said: "Wow, you Catholics really got something there. The music is so bad, the preaching is so boring, and all those people are there!"

Unfortunately, we can no longer count on 75% of the Catholic population fulfilling the Sunday Mass obligation. We must prepare people to be part of a worshipping community. Many years ago, as Bishop of the Virgin Islands, I was invited to visit the local synagogue by the rabbi. It is a beautiful West Indian building with white sand on the floor. It is over 300 years old. Walking around the synagogue I picked up an old Jewish prayer book, and it happened to open to a beautiful prayer that begins with the words: "More than Israel has kept the Sabbath, the Sabbath has kept Israel." I thought to myself: "What a great truth that is! We Catholics can say the same thing: more than we have kept the Sunday Mass obligation, it has kept us a people, a church, focused on God, His word, and the mission He has entrusted to us."

In a culture addicted to entertainment, our young Catholics often find Sunday Mass a rather unsatisfying experience, like Flannery O'Connor's Baptist girlfriend. Our challenge is to be teachers of prayer: to help our young Catholics experience prayer so that when they gather for the Sunday Eucharist, they have a notion of why they are there and how to pray.

There can be no Catholic life, no holiness, no discipleship without prayer. Every Catholic school, every religious education program must have a prayer component that will help our young Catholics be part of a worshipping community. It is gathered around the altar that we recognize Christ in the breaking of the bread, and where by partaking of the Eucharist we become one with Christ and with each other.

It is important for us to appreciate other faiths, but generic Christianity and comparative-religion courses can have disastrous effects in our attempts to pass on the Catholic faith to new generations. Today's religious climate demands that we incorporate apologetics into our catechesis. Americans want to know "the why" of our teachings. In the past we have often been quick to present conclusions without showing how our doctrines fit together. In the highly personalized religious atmosphere of today many of our young people could say: "My karma ran over my dogma." But we are a people of the Book, of the Creed, and of the living Magisterium.

Dean Hoge, in his *Young Adult Catholics: Religion in a Culture of Choice*, urges us to promote the distinctiveness of Catholic identity. I would concur and say that we need to stress the centrality of the Eucharist, the sacrament of Confession as an experience of God's mercy and as a means of conversion and spiritual growth, Marian piety, and the importance of the universal ministry of Peter in the papacy, and our emphasis on community and the social teaching of the Church. These things are uniquely Catholic and understanding this helps bind young people to the Church.

Bringing our young people together in large numbers where they can witness to each other is also a valuable exercise. It is always a joy to see our young Catholics at the March for Life in Washington. They are truly energized by the experience of faith and of the Gospel of Life in the company of thousands of their peers. Combined with a visit to the John Paul II Cultural Center and the Holocaust Museum, it can be a marvelous learning event for our young Catholics. We need to do things out of the classroom setting, to give them a chance to see that what they learn about in class has repercussions in the way believers live and interact.

Andrew Greeley has said that "at every level Church leaders and teachers should realize that Beauty (by which Goodness and Truth are present) is their strongest tool . . . for drawing the faithful closer to the Church and to the God for which the Church is a sacrament."

Our challenge is to help our people glimpse the beauty of God, the beauty of the Gospel. Pope John Paul II in his *Letter to Artists* wrote, "Beauty is a key to the mystery and a call to transcendence. It is an invitation to savor life and to dream of the future. This is why the beauty of created things can never fully satisfy. It stirs that hidden nostalgia for God which a lover of beauty like Saint Augustine could express in incomparable terms: "Late have I loved you, beauty so old and so new: late have I loved you!" (no. 16).

It is that beauty that we want to help our people to experience. We must experience it ourselves in our own interior life. A teacher of the faith must first be a disciple to Christ, the Master Teacher. We must love the Church. Jesus is the Bridegroom, not the widower. He does not exist separate from His Bride. I have always liked the ancient Christian text, the *Shepherd of Hermas*. It is a book of revelations granted to Hermas in Rome by agency of two heavenly figures, the first an old woman and the second an angel in the form of a shepherd. The old woman represents the Church. In successive visions she becomes younger and more beautiful. As Hermas moves on the path of conversion, the vision of the Church's beauty becomes more apparent to him.

The path to holiness is a path to the source of all goodness and truth, of absolute beauty. The character Prince Myshkin in Dostoyevsky's *The Idiot* puts it so well: "Beauty will save the world."

We want to share with new generations what we have discovered: namely, that being a Catholic with a sense of personal vocation and a communal mission is a beautiful life. Our mission is about helping people catch a glimpse of the Beauty that saves and to have an appetite for that Beauty.

Doctrine and Catechetics

FATHER THOMAS WEINANDY, O.F.M. CAP.

Before I take up the topic of this essay I would like to pay tribute to Father Ronald Lawler. I first came to know Father Ronald when I was a seminarian in the 1960s at Saint Fidelis Seminary and College, Herman, Pennsylvania. The high-school students did not have much contact with Father Ronald, since he taught exclusively college students and was at the time president of the college. However, his reputation as possessing a keen mind and being an excellent philosophy teacher (if one was into philosophy) trickled down to us on the high-school level. It was in my freshman year in the college that I came into immediate contact with Father Ronald, and over the following years of college, I came to appreciate him immensely as a teacher and as a friar.

Father Ronald taught us the whole of the history of philosophy—four semesters, which encompassed ancient, medieval, modern, and contemporary. He also offered, as electives, the Philosophy of Religion and Political Philosophy. (I attended Saint Fidelis College at the height of its academic excellence. Not only did we have two other excellent philosophy teachers, Father Vincent Rohr and Dr. Joseph Boyle, but also outstanding teachers in history, English, theology, psychology, Greek, and Latin. I am not hesitant to claim that the students of Saint Fidelis College received one of the best liberal arts educations in the country at that time.)

While we did not have Father Ronald for epistemology and metaphysics, these subjects were very important throughout the whole of

Rev. Thomas Weinandy, O.F.M. Cap., is executive director of the Secretariat for Doctrine and Pastoral Practices of the U.S. Conference of Catholic Bishops.

what he taught. Father Ronald was ardent in his conviction that human beings had the intellectual ability to know the truth, and that such ability was absolutely essential for living a truly human life. Moreover, this realist epistemology was founded upon a metaphysical anthropology—human beings were composed of body and soul, and thus, through the material senses, the immaterial intellect could grasp the true nature and reality of the world around it. In all of this Father Ronald, though a Capuchin Franciscan, was a true son of Saint Thomas Aquinas.

From such teaching and the authors Father Ronald had us read, such as Gilson, Maritain, Copleston, Pieper, and Mascall, I came to appreciate (an appreciation I continue to this day) the extreme importance, the necessity, of metaphysics and epistemology, and I too, philosophically and theologically, have always been loyal to my Thomistic roots. (Though as college freshmen, merely beginning our philosophical training, we heard that Father Ronald was to be away for a few days to attend a "Conference on Metaphysics." In our youthful playfulness, ignorance, and pride, we laughed and joked about how it could be possible to spend days talking about metaphysics. What was there to talk about, for the subject matter was "being" in and of itself? Little did I know that I would spend a huge amount of life pondering and teaching and writing about things metaphysical!)

However, Father Ronald was not merely interested in man's ability to know the world around him, but equally, and ever more so, that such intellectual ability provided the opening for human beings, created in God's own image and likeness, to know God and the revelation of God, and so come to love the God who knows and loves human beings.

It is here that the topic of this essay begins; for Father Ronald knew, in faith, that God had acted in time and space. Those events not only revealed to human beings things that they would not have otherwise known, but that such divine actions radically changed the manner in which God related to human beings and human beings could relate to God. Those revealed mysteries of the faith, those divine actions, have been embodied in human words, and those human words give access to the realities that they express.

Enunciated and articulated Christian doctrine, for Father Ronald, as for the Church, expresses the truth of who God is and what He has done and is presently doing.

Thus, in keeping with his high metaphysics and realist epistemology, Father Ronald realized that Christian doctrine could not simply be taught and known, but that in coming to know Christian doctrine one could enter into the very reality of that which doctrine proclaimed. Thus doctrine, for Father Ronald, was always at the heart of Catholic catechesis, not simply because it was an authoritative ancient letter, but because it provided one entrance into the very life-saving mysteries of God which would come to fruition in heaven.

In the remainder of this essay I will examine, first, the nature of Christian doctrine, and then a number of doctrines in order to highlight their catechetical importance.

The Awesome Incomprehensible Nature of Doctrine

It has been said (and still is sometimes said, given much of the past and the present catechetical mood within the Church) that doctrines, because they are so unambiguous, evacuate the Gospel of its mystery. Moreover, since they are often written in a language and employ concepts that go back centuries, doctrines have become the dry bones of a lifeless Christianity.

However, precisely the opposite is the case. The very nature of doctrine—and the history of the development of doctrine bears this out—is to preserve the mystery, and in so preserving the mystery preserve the salvific life that resides in that mystery. It is heresy, doctrinal error, that deprives the Gospel of its mystery, and in so doing deprives it of its salvific life.

For example, the New Testament, following upon the Old, proclaimed that there is one God, and yet it equally proclaimed that the Father, the Son, and the Holy Spirit all acted in such a manner so as to identify them as God. Jesus spoke of His Father. Jesus spoke of Himself as the Father's only Son and did things that only someone who was truly divine could do, such as teach divine truths on His own authority, forgive sins, promise eternal life, demand faith in Himself, work miracles, etc. The Father raised Jesus gloriously and bodily from the dead, and so He now is the divine Lord and Savior of all. Jesus promised the outpouring of the Holy Spirit, the Spirit of Truth sent by the Father through Him. The arrival of that Holy Spirit engendered faith, allowed those who believed to do what Jesus Himself did, though now in His divine name; transformed them from being sinners into being holy children of the Father in the likeness of Jesus the Son; and was the guarantee and first down payment for their own bodily resurrection. All such actions and more manifested the divine status of the Holy Spirit. In the midst of all of this the New Testament nonetheless insisted that there was but one true God. We are in the midst of a mystery—the mystery of God's very being!

The history of the early Church is not only the history of faith seeking to grasp the reality of the mystery of God, but equally the refutation of heresies that would destroy the mystery of God. Actually, it was in the refutation of the various heresies that the early Church came to articulate clearly what the mystery of the one God is—a Trinity of Persons.

When Arius, in his desire to preserve the oneness of God, denied that the Son was truly divine and instead proposed that He was the first of all creatures, he sought to deprive God of His mystery. It was the Church at the Council of Nicea (325), in proclaiming that the Son was "one in being with the Father," who preserved the mystery of God. When the divinity of the Holy Spirit was later denied, it was the First Council of Constantinople (381) that assured all believers that He is indeed "the Lord, the Giver of Life, who proceeds from the Father and together with the Father and Son is worshiped and glorified," and in so doing preserved the mystery of God.

Now some might protest at this juncture, as suggested above, and say: "Having articulated with such clarity that the one Being of God is the three Persons of the Trinity, does this not make our under-standing of God clearer and so more knowable and thus less mysteri-ous?" Here a very important distinction must be made with regard to the nature of Christian doctrine and its importance for catechetics.

Yes, it is true that Christian doctrine does enhance the clarity and thus the knowability of the mysteries of faith. However, in so doing the mysteries themselves become even more mysterious. To illustrate this, let us return to the Christian doctrine of God.

The early descendents of Abraham believed in one God, as opposed to the multiplicity of the pagan gods. However, Moses was not content with this simple knowledge. At the burning bush he asked this one God what was His name. He wanted to know more about God, and so in obtaining God's name he would obtain more knowledge. God answered Moses' query, but He must have done so with a smile. In telling Moses that He is "I Am Who Am" God did provide Moses with further knowledge of Himself, but in so doing He actually made Himself even more mysterious. Thus Moses did know more about who God is than he knew before he asked the question, but what he now knew enhanced the very mystery of God's being as the One who simply "is."

Similarly, the New Testament revelation that the one God is the Father, the Son, and the Holy Spirit provided an even greater understanding of the very nature of God's being, but, again, in so doing God became even more mysterious. The development of the doctrine of the Trinity, that the one God is three distinct inter-related Persons or subjects (three "who's"), sharpens the focus of this mystery, and in so doing the mystery of the Trinity assumes an awesomeness that is beyond human comprehension.

A similar pattern can be discerned within the doctrine of the Incarnation. The New Testament proclaims that the man Jesus, while being truly human, said and did things that manifested that He was God. The Gospel of John simply proclaimed that "the Word became flesh and dwelt among us." The history of the doctrinal controversies surrounding the reality of Christ demonstrates that the Church was adamant in preserving three incarnational truths. Against the Docetists and the Apollinarians, the Church affirmed that Jesus is truly and fully human. Against the Arians it insisted upon his full divinity. Against Nestorius, who, while upholding the full humanity and the full divinity, could conceive and articulate only a moral union between them, the Church stipulated that the incarnational union was truly ontological. The Son of God did actually come to exist as man, and so the Son actually lived a fully and truly human life, for it was He who actually was born, suffered, and died. Thus the Christian doctrine of the Incarnation, that one and the same Son exists in two natures, that is, as God and as man, again provides clarity and depth to this mystery and in so doing underscores the astounding nature of the mystery.

The axiom then of all Christian revelation is that the more God reveals about Himself, and so the more we come to know Him in faith, the more mysterious He becomes. Now, the conclusion to be drawn from this is that, while Christian doctrines, in their turn, provide even greater knowledge of the divine mysteries, yet in so doing they specify more clearly the exact nature of those mysteries. Christian doctrine allows one to know more clearly what the mysteries of faith are, but it does not allow one to comprehend the mysteries. They retain their mystery and can even become more mysterious. Even in heaven, where we will see God face to face, we will know God as He is, but He will be fully known as the absolutely incomprehensible mystery of his triune being. This will be the splendid glory and utmost joy of heaven itself.

Participation in the Christian Doctrines

Now the goal of catechetics is to allow the students, young or old, to grasp the mysteries of faith, that is, that they come to know exactly what the mysteries of faith are. Yet, in so doing, they are to equally stand before these mysteries of faith not with a mind of hopeless frustration that they do not fully comprehend them—for example, that the one God is a trinity of interrelated Persons—but rather with a mind that glories in the awesomeness, grandeur, and splendor of what has been revealed. Moreover, they must recognize that through the grace that is channeled through faith, prayer, the sacraments, and virtuous acts they actually come to participate and so share in the realities of these mysteries of faith. The awesome mystery of the triune God becomes their life.

Here again we are confronted with the importance of Christian doctrine in relationship to catechetics. Some Christian doctrines articulate the Christian mysteries of faith that stand outside of ourselves or over against us, such as the doctrine of the Trinity or the Incarnation. However, other Christian doctrines express the

Christian mysteries of faith that allow the believer to participate and share in these central mysteries.

I just stated that grace allows one to participate in the mysteries of faith: that is, one becomes a member of Christ's Body, the Church, and in so doing one comes to live in union with the Trinity. However, grace itself is a mystery, and the doctrine of grace professes that mystery. The doctrine of grace specifies that, through the indwelling of the Holy Spirit, a person is united to the risen and glorious incarnate Jesus and so is transformed into His likeness as Son, thus becoming a child of the Father. In so doing, a Christian comes to relate, in Christ, to the Persons of the Trinity, from the standpoint of Jesus the Son, as the Persons themselves relate to one another. The Christian lives, literally, within the life of the Trinity. This is again an awesome mystery, and, while it can be conceived and articulated, it cannot be fully comprehended. Nonetheless, catechetics is, through the teaching of this doctrine, to bring its students not simply to an objective knowledge of the doctrine of grace, but also to an experience of it in their lives through prayer and the sacraments. In so doing, the student will, in the face of such a mystery, rejoice in its grandeur and be overwhelmed that he or she possesses the dignity of participating in it.

Now this leads me to another Christian doctrine—the Liturgy of the Eucharist. There are at least two doctrines contained here that are important for catechetics.

First, the Mass is the making present of the one sacrifice of Jesus on the cross, and, in so making this sacrifice present, those who participate in the liturgy are actually united to that sacrifice and so reap its benefits—the forgiveness of sins and reconciliation with the Father through the outpouring of the Holy Spirit. This is once more an awesome and marvelous mystery, but one that students need to grasp and so be able to participate fruitfully in it.

The second is the doctrine of Transubstantiation. This doctrine clearly specifies that the bread and wine cease to be such and become the actual risen Body and Blood of Jesus and, thus, those who partake of the Eucharist are in literal communion with the risen Lord Jesus, and so share in His risen and divine life. In turn, it is through the Eucharist that one comes to share as fully as possible here on earth the life of loving communion with the Father through the Holy Spirit. We may not be able to comprehend such a great mystery, but it is this mystery, in all of its wonder, that the doctrine of Transubstantiation articulates, a doctrine that can only bring joy to the Catholic believer.

Allow me to conclude by speaking briefly on a Christian doctrine, a Christian mystery, that was so dear to the heart and mind of Father Ronald—the Church. All that was said above finds its home within the Church; for here the truth of Christian doctrine is authentically proclaimed in all its splendor and awesomeness under the apostolic authority of Peter and the apostles. Here, too, within the Church, one is able to participate in all those Christian mysteries of faith; for only within the Church does one become a member of the Body of Christ, and so fully and truly participates in the very life of the triune God through prayer and the sacraments. The Church is that mystery which is the great meeting place in Christ through the Spirit between the Father and human beings, and thus it is central and essential to the Christian faith. Thus, the doctrine of the Church is equally central to all catechetics. Only as the student comes to love the Church and participate in the life of the Church will he or she come to love Jesus and rejoice in the Father through the indwelling of the Holy Spirit.

This is why Father Ronald agonized so over the present state of the Church. For him, many in the Church were not clearly proclaiming Christian and Catholic doctrine, and equally, then, many were not allowing the faithful of the Church to participate authentically, and so fully, in the life and sacraments of the Church. For Father Ronald, the Church was the home of divine truth and the home of divine life, and when that home becomes dysfunctional all its members suffer. Father Ronald spent his life, through his own loyal proclamation of Catholic doctrine, to bring healing and life to the Church of today, and I am confident that he is doing so to this day, though now in the much more congenial atmosphere of the glory of Jesus and of the saints that he loved.

Confirmation: An Increase and Deepening of Baptismal Grace

KATRINA ZENO

ighteen years ago I set about to design a Confirmation program for my college thesis. It never happened. As I delved into the history of Confirmation, a tangled body of theological opinions emerged. I quickly realized the sacrament of Confirmation was still in its theological adolescence (or perhaps mid-life crisis!), searching for its unique identity. Before I could design a program, I had to nail down its distinctive theology.

Not much has changed in eighteen years. Today, most Catholics vaguely know Confirmation has something to do with the Holy Spirit and receiving "more," but beyond that, the sacrament's identity seems shrouded in uncertainty. Is it making an "adult" commitment to the faith and therefore to be administered in adolescence? Is it a dimension of the *Rite of Baptism* and therefore to be given in close time proximity to Baptism? Is it an infusion of grace, like a booster shot, which should be conferred advantageously before the tumultuous onset of adolescence? As a Confirmation catechist, I've been confronted with all three perspectives courtesy of pastors, priests, and parents.

At the risk of belaboring the point, a review of the historical and theological development of the sacrament of Confirmation is in order. This review, I trust, will illuminate a legitimate theology of Confirmation as well as the theological riches of this sacrament, which deals with the very mystery of salvation and our participation in Trinitarian life.

Katrina Zeno is founder of *Women of the Third Millennium.*

The earliest explicit literature detailing the rite of Christian initiation is the *Apostolic Tradition* of Saint Hippolytus. Written around the turn of the third century, this document is concerned with preserving Church traditions that were under attack. The rich liturgical ceremony for initiation described by Hippolytus discloses three important data:

1. The rites of initiation consisted of Baptism with water, anointing with oil, and first communion in connection with the Easter Vigil.
2. Two separate anointings with oil occurred after immersion in water, one by the presbyter and one by the bishop.
3. The threefold invocation of the Father, Son, and Spirit was used by the bishop during his chrismation.

The general pre-Nicene understanding of initiation encompassed one rite that involved both an immersion in water for the remission of sins and the sealing of oil and imposition of hands for the imparting of the Spirit. Furthermore, the candidates were considered to be of adult stature, since they were required to be catechumens of up to three years' duration, live exemplary lives, and prepare for initiation through fasting, prayer, and participation in the Easter Vigil. In short, the primary mode of initiation in the early Church was conferral of Baptism with water, anointing with oil, and reception of the Eucharist only after the candidates exhibited a readiness to live the Christian life through renunciation of sin and moral instruction.

If one takes the early Church model as the definitive guide for celebrating the sacraments of initiation, then obviously the current time-split between Baptism and Confirmation is an aberration. However, we must be careful to discern not only the initial celebration and expressions of formulae of faith, but to also trace their theological and historical development. Jumping back to the third-century ecclesial practices and insisting on these as normative would ignore 1,800 years of ecclesial and theological development.

Central to the bifurcation of Baptism and Confirmation is the theological development of original sin. The writings of Origen (d. 254 AD) represent a significant departure from earlier Church fathers, who emphasized the innocence of newborn children. Origen fleshed out the need for newborns to receive the remission of sins (i.e. infant Baptism), even though they had never committed a personal sin.

The theological development of original sin naturally led to a development in ritual: water Baptism (by a priest) emerged as a separate rite from anointing with chrism and the imposition of hands (by the bishop). The fourth century marks a significant turning point in the history of Christian initiation—the acceptance of infant Baptism as normative resulting in the separation of Baptism of water from Baptism in the Spirit.

Consequently, the fifth through twelfth centuries are filled with writers and theologians attempting to unravel this sacramental mystery. Was Baptism efficacious in and of itself? If so, what was the necessity of *confirmatio*, "Confirmation," as it came to be called in the West?

Eusebius of Emesa, writing in the late fifth century, articulated this answer: "The Holy Ghost bestows at the font [i.e. at Baptism] absolutely all that is needed to restore innocence. In Confirmation He provides an increase in grace. . . . In Baptism we are born to new life, after Baptism we are confirmed for combat." Eusebius appeals to the image of strengthening and equipping for war used by Saint John Chrysostom and others to give validity to the rite of Confirmation.

In the ninth century, Rabanus Maurus advanced the theology of Confirmation another step. Prompted by the Carolingian reforms in Gaul (which insisted upon an episcopal anointing as well as a presbyteral anointing), he undertook the monumental task of explaining the theological difference between these two anointings. Nathan Mitchell, in his article "Dissolution of the Rite of Christian Initiation," paraphrases Maurus' theological development:

> The first anointing after Baptism, done by the presbyter, effects the descent of the Spirit and the consecration of the Christian; the second anointing, the episcopal chrismation and laying on of hands, brings the grace of the Spirit into the baptized with all the fullness of sanctity, knowledge, and power.[1]

The theological vocabulary that emerged to describe Confirmation as a separate rite from Baptism clustered around strengthening, increase, empowering, and fullness. Confirmation strengthens and empowers the baptized to preach to others the same gift he or she has received in Baptism and equips the believer for combat.

With the advent of medieval scholasticism and the codifying of centuries of theological development in the writings of Saint Thomas Aquinas and others, the sacrament of Confirmation appeared to arrive at a more secure identity. In particular, Aquinas augmented the theology of Confirmation with his own anthropological model: by comparing the sacramental life to human bodily life, he described the baptismal character as corresponding to spiritual childhood while the character of Confirmation pertained to spiritual maturity.[2] By using the notion of spiritual adulthood, Aquinas defined, analogically, what happened in Confirmation: "The Christian, justified in Baptism, is given the fullness of grace 'in Confirmation.'"[3]

Not only is Aquinas' sacramental theology the basis for our current theological tradition, but his ecclesial understanding undergirds the contemporary view of sacraments as well. For Aquinas, the sacraments are not rarified rituals applied to isolated individuals, but dynamic events mediated through the Church that put the believer into contact with Christ and His Body. Baptism is a relational act that establishes a permanent connection between Christ, the believer, and the worshipping body.

With the upheaval of the Reformation era, a new concern leapt to the forefront with regard to Confirmation—the element of conscious faith. In the sixteenth century, Erasmus proposed a post-baptismal catechesis by introducing a catechumenate for the baptized that culminated in Confirmation. Following suit, the Council of Cologne suggested for the first time that a child should not be confirmed before the age of seven in order that he understand what is being done.[4]

The reformers Wycliffe and Hus stressed even further the element of conscious faith in connection to the apostolic laying on of hands:

> Whoever being baptized has come to the true faith and pro-
> poses to portray it in action, in adversities, and reproaches,
> to the intent that the new birth may be seen revealed in his
> spiritual life and thankfulness, such a one ought to be
> brought to the bishop, or priest, and be confirmed . . . so that
> there may come to him an increase of the gifts of the Holy
> Spirit for the steadfastness and the welfare of the future.[5]

The medieval tradition of Confirmation as an increase in grace is coupled with the conscious consent of the believer to carry out his faith through a concrete and visible witness.

The rise of the Anabaptist tradition stressed even further the element of conscious faith to the point of transferring Baptism from the economy of salvation to the economy of obedience. Baptism became something sought by one who had already become a Christian by conversion rather than a sacramental ritual "done" to the individual.

The importance of the Reformation period lies in its revival of catechetical instruction linked to a mature assimilation of Christian values and piety. The trend in Protestant catechesis was to regard Confirmation as the "culmination of a period of concentrated preparation and teaching and an occasion of religious crisis, decision making, or public commitment."[6] Although baptized persons bore the sign of Baptism, they needed to be reawakened from sin and complacency and brought to real faith.

The process by which this "real" faith came about became the distinguishing feature of the different lines of Christian tradition—from those who believe in a two-stage initiation (Baptism and Confirmation—Roman Catholic and Mainline Protestant), to a one-stage initiation (Eastern Orthodox and Anabaptist) to dispensing with rites altogether (Quaker and other Protestant denominations).

From this historical and theological review, a precedent for both a unified rite of initiation and a twofold rite of Baptism and Confirmation is evident. This is why the Roman Catholic Church continues to employ three means for full initiation into the Body of Christ: Baptism and Confirmation of adults (RCIA); Baptism and Confirmation of infants (Eastern Rite Churches); and Baptism of infants with an intervening time period before Confirmation (Roman Rite).

While an exhaustive analysis of Confirmation would treat all three expressions, the purpose of this chapter is to investigate the latter—Baptism of infants and confirmation of pre-teens or young adults. The restoration of the Rite of Christian Initiation of Adults since Vatican II wonderfully restored the practice of the early Church, which offered an extensive pre-Baptismal catechumenate culminating in a sacramental celebration that is experiential for those who are initiated as well as the entire believing body. The emphasis is on conscious incorporation of the catechumen into the worshiping community that is *fully* conscious of its identity as the community of the Risen Lord.

As a living Body and light to the world, the Roman Catholic Church joyfully provides for those who respond to that light as adults. However, she also continues to provide for those who are born into it. Rather than requiring conscious faith as the prerequisite for Baptism, infant Baptism emphasizes, as Saint Thomas noted, the relational act that establishes a permanent connection between Christ, the believer, and the worshipping body. The individual is restored to communion with God through Jesus Christ; infant Baptism makes the infusion of this divine relationship possible from the earliest moments of human life.

In his book *Infant Baptism and Adult Conversion*, O. Hallesby insightfully argues that an infant should not be denied Baptism merely because of his or her inability to make a "conscious decision." The developing human person should not be left prey to the singular influence of sin. God's life should also be made available to the child:

> It is this inherited sinful life that God meets by regenerating the child, that is, giving it relationship with a life of an entirely different kind, with the good life, with God's own life. The evil life is not to be permitted to work alone in the child.[7]

Through the practice of infant Baptism, even the youngest members receive full membership in the one Body of Christ. This capacity for full participation is not reserved in one lump sum for a later age, but is gradually appropriated as the baptized matures. The responsible living out of the full Christian life by each individual is the responsibility of the corporate Church body.

To deepen our understanding of Confirmation, then, is to deepen our understanding of salvation. Infant Baptism and adolescent Confirmation emphasize both the gratuitousness of God's grace and the role of free will in responding to the gift. This is why the *Catechism of the Catholic Church* speaks of Confirmation as bringing an increase and deepening of Baptismal grace: "It must be explained to the faithful that the reception of the sacrament of Confirmation is necessary for the completion of Baptismal grace. For 'by the sacrament of Confirmation, [the baptized] are more perfectly bound to the church and are enriched with a special strength of the Holy Spirit'" (1285).

The effects of the sacrament of Confirmation, according to the *Catechism* (1303), are fivefold:

1. It roots us more deeply in the divine filiation which makes us cry "Abba, Father!"
2. It unites us more firmly to Christ.
3. It increases the gift of the Holy Spirit in us.
4. It renders our bond with the Church more perfect.
5. It gives us a special strength to spread and defend the faith by word and actions as true witnesses of Christ.

Consequently, the *Catechism* states four aims for Confirmation catechesis: to lead the Christian toward 1) a more intimate union with Christ; 2) a more lively familiarity with the Holy Spirit; 3) a greater capability of assuming apostolic responsibilities; 4) a sense of belonging to the Church of Jesus Christ as well as the parish community.

Finally, it's important to note the overall purpose of the sacraments is to "manifest and communicate to men, above all in the Eucharist, the mystery of communion with the God who is love, one in three Persons" (CCC 1118). This mystery of communion is again emphasized in paragraph 1129: "The fruit of the sacramental life is that the Spirit of adoption makes the faithful partakers in the divine nature by uniting them in a living union with the only Son, the Savior."

With this background, I would like to conclude this chapter with my eighteen-year-old goal—identifying specific catechetical content for a Confirmation program.

Since Confirmation is an increase and deepening of Baptismal grace, the relational miracle of Baptism must occupy a central place in Confirmation catechesis. For this goal, the Catholic Church has received a most surprising and underutilized gift in recent years: Pope John Paul II's "Theology of the Body."

Whenever I mention that I have developed a Confirmation curriculum based on the theology of the body, people usually react with mild surprise or shock: "How could the theology of the body have anything to do with Confirmation?" For most people, theology of the body is synonymous with sex and marriage, not sacraments and Confirmation.

While Pope John Paul II indeed addresses the meaning of marital union and marriage, these concerns occupy only two "cycles" of his 129 Wednesday audiences. Even more fundamental to theology of the body is a theological anthropology—a carefully constructed vision of the human person made in the image and likeness of God. In this vision, the human person fulfills the meaning of his being and existence by living in union and communion with God and others through a sincere gift of self—what Pope John Paul II affectionately calls *communio personarum*.

This anthropological vision dovetails exquisitely with the sacrament of Confirmation as the completion of Baptism. By first walking my 11- and 12-year-old Confirmation candidates through Genesis 1 and 2, they come to see (with Pope John Paul II's help) God's original intention "from the beginning": 1) to be made in His image and likeness; 2) to be made of body and spirit; 3) not to be alone; and 4) to live in union and communion with God and others through a sincere gift of self.

This foundational anthropology sets the stage for the tragedy of original sin—deliberately disobeying God, with the result that our communion with God is shattered. We are born into the world separated from God, separated from each other, separated from the world around us, and separated within ourselves between body and spirit.

With this background, the miracle of Baptism takes on new meaning for the Confirmation candidates. They understand more concretely the consequence of sin as separation and the miracle of Baptism as union—or better, reunion—with God, with others, with the world around them, and within themselves between body and spirit. The link between theology of the body and Confirmation is easily seen: the Holy Spirit, whom we forfeited in original sin, is precisely the One who brings about this marvelous reunion, the same Spirit they will receive "more" of in Confirmation.

From here, the catechetical focus shifts more specifically to the Holy Spirit. By looking at references to the "spirit of God" in the Old Testament and the "Spirit" and "Holy Spirit" in the New Testament, a tapestry of the Third Person of the Trinity emerges. His presence in history and His action in individuals' lives and the life of the Church as portrayed in Scripture helps the candidates to develop a more "lively familiarity" with the Holy Spirit. This section culminates with the descent of the Holy Spirit on Pentecost as the "Gift and Promise."

Having laid the anthropological and pneumatic foundations for a "life in the Spirit," the final catechetical emphasis is sacramental. For young people, the meaning and power of Sacraments as efficacious signs need to be reiterated with the same regularity as "please" and "thank you." Only when they grasp the difference between a sign and a sacrament do infant Baptism and Confirmation as its completion make sense as ritual celebrations. Indeed, this is the point to which Confirmation catechesis has been tending thus far—that the sacrament is an encounter with Christ for the increase of divine life within them.

At this point, my favorite image is introduced—that of a temple. I draw for the candidates the foundational floor (Baptism), which is being sealed in Confirmation. I then draw the sides of the "temple" as two lines coming down, indicating what God does for us in the sacramental rite—strengthening us with the gifts of the Holy Spirit from Isaiah 11 and releasing in us the fruits of the Spirit from Galatians 5 and the charismatic gifts of the Spirit from 1 Corinthians 12.

Confirmation, however, is not only what God does in us, but our response back to God, since the *Catechism* says, "the fruits of the sacraments also depend on the disposition of the one who receives them" (1128). Our response to God, therefore, represents the two sides of the roof: On the one side, we *confirm* our "yes" back to God, just as Mary did at the Annunciation. This is the element of conscious faith so critical to the reformers. One the other side, we *commit* ourselves to the moral life of holiness, which the *Catechism* says is sustained by the gifts of the Spirit (see CCC 1830). Where the two lines of the "roof" come together at the peak, I draw a cross to indicate how this all happens "under the cross." Thus we are "temples of the Holy Spirit."

The final element in catechetical preparation is that of mission. In the Rite of Confirmation, the *bishop* confers the anointing as a symbol of his link with the apostles and their apostolic mission. This episcopal anointing has been preserved until the present time to highlight "a greater capability of assuming apostolic responsibilities" and the "special strength to spread and defend the faith by word and actions as true witnesses of Christ."

Regardless of what is experienced or not experienced at the moment of sealing, the sacramental character of Confirmation is infallibly imparted. The specific grace of this "character" is linked with the "power to profess faith in Christ publicly and as it were officially" (CCC 1305). This is the grace of apostolic mission, a grace that is meant to blossom over the lifetime of the confirmed as he or she becomes more consciously identified with the Church as the Body of Christ and therefore with the salvific mission of Christ on earth. This particularly potent dimension of the sacrament of Confirmation, which Pope John Paul II described as the "spirituality of Pentecost" and the "new evangelization," has yet to be fully mined in Confirmation preparation and in the Church.

The catechetical approach above can be outlined as follows:

1. Overview of Confirmation: scriptural basis, sealing with the Holy Spirit.
2. Life before original sin ("in the beginning").
3. Our call to live in union and communion through a sincere gift of self.
4. Sacramental view of reality (the divine vision).

5. Original innocence and holiness (from the *Catechism*).
6. Analysis of original sin.
7. Consequences of original sin from John Paul II and the *Catechism*.
8. Overview of the Jesse Tree (Advent).
9. Significance of the Holy Spirit to bring about union.
10. The Holy Spirit in the Old Testament.
11. The Holy Spirit in the New Testament.
12. The Holy Spirit as the gift and the promise (Pentecost).
13. Confirmation as a sacrament (Sacramental theology).
14. Confirmation as the completion of Baptism.
15. Significance of Baptism in Scripture and the *Catechism*.
16. Confirmation as the grace of mission.
17. Planning of Confirmation liturgy.

Other catechetical elements of the program attempt to make the preparation period experiential for the entire family (i.e. the believing Body). These include:

1. The Family Table—A sheet sent home with the candidate after every class with discussion questions and activities for the family to do at home.
2. Homework—This involves memorization of Scripture and the *Catechism* as well as activities, studying for quizzes, and reading Scripture.
3. Holy Spirit Prayers—These are prayers for the sevenfold gifts of the Spirit from Isaiah 11 that are suggested to be prayed by the family. Every month a different gift is prayed for (wisdom, knowledge, etc.).
4. Confirmation Retreat—This is a one-day retreat (9 am to 4 pm) attended by the Confirmation candidate and his/her sponsor or one parent. The theme of the retreat is "Bursting Your Baptismal Graces: Priest, Prophet, and King."
5. Chrism Mass—The Confirmation class attends the Chrism Mass during Holy Week, in which the bishop blesses the oil that will be used to anoint the candidates during the actual Confirmation rite.

The privilege of teaching Confirmation lies in the privilege of re-presenting the Christian mystery as a journey from woundedness resulting from original sin to life in the Spirit as the fruit of the Paschal Mystery. The time lapse between infant Baptism and adolescent Confirmation allows the providential opportunity for each Christian to re-encounter the mysteries of the faith in an ever-deepening and more intellectually satisfying manner. In fact, the *Catechism* states, "By its very nature infant Baptism requires a *post-Baptismal catechumenate.* Not only is there a need for instruction after Baptism, but also for the necessary flowering of Baptismal grace in personal growth" (CCC 1231).

Pope John Paul II's theology of the body offers an ideal tool for drawing together the multi-dimensional meaning of Confirmation. His theological anthropology provides the integrating principle for a post-Baptismal catechumenate based on a deepened understanding of Baptism and our free-will response to God. In this way, the seminal Christian life conferred in Baptism can be nourished and brought to bear fruit for the benefit of the Church and the world.

May we continue to pray with the universal Church for the full flowering of this apostolic and Pentecostal grace: "Come, Holy Spirit!"

Notes

[1] Nathan Mitchell, "Dissolution of the Rite of Christian Initiation," in *Made Not Born* (Notre Dame, IN: University of Notre Dame Press, 1976), 54.

[2] *Summa Theologica*, IIIa, 72, 5, cited by Leonel Mitchell in "Christian Initiation: The Reformation Period," in *Made Not Born* (Notre Dame, IN: University of Notre Dame Press, 1976), 68.

[3] Ibid., 69.

[4] Leonel Mitchell, "Christian Initiation: The Reformation Period," 85.

[5] Ibid., 85.

[6] Daniel Stevick, "Christian Initiation: Post-Reformation to the Present Era," *Made Not Born* (Notre Dame, IN: University of Notre Dame Press, 1976), 109.

[7] O. Hallesby, *Infant Baptism and Adult Conversion* (Minneapolis, MN: Augsburg Publishing House, 1924), 39.

Catechesis for Personal Vocation

RUSSELL SHAW

Let me begin by saying something I've said many times and am always happy to say again: There is no vocation shortage in the Catholic Church. As a matter of fact, a shortage of vocations is impossible. What we have instead is a shortage of vocational discernment, and although that is a serious problem, it's a problem of a very different sort. Here is the heart of the message Germain Grisez and I have attempted to communicate and explain in our book *Personal Vocation: God Calls Everyone By Name* (Our Sunday Visitor, 2003).

This message is very good news. And it is news that I've found many people are very glad to hear. If there were a shortage of vocations—which isn't possible, but let's suppose it was—then the shortage would be from God. In that case, there would be nothing to do about it except pray.

But because the shortage is a shortage of discernment, we can be sure it comes from *us*. Prayer is still needed, of course, but there are a lot of other things we can and should be doing along with praying.

The first thing is to acquire a clear understanding of the meaning of "vocation." Once people get the hang of it, they often find it genuinely exciting.

The reality of vocation is like a set of concentric circles.

At the center is the common Christian vocation. It arises from Baptism and is shared by all members of the Church. In general terms, it consists of the commitment of faith and what follows from

Russell Shaw *is the author of many books and a retired official of the Knights of Columbus and the U.S. Catholic Conference.*

it—to love and serve God above all things, to love and serve neighbor as one would love and serve oneself, and in this way to collaborate in continuing the redemptive work of Christ which is the mission of the Church.

The first concentric circle, radiating from this central point, is vocation in the sense of state in life. The clerical state that comes from Holy Orders, the consecrated life, the state of marriage, the single lay state in the world—these are all states in life. A "state" is a specification of the common vocation—it makes it more definite and concrete. It is a broad, overarching commitment to a lifestyle that sets a person on a path that will fundamentally shape his or her life through the countless choices and actions required to travel it to the end.

The outer circle—and the third meaning of vocation—is personal vocation. This is the unique combination of commitments, relationships, obligations, opportunities, strengths, and weaknesses in and through which the common Christian vocation and a state in life are concretely expressed in the life of somebody trying to know, accept, and live out God's will for him or her. It is the unique, unrepeatable role in God's redemptive plan that God intends for each one of us. "Every life is a vocation," Pope John Paul II said.[1] And indeed it is— a *personal* vocation.

Usually, when Catholics say "vocation," they mean vocation only in the second sense—state in life. And usually, in speaking of vocation in this sense, they mean only a calling to the priesthood or the religious life. For instance, when we are asked to pray for vocations, ordinarily we are being asked to pray that more people will become priests or religious; a vocations program or vocations office is a program or office that recruits and screens candidates for the seminary or novitiate; a vocations director is someone who does this kind of work.

And very important work it is. In no way do Grisez and I—and Pope John Paul II—suggest otherwise. Still, we do say "vocation" has a broader sense. And that personal vocation is a foundational part of the structure of any true vocation. And that until more people grasp the idea of personal vocation and act upon it, the present "vocations crisis"—the shortfall of new candidates for the priesthood and consecrated life—will not be solved. (To be strictly accurate, it is Grisez and I who say *that*. Pope John Paul II, as far as I know, was silent on the point.)

Not only will we not solve the vocation crisis, but we also will be inviting continued confusion about their identity and role as Christians on the part of Catholic lay people.

This is hardly a new problem. Flannery O'Connor got to the heart of it years ago. Somebody asked her why she, a Catholic, wrote about Protestants instead of her fellow Catholics. In reply, she said in part:

> To a lot of Protestants I know, monks and nuns are fanatics, none greater. And to a lot of the monks and nuns I know, my Protestant prophets are fanatics. For my part, I think the only difference between them is that if you are a Catholic and have this intensity of belief you join the convent and are heard from no more; whereas if you are a Protestant and have it, there is no convent for you to join and you go about in the world, getting into all sorts of trouble and drawing the wrath of people who don't believe anything much at all down on your head.[2]

O'Connor may not have written much about her fellow Catholics, but she was a shrewd observer of them. This is a good example. Here was the idea of vocation she found among Catholics: "If you are a Catholic and have . . . intensity of belief you join the convent." Not much encouragement there for deeply committed lay people like herself.

And of course thinking this way about vocation discourages people who don't feel immediately called to the clerical state or the consecrated life from engaging in vocational discernment to learn what God wants them to do—discernment that just might lead to the realization that the clerical state or the consecrated life is just what God has in mind for them.

So, what is vocational discernment?

After I gave a talk on personal vocation, a woman told me that until recently she'd been a tenured professor. Convinced that God wanted her to do something else with her life, she had recently quit her job. Now she was trying to decide what came next.

"I used to be the professor, the one who told the students," she said. "Now I'm waiting for somebody to tell me."

I am not suggesting that everyone who wants to do God's will needs to quit his or her job. I am not even suggesting that this particular woman did the right thing in quitting hers. I can't pretend to know whether she did or did not. I am only saying that, having taken that step—rightly or wrongly—she faced an urgent need to reorganize her life in light of the new circumstances she had brought about.

What she needed to do, of course, was engage in discernment.

Discerning our vocations is something we all need to do. Pope John Paul II calls ongoing vocational discernment "the fundamental objective of the formation of the lay faithful."[3]

It is the process of prayerfully reflecting on our strengths and weaknesses, our existing commitments and relationships and obligations—indeed, *all* the circumstances of our lives—and comparing these with the needs and the opportunities for service in the Church and in the world around us.

The question discernment seeks to answer is not "What do *I* want from life?" It's "What does *God* want from me?"

This idea of personal vocation is not so very new. There are hints of it here and there in well-established masters of the spiritual life like Saint Ignatius of Loyola, Saint Francis de Sales, Jean-Pierre de Caussade, S.J., and John Henry Newman. In one of his Anglican sermons, for instance, Newman remarks:

> For in truth we are not called once only, but many times; all through life Christ is calling us. He called us first in Baptism; but afterwards also; whether we obey or not, He graciously calls us still. . . . [W]e are all in course of calling, on and on, from one thing to another, having no resting-place, but mounting towards our eternal rest, and obeying one command only to have another put upon us. He calls us again and again, in order to justify us again and again—and again and again, and more and more, to sanctify and glorify us.[4]

Discernment is not something merely subjective.

The process is guided, and the result is measured, by the teaching and law of the Church and the decisions of legitimate authority.

It also involves consultation with trustworthy spiritual directors and level-headed friends who are willing to call to our attention things about us—good things and bad things, both—that we may not be fully aware of ourselves.

Although certain periods in a person's life are more critical than others from the standpoint of vocational decision-making, the fact is that discernment is an ongoing, daily project for a serious Christian. It is closely linked to the universal call to holiness of which the Second Vatican Council speaks,[5] since it involves trying to know and do God's will for us in regard to everything in our lives.

Father Walter Ciszek, S.J., the courageous priest who spent many years in prisons and prison camps in the Soviet Union during and after World War II, put it like this:

God has a special purpose, a special love, a special providence for all those He has created. God cares for each of us individually, watches over us, provides for us. The circumstances of each day of our lives, of every moment of every day, are provided for us by Him. . . . [This] means . . . that every moment of our life has a purpose, that every action of ours, no matter how dull or routine or trivial it may seem in itself, has a dignity and a worth beyond human understanding. No man's life is insignificant in God's sight.[6]

We find our personal vocations, and we accept or reject them, live them out or fail to do that, in "the circumstances of each day of our lives, of every moment of every day." And finding God's will, accepting it, and living it out is, of course, holiness.

Many things follow from this view of personal vocation. One is that we need to make our homes, our parishes, our schools and institutions and organizations and programs of all sorts schools of vocational discernment. That is to say, we need continuing, universal catechesis for personal vocation.

At a book-signing, a lady told me that she'd formerly been a Protestant evangelical but now was a Catholic. She was happy with her choice, she said, but she had a problem: She wanted to hand on her faith and her commitment to her children, but she didn't find the resources in the Catholic community that she'd found as a Protestant. So, what should she do?

One thing she *shouldn't* do, I replied, was to make the mistake that many people do make, and hand off the responsibility for the religious and vocational formation of her children to somebody else—the parish, the school, the CCD program, whatever it might be. This is something that parents definitely need to do—though certainly with all the help they can possibly get from other sources. Central to the formation they give their children should be catechesis in vocational discernment.

Note that the objective must be discernment, not recruitment. There should be no coercion or pressure of any sort. No one can discern a vocation for anyone else. No one should try.

But we do need to encourage a far more widespread practice of vocational discernment, in many church settings, than is now the case. Vocational discernment should become an ordinary part of our lives as Catholics. And that will require much more than an occasional "vocations" assembly in school or praying for new priestly and religious vocations in the prayers of the faithful, good and important though these things are.

In concluding, I want to return to a possible objection mentioned earlier—that by talking too much about the personal vocations of *all* members of the Church, without exception, we risk discouraging *some* members from recognizing and accepting *their* vocations to be priests and religious.

The answer is that it will work just the other way around. The more Catholics pray and reflect upon what God is calling them to, the greater will be the number who discover that God is calling them to be priests and religious, while the rest—far and away the larger number, of course—will discern their callings to other forms of participation in the mission of the Church. Personal vocation, in other words, will not make the vocations crisis worse, but will help to resolve it.

Every year, as you know, the Church celebrates a World Day of Prayer for Vocations, and every year the Holy Father issues a message to mark the occasion. The message in 2003 was especially notable.

Just as service, vocation, and redemption were central in the life of Jesus, John Paul II remarked, so also they are central in the lives of Christians. And not just "vocation" in a generic sense, but vocation in a sense that is special for each individual.

How can one not read in the story of the "servant Jesus" the story of every vocation: the story that the Creator has planned for every human being, the story that inevitably passes through the call to serve and culminates in the discovery of the new name, designed by God for each individual? In these "names," people can grasp their own identity, directing themselves to that self-fulfillment which makes them free and happy.[7]

It hardly needs saying that these "names" of which Pope John Paul II spoke so movingly are our personal vocations.

Notes

[1] Pope John Paul II, "Message for World Day of Prayer for Vocations," 2001.

[2] Flannery O'Connor, "Letter to Sister Mariella Gable," in *Flannery O'Connor: Collected Works* (New York: The Library of America), 1183.

[3] Pope John Paul II, Post-Synodal Apostolic Exhortation *Christifideles Laici* on the Vocation and the Mission of the Lay Faithful in the Church and in the World (December 30, 1988), n. 58.

[4] John Henry Newman, "Divine Calls," in *Parochial and Plain Sermons* (San Francisco: Ignatius Press, 1987), 1569-1570.

[5] See Second Vatican Council, Dogmatic Constitution on the Church *Lumen Gentium* (November 21, 1964), no. 5.

[6] Walter Ciszek, S.J., *He Leadeth Me* (Garden City, NY: Doubleday Image Books, 1975), 231.

[7] Pope John Paul II, "Message for World Day of Prayer for Vocations," 2003.

The Paternal Order of Priests: An Open Letter to the Clergy on Their Continuing Education

SCOTT HAHN

My Dear Fathers,

There is a famous homily of Saint Augustine in which he refers to the fathers in his audience as "my fellow bishops."[1] He startles his congregation, which certainly included many busy fathers of families, by telling them to be faithful to the duties of the priesthood.

"Fulfill my office in your own homes," he says. The word "bishop" means supervisor, and since "a man is called a bishop because he supervises and takes care of others, every man who heads a household also holds the office of bishop—supervising the way his people believe, and seeing that none of them fall into heresy, not his wife, or son, or daughter, or even his servant."[2]

Augustine spoke these words as the Church faced its first real wave of clericalism. Christianity had been legal for almost a century and compulsory for almost a generation. The clergy, who had once been reviled and persecuted in the empire, were now respected and even exalted. This newfound respect was welcome, of course, and it was their due as priests of Jesus Christ.

Clericalism and Its Discontents

But clerical exaltation had a downside, too. In fact, the empire so revered the clergy that the lay state seemed insignificant by contrast.

Scott Hahn is professor of biblical theology at Franciscan University of Steubenville and Saint Vincent Seminary.

Augustine's modern biographer Peter Brown spoke of the "widening gulf between an ascetic elite" (meaning the celibate clergy and monks) and "a passive rank and file"[3] (meaning the married laity). As great a churchman as Saint Jerome once quipped that he approved of marriage, but mostly because it was the breeding ground for future celibates.[4] So it's little wonder that ordinary Christians began to lose sight of the sacramentality of marriage and the sacred vocation to family life.

Imagine, then, the shock when Augustine addressed those over-worked and under-appreciated married men as "my fellow bishops." In an age of rising clericalism, such words must have seemed so exaggerated as to be scandalous.

Today, we live in a different sort of world. It's almost an inversion of Augustine's world. While he faced a budding clericalism, we're looking at a full-grown *anti*-clericalism. While his contemporaries felt free to sneer at marriage and treat it as an occasion of sin, our contemporaries miss no opportunity to sneer at celibacy and treat it as an occasion of sin.

Our world is Augustine's world turned upside-down. Yet I think we can learn much from Augustine's approach. He could speak so truly of priesthood and fatherhood because he could see a reality beyond the visible. That is the very definition of a Catholic world-view, a sacramental worldview. And so today, in the spirit of Augustine, I want to address ordained priests as "my fellow fathers."

No Small Change

One of the marvels of God's plan is that He has given fathers a priesthood and priests a fatherhood. Within the family, the father stands before God as a priest and mediator. Within the Church, the priest stands before his parish as a father. A priest's fatherhood is not merely metaphorical. It is something metaphysical. It is a supernatural participation in God's fatherhood and in Christ's high-priesthood. How did Christ exercise His high-priesthood? He became the New Adam, the father of a new human family in the Church; in doing this, He became the perfect image of the Father on earth.

As priests of the New Covenant, you are conformed to Christ in a unique and powerful way. Christian tradition speaks of ordination in the most astonishing terms. It is a commonplace of Catholic speech to say that the priest is *alter Christus*, another Christ. The *Catechism of the Catholic Church* tells us, further, that the priest acts "in the person of Christ" and, like Christ, he is a "living image of God the Father" (CCC 1548-9). Through the ministry of ordained priests, the presence of Jesus Christ "is made visible in the midst of the community of believers."

Theologians refer to the ontological change—a change in the man's very being—that occurs with the sacrament of Holy Orders. Ordination "confers an indelible spiritual character" that is permanent and "imprinted . . . for ever" (CCC 1582-3). In the words of Scripture: once ordained, "You are a priest forever" (Heb. 5:6; Ps. 110:4). And as a priest you are a father. Saint Paul considered himself to be a father. He addressed Timothy as "my son" (1 Tim. 1:18) and "my beloved child" (2 Tim. 1:2). He called Titus "my true child" (Tit. 1:4). And he speaks of himself as the father of the slave Onesimus (Philem. 10). But his most beautiful expression of paternity he addresses to the entire Church of Corinth: "I do not write this to make you ashamed, but to admonish you as my beloved children. For though you have countless guides in Christ, you do not have many fathers. For I became your father in Christ Jesus through the gospel" (1 Cor. 4:14-15). Paul became a father when he became a priest.

We know from his Letter to the Romans that Paul considered his vocation to be priestly. There, he speaks of "the grace given me by God to be a minister of Christ Jesus to the Gentiles in the priestly service of the gospel of God" (Rom. 15:15-16). And what was that grace if not the sacramental character of his priesthood? Ordained a priest forever, Paul had undergone an essential change, a sacramental change. Ever afterward, he spoke as a father because he spoke as a priest—a man who participates in the paternity of God, who is "everlasting Father" (Is. 9:6).

The great Cappadocian Father Gregory of Nyssa compared this sacramental change to the transubstantiation that occurs in the Eucharist. "The bread," he explains, "is at first common bread. But

when the sacramental action consecrates it, it is called the Body of
Christ, for it becomes the Body of Christ. . . . The same power of the
word makes the priest worthy of veneration and honor. The new
blessing separates him from common, ordinary life. Yesterday he
was one of the crowd, one of the people. Now, suddenly, he has
become a guide, a leader, a teacher of righteousness, an instructor
in hidden mysteries. And this he does without any change in body
or form. But, while he appears to be the man he was before, his
invisible soul has really been transformed to a higher condition by
some invisible power and grace."[5]

This permanent character—this communion with Christ—this
share of God's fatherhood—is not merely metaphorical. Indeed, it
would be more accurate to say that *my* fatherhood is metaphorical.
The truth is that both priests and dads are fathers; and, in different
ways, their fatherhood is a metaphysical and theological reality. It is
something sacramental, a living sign of God's presence and power.

Family Ties

If this comes as news today, it is only because so many of us have
unwittingly become religious empiricists. Since a sacramental
character is invisible, we may be tempted to think of it as less real,
less permanent, merely propositional. But, again, I say that, because
it is sacramental, it is more real, more permanent, and much more
than propositional.

This demands of us a deep faith, an act of faith sustained over a
lifetime. Saint Thomas Aquinas said: "We do not believe in formu-
las, but in those realities they express, which faith allows us to
touch. The believer's act of faith does not terminate in the propositions, but in the realities which they express" (quoted in CCC 170).
We do not put our faith in theories or abstractions, but in realities.

The New Covenant is itself a sacramental economy of the
supernatural order that is more real than the world we see around
us. The reality of your fatherhood, like the reality of my fatherhood,
should be more real to us than an oncoming tractor-trailer. Such
realities are powerful. They demand our attention. We ignore them
at our peril.

My fellow fathers: put faith in your fatherhood. Pope John Paul II wrote: "The great family which is the Church . . . finds concrete expression in the diocesan and the parish family. . . . No one is without a family in this world: the Church is a home and family for everyone" (*Familiaris Consortio* 85). As priests, you must be fathers to that "great family"—what an overwhelming task![6]

To my six children, I am a father. What that means is that I provide for them. I give them a name, a home, and food to sustain them. I teach them, guide them, and discipline them. I love them unconditionally; I forgive them for the trouble they cause. I pray for them daily. And all that is true of my fatherhood must be much more true—not less—in your life as ordained priests. Go back to Aristotle, and you'll see that philosophers have always understood paternity as the highest degree of causality, the very communication of one's own nature and life.

If this is true of natural fatherhood, it is more true of a priest's supernatural fatherhood. As a natural father, I've communicated biological human life—but by administering the sacraments of Baptism and Eucharist, you communicate *divine life*, the very *supernatural grace* of Christ's own divine sonship.

You must be father to a much larger family than mine. And your fatherhood, like mine, means far more than mere begetting. Like any father, you must take responsibility for the souls to whom you've given life—those thousands of souls in hundreds of households. You must provide for them, teach them, exhort them, discipline them, guide them, correct them, and forgive them. You are their father. Spiritually speaking, the buck stops with you. In my home, I expect my children to assume responsibilities as they grow older; but as their father, I am the one who has to assume ultimate responsibility for them and for my household.

My fellow fathers: We will be called to account for this. The thought of that makes me tremble for my fatherhood. It should make you tremble for yours. I cannot be a good father unless I make a constant effort to learn, to study. As head of a household, I have had to educate myself in many remote and obscure corners of unfamiliar academic disciplines. To take on a mortgage responsibly, I had to become something of an economist. To stand responsibly by a child's sickbed, I had to become an amateur physician. To keep it all together, day after day, I've had to read as deeply as I could in the doctors of prayer and morals.

You, too, need to immerse yourself in study. You cannot be a good father without ongoing education. If you haven't made the most of your time up till now, make an Act of Contrition and start your life over tomorrow. Roll up your sleeves, open your books, get down on your knees and pray.

Your priesthood and your fatherhood will demand a wealth of knowledge and wisdom that you may not have right now. In prayer, you'll prepare to draw on the infinite wisdom of God—and that's indispensable, but it's not everything. God gives us grace with our vocation, but He expects us to correspond to that grace in an active way, with our work and our study.

Remember the old adage: Grace does not destroy nature, but builds on it, to perfect and elevate it. Yes, you need prayer; but you also need to study. God has given you a mind. You must put it to good use, and give Him something to build on.

Heed the words of an experienced teacher and a former student: If you're not studying right, you can't be praying well. If you're praying right, you're going to study better. And if you're studying right, you're going to pray better.

So pray well. Study well. And you'll create a kind of feedback loop.

That loop, I might add, pretty much describes the life of the man to whom this volume is dedicated, Father Ronald Lawler.

Here Comes the Bride

I'd like to pass on one secret of good fatherhood before I leave you for now.

The secret is this: strive to fall more in love with your bride every day, and with the children she has given you. By now, you are grown men, and you have probably known many married couples who have "fallen out of love." You have also known workaholic or self-absorbed fathers who live lives detached from the cares of their children. There are no newlyweds, no new parents, who plan for this to happen. No couple embarks upon marriage with the hope that they can make each other miserable, and share that misery with many others.

But misery descends upon a staggering number of families today. Some of them you can tally up in divorce statistics; others stay together, though in separate and distant orbits. The analogy applies just as well to the priestly fathers who abandon their bride, the Church, and her children—and to those who stay with her, grudgingly and in misery. Falling in love is usually involuntary. Staying in love, however, demands will and work and help from almighty God. But the rewards are well worth our effort.

As the years go by, I find myself falling more in love with my wife Kimberly. We've spent a quarter-century together, and I suppose I know her faults better than anyone alive. But I've come to know that I never go wrong in trusting her. I always go wrong in distrusting her. My fellow fathers, my bride is lovely, but your bride the Church is still lovelier. My bride is trustworthy and faithful, but yours is ever more so. Gaze upon the Church supernaturally. Walk beside her, by faith and not by sight.

For your priesthood, like my fatherhood, is not a job; it's not an administrative role. It's a vocation from God. There's a big difference between a job and a vocation, and it manifests itself in countless ways. Every year I take a vacation from my job, but I never take leave of my family. In fact, when I go on vacation, my family goes with me.

Though you will often take your restful time away from parish life, you must always take your priesthood and fatherhood with you. For your family is larger than mine. Your family is everywhere. Wherever you go, you must always be a father to the great family of the Church.

True priestly fatherhood is the only sure antidote to the recurring ecclesiastical illness called clericalism. We must always remember—you and I—that we are not bosses, not managers, and not administrators. We are fathers. So what's the difference? A boss can be threatened by the achievements of his subordinates. But a father finds only fulfillment in the successes of his sons and daughters.

I often tell my kids that I'm not just raising children; I'm raising up brothers and sisters. I am a rung in the ladder that they must climb in order to reach the one true Father of us all. If your priesthood is fatherly, you will raise up sons and daughters to be your brothers and sisters in Christ. As fathers, we must not create and sustain dependency in our children. We must be dependable so that they can depend ever more on the Lord. For it is from Him that "all fatherhood in heaven and earth receives its name" (Eph. 3:15). Our fatherhood is great, but it is only an image of His, only a share He has granted us by grace.

My fellow fathers: Like Augustine before you, like Gregory of Nyssa before you, like Ronald Lawler before you, you must strive to be a realist. Be a man who knows he is a father, and knows that his fatherhood is something real, something metaphysical, something theological, something permanent.

Why Did God Make You?

The world needs your priesthood and your fatherhood, as never before.

In your heart, hear the call that is as old as the Old Covenant. For the priesthood of the New Covenant is not an innovation. It stands in continuity with the priesthood of the Jerusalem temple, the priesthood of the tabernacle in the desert, and, most importantly, the priestly fatherhood of every household in the time of the patriarchs. Priestly fatherhood and fatherly priesthood are timeless covenant structures of the family of God. Yet they are ever in need of renewal; for we do not father as we should.

In the Book of Judges, we read that, when a Levite appeared at the door of Micah, Micah pleaded, "Stay with me, and be to me a father and a priest" (Judg. 17:10). A chapter later, Micah's plea was echoed, almost verbatim, by the Danites as they invited the Levite to be priest for their entire tribe: "Come with us, and be to us a father and a priest" (Judg. 18:19). That call echoes still today, in your hometown and in distant mission lands.

A father and a priest: God made you for this.[7]

Notes

1 "Domini fratres et coepiscopi mei." Saint Augustine, Sermon 94 in *Patrologia Latina* 38. All translations used in this article are original or composite.

2 Ibid.

3 Peter Brown, *Augustine of Hippo* (Berkeley: University of California, 2000), 244-245.

4 Saint Jerome, Letter 22.20-21, to Eustochium. "I praise wedlock, I praise marriage—but it is because they produce virgins for me."

5 Gregory of Nyssa, quoted in Scott Hahn and Mike Aquilina, *Living the Mysteries* (Huntington, IN.: Our Sunday Visitor, 2003), 43-45.

6 Hear Augustine again: "The apostles were sent as fathers; to replace those apostles, sons were born to you who were constituted bishops. . . . The Church calls them fathers. . . . Such is the Catholic Church. She has given birth to sons who, through all the earth, continue the word of her first Fathers." From his *Expositions on the Psalms* 44.32, quoted in Henri de Lubac, *The Motherhood of the Church* (San Francisco: Ignatius Press, 1982), 90.

7 For a profound meditation on "The Priest as Spiritual Father," see Fr. Pablo Gadenz in *Catholic for a Reason*, vol. 1: *Scripture and the Mystery of the Family of God* (Steubenville, OH: Emmaus Road Publishing, 1998), 207 ff.

Human Dignity: The Heart of Catholic Social Teaching

JANET AND J. BRIAN BENESTAD

I t is a privilege and pleasure to be contributors to this collection of essays in honor of Father Ronald Lawler. He was a great storyteller and a man of delightful wit, a warm and encouraging colleague and a friend to all who love the Catholic Church. Father Lawler's work, as well as his remarkable insight and courage in the teaching of the faith, are held in high esteem in Catholic academic and catechetical circles.

We were asked to deal with Catholic social teaching, a subject which was very dear to Father Lawler's heart. While he did not publish in the field of Catholic social teaching *per se*, Father Lawler's life and loves go to the very heart of what the social teaching of the Church is all about.

It is in that spirit that this essay will deal, first, with a brief overview of some of the limitations of the "social justice" approach to Catholic social teaching. Second, it will show how an expanded view of the dignity of the human person might help individual Catholics to understand Catholic social teaching better. Third—and no essay in honor of Father Lawler could do any less—it will offer some reflections on the catechetical implications for what has gone before.

Janet Benestad is secretary for parish life and evangelization in the Diocese of Scranton. J. Brian Benestad is professor of theology at the University of Scranton.

The Limitations of the "Social Justice" View of Catholic Social Teaching

Despite prodigious efforts, the Catholic Church since Vatican II has had little success in making Catholic social teaching well known. There is a great deal of talk in Catholic schools and parishes about social justice. Many a Catholic college graduate can produce an impressive list of volunteer activities as part of his or her resume. Hardly a child receives Confirmation who hasn't completed a number of service hours, and most Catholic high school graduates can reflect at length on the benefit of such activities as visiting the nursing home, cleaning up the local playground, etc. Nevertheless, hardly anyone would argue that young Catholic men and women have been well formed in the principles of Catholic social teaching.

One reason is that those principles are rarely fully expounded even by Catholic bishops. Since the mid-sixties the American bishops, as a national conference, have directed most of their efforts regarding social doctrine to taking positions on public policy. In 1998, however, the bishops' conference sounded an alarm about ignorance of Catholic social teaching. Specifically, they said, "Our social heritage is unknown by many Catholics. Sadly our social doctrine is not shared or taught in a consistent and comprehensive way in too many of our schools, seminaries, religious education programs, colleges and universities."[1] As part of their proposed solutions, the bishops called for sweeping changes in the curriculum of seminaries and in Catholic schools from kindergarten through college.

In the same statement, the bishops offered a summary of the principles and themes of Catholic social teaching under the following headings:

- The sacredness of life and the dignity of the human person;
- The social character of the human person (call to family, community, and participation);
- Rights and responsibilities;
- The option for the poor and vulnerable;
- The dignity of work and the rights of workers;
- International solidarity;
- Care for creation.

The bishops also cite subsidiarity (relying on the individual, private groups, and lower level of government to accomplish tasks) and the common good as themes.

Included in the 1998 statement were two comments about Catholic social teaching that had not been in the bishops' 1990 statement.

First, they said, "Our commitment to the Catholic social mission must be rooted in and strengthened by our spiritual lives. In our relationship with God we experience the conversion of heart that is necessary to truly love one another as God has loved us."[2] Until 1998, this obvious fact, that understanding and living Catholic social teaching depends upon living the whole of the Christian faith, was hardly ever mentioned in episcopal documents. This is odd, since it cannot be emphasized enough that it is from their faith that most people begin to learn about the meaning of virtue and justice. In fact, educating peoples' minds and hearts in the truths of the faith is the first and most basic contribution that the Catholic family, school, and parish make to the common good. "We shall reach justice through evangelization," Pope John Paul II said to the Latin American Bishops early in 1979.

The second point made in the 1998 statement came under the heading "life and dignity of the human person." The text included the evils of abortion, assisted suicide, the death penalty, cloning, and proposals to "perfect" human beings by genetic engineering. These things were not mentioned under the same heading in the 1990 statement.

These two statements from the 1998 bishops' pastoral taken together send an important message regarding Catholic social doctrine that had been missing from episcopal documents. That message may be summed up in the following way: first, spiritual conversion is as necessary to effecting the Church's social mission as political action; and, second, the culture of death produced by acceptance of such evils as abortion and euthanasia poses fundamentally unacceptable threats to human dignity.

Another way of analyzing the effect of the 1998 statement is to look at the impact that pre-1998 episcopal statements had on Catholic thinking. Monsignor George Kelly, a very dear friend of Father Lawler's, does exactly that. The Church's "political role in secular society," said Monsignor Kelly, "was weakened once her hold on the conscience of her people was attenuated."[3] Two rhetorical questions in Monsignor Kelly's autobiography make the same point with added nuance: "How does one intensify Catholic social consciousness on the basis of Church teaching while exalting the sanctity of the individual conscience against Church teaching? How can the Church impose new social obligations on a people being retrained to pick and choose their way through the demands of the universal faith?"[4] In other words, the Church can hardly expect to transform society by issuing policy statements, or even encouragements to practice social doctrine, if large numbers of Catholics are no longer committed to understanding and practicing the faith as a whole.

Put yet another way, if Catholics are going to learn about Catholic social teaching, the social-justice paradigm most often used by bishops, social activists, and academics needs to be supplemented in at least two ways.

First, it must be taught in season and out of season that the knowledge and practice of the faith as a whole is the indispensable condition for the reception and practice of Catholic social doctrine. There simply is no substitute for wisdom and virtue in the citizens of a nation.

Second, a renewal of Catholic social teaching must include a thorough explanation of all the major themes of Catholic social doctrine in dialogue with the disciplines that are an essential part of a liberal education. This requires, at least, knowledge of the Bible, the Fathers of the Church (especially Augustine and Aquinas), the papal social encyclicals, documents of Vatican II, the *Catechism of the Catholic Church*, and the tradition of political philosophy.

An Expanded View of the Dignity of the Human Person

Liberalism and liberal democracy incline citizens to think about morality to a great degree in terms of rights or subjective values. This in turn leads to a fixation on choice and autonomy as ends in themselves and about the goods of the body: safety, health, pleasure, and prosperity. The liberal temper is anything but neutral in the moral tone it sets for citizens. It supposedly encourages openness to all human possibilities, but today's version of openness encourages not the pursuit of truth, but rather subservience to public opinion, a preoccupation with having things, the exercise of will divorced from the guidance of right reason or faith, and a reshaping of religion to suit the temper of the times.

Because of the emphasis on autonomy and rights, liberal regimes dispose citizens to have an incomplete understanding of human dignity. Persons are said to have dignity because they are autonomous and capable of making choices. According to the most common opinion in contemporary society, the dignity of the human person is especially secured by insuring the protection of rights. The initial and primary emphasis on rights is, of course, a logical step, since the autonomous exercise of choice requires the possession of rights.

Another consequence of understanding dignity as constituted by human autonomy is linking the assessment of human dignity to a person's quality of life, especially the capacity to make autonomous choices. It is now commonly thought that a person's dignity diminishes with his declining quality of life. Physical and mental deterioration, as well as suffering, supposedly diminishes human dignity. In *Quill* v. *Vacco* (1997) the Second Circuit Court of Appeals said the following about legal obligations toward the terminally ill: "The state's interest lessens as the potential for life diminishes."[5] The presence of this ominous statement in a decision by an Appeals Court surely indicates a trend toward regarding persons with diminished physical capacity as less than fully human. Some argue that they are not entitled to the same rights as healthy individuals.

Pope John Paul II refers to the contemporary assault on the traditional understanding of human dignity in his *Gospel of Life*:

We must also mention the mentality which tends to equate personal dignity with the capacity for verbal and explicit, or at least perceptible communication. It is clear that on the basis of these presuppositions there is no place in the world for anyone who, like the unborn or the dying, is a weak element in the social structure, or for anyone who appears completely at the mercy of others and radically dependent on them, and can only communicate through the silent language of a profound sharing of affection.[6]

This way of understanding the human person is highly individualistic and fails to appreciate the rhythm of life, in which a person moves from the weakness and dependence of the unborn, to the strength of adulthood, to the weakness of old age. Even during the time when a person is most strong, he or she is dependent in various ways for physical, intellectual, and spiritual care. In the Catholic mind, human beings retain their dignity when they are receiving care and may even grow in dignity. Think of the person who accepts his dependence and suffering as a way of identifying with the passion of Christ.

The liberal understanding of dignity is a challenge to the Catholic Church, both in the area of ordinary catechetics and Catholic social thought. Careful education is necessary for Catholics to understand that the dignity of the human person is not essentially constituted by the ability to make choices. According to Catholic teaching, people have dignity because they are created in the image and likeness of God, redeemed by Jesus Christ, and destined for eternal life in communion with God. In Pope John Paul II's words, "The dignity of the person is manifested in all its radiance when the person's origin and destiny are considered: created by God in his image and likeness as well as redeemed by the most precious blood of Christ, the person is called to be a 'child in the Son' and a living temple of the Spirit, destined for eternal life of blessed communion with God."[7]

As Vatican Council II puts it, "The principal cause of human dignity lies in the call of human beings to communion with God."[8] Being created in the image of God and redeemed by Jesus Christ makes it possible for everyone to respond to God's invitation to communion with Him. This threefold foundation for human dignity—creation, Redemption, and eternal life—is both inviolable and instructive. No act of the human person can remove this foundation. Even when people commit the worst sins and crimes, and suffer diminished physical and spiritual capacities, they retain human dignity. This teaching about the permanence of human dignity from conception to natural death is a well-known theme among informed Catholics. Less widely understood, however, is another aspect of the teaching on human dignity.

Consider once more the threefold formulation of human dignity—that everyone is created in God's image, redeemed by Jesus Christ, and destined for eternal communion with God. Consider also the reality of sin. It logically follows that all will have to strive and strain to reach their ultimate goal, communion with the triune God. All human beings are able to do this because God "willed to leave man 'in the power of his own counsel' (cf. Sir. 15:14), so that he would seek his Creator of his own accord and would fully arrive at full and blessed perfection by cleaving to God (GS 17)."[9]

Christians continually *achieve*, or realize, their dignity by seeking truth, resisting sin, practicing virtue, and repenting when they succumb to temptation. In other words, dignity is more than a quality endowed when life begins, unaffected by the way people live. For example, one person's dignity may be diminished by a life of sin, and another person's dignity may be continuously appropriated over a lifetime of virtue. This is the "radiance" to which the Holy Father refers in the quote above.

In *Rerum Novarum* Pope Leo XIII made the same point using language characteristic of Thomas Aquinas: "true dignity and excellence in men resides in moral living, that is, in virtue . . . ."[10] Saint Leo the Great's famous Christmas sermon states this point in a memorable way: "Christian, recognize your dignity, and now that you share in God's own nature, do not return by sin to your former base condition."[11] It is significant that this quotation stands as the first sentence in the section on morality in the *Catechism of the Catholic Church*. It immediately directs attention to the necessity of achieving human dignity by living without sin.

Gaudium et Spes says that "man achieves [the dignity to which he is called] when emancipating himself from all captivity to passion, he pursues his goal in a spontaneous choice of what is good, and procures for himself through effective and skillful action, apt means to that end. Since man's freedom has been damaged by sin, only by the help of God's grace can he bring such a relationship with God to full flower."[12]

Pope John Paul II argues that "genuine freedom is an outstanding manifestation of the divine image in man."[13] By "genuine freedom" the pope means freedom that takes its bearing by what is true and good, not the freedom that is indistinguishable from license. In other words, people who understand freedom as license will diminish their dignity by committing sin. Conversely, people increase their dignity by living virtuously. Pope John Paul II goes so far as to say that martyrdom is "the supreme glorification of human dignity."[14] This statement makes eminent sense because martyrs achieve the summit of human dignity by laying down their lives for God and neighbor. This is the reason why martyrs are held in such high regard by Christians.

In *Centesimus Annus* Pope John Paul II provides a perfect commentary on the importance of understanding human dignity correctly in order to understand Catholic social teaching. "The guiding principle of Pope Leo's encyclical, [*Rerum Novarum*], and of all of the Church's social doctrine, is a *correct view of the human person* and of his unique value, inasmuch as 'man . . . is the only creature on earth which God willed for itself.'"[15] On the basis of faith and reason the Church proclaims the dignity of the human person as the foundation of Catholic social teaching.

Nonetheless, there is still disagreement over the meaning of this key concept. Consider the following statements made by the U.S. Bishops in 1990 and 1998.

In a world warped by materialism and declining respect for human life, the Catholic Church proclaims that human life is sacred and that the dignity of the human person is the foundation of a moral vision for society [and] . . . the foundation of all the principles of our social teaching. . . . We believe that every person is precious, that people are more important than things, and that the measure of every institution is whether it threatens or enhances the life and dignity of the human person.[16]

Each person possesses a basic dignity that comes from God, not from any human quality or accomplishment, not from race or gender, or age, or economic status.[17]

In these statements, the bishops focus on the fact that every person possesses an inalienable and inviolable human dignity. They do this in order to protect vulnerable human beings from being declared unworthy of respect or of the law's protection because of poor quality of life. The unborn child, for example, is particularly vulnerable because people can argue that it can't make choices and therefore lacks dignity. The bishops make this point precisely because of the tendency in liberal regimes to link dignity with autonomy and the ability to make choices.

Nevertheless, the bishops' statements do not do justice to the full range of Catholic teaching on the subject. Pope Leo XIII, Vatican Council II, and the *Catechism of the Catholic Church*, as we observed above, unambiguously teach that human dignity comprises both a person's origin and destiny. In fact, the whole Catholic tradition teaches the same point. The relatively recent Vatican *Guidelines for the Study and Teaching of the Church's Social Doctrine in the Formation of the Faith* reinforce the constant teaching of the Church. They say that human advancement depends on "ennobling the human person in all the dimensions of the natural and supernatural order" and that "man's true dignity is found in a spirit liberated from evil and renewed by Christ's redeeming grace."[18]

This means that Catholic social teaching must assume both senses of the term "dignity of the human person" in order to be complete. Without teaching the twofold character of human dignity, the very keystone of Catholic social teaching is not accurately described. Without that full description, Catholic teaching is not quite up to the task of elaborating the other important themes in the discipline.

As Pope John Paul II said in *Centesimus Annus*, "From the Christian vision of the human person there necessarily follows a correct picture of society."[19] It therefore follows that an incomplete understanding of human dignity will lead to a misunderstanding of life in society.

If human dignity is something one achieves on the road to holiness, then the family, mediating institutions, and the law all have a role to play in helping individuals to acquire that dignity. For example, the education a mother and father give will help their children recognize and achieve their dignity. The law can encourage people not to act "beneath their dignity" by driving drunk or by discriminating against racial or ethnic minorities. In other words, a correct conception of the human person would enable citizens to recognize the moral principles that must be observed in order to have a good democracy.

Because of his vision of the human person, Pope John Paul II said this about the democratic way of life. "Democracy cannot be sustained without a shared commitment to certain moral truths about the human person and the human community. The basic question before a democratic society is 'How ought we to live together?' In seeking an answer to this question, can society exclude moral reasoning . . .? Every generation . . . needs to know that freedom consists not in doing what we like, but in having the right to do what we ought."[20] It is a correct view of the human person that limits and guides freedom.

Another way to approach the understanding of human dignity is to reflect on the primacy of receptivity, a theme explained in the justly famous *Introduction to Christianity* by Cardinal Ratzinger (now Pope Benedict XVI). He writes, "From the point of view of the Christian faith, man comes in the profoundest sense to himself not through what he does but through what he receives (or accepts). . . . And one cannot become *wholly* man in any other way than by being loved, by letting oneself be loved."[21] Otherwise stated, Mary's fiat is the model for the person who wants to live as a Christian: "Let it be done to me according to your word."

Persons who desire to realize their dignity must be receptive to instruction, exhortation and grace in the various communities in which they live. Especially important are the family, Church, and school. But voluntary associations and even the law play a role in creating and developing receptivity in people.

In various parts of his autobiography, Monsignor George Kelly captures the laborious struggle of the nuns in Catholic schools to educate young people to act in accord with their God-given dignity. At the very beginning of his story he tells of a meeting that he had with twenty-five of his former altar boys after addressing the New York City Police Holy Name Society. The police commissioner surprised Monsignor Kelly by bringing him into a VIP room to meet the twenty-five former altar servers who had become New York City policemen, even lieutenants and captains. "As I approached them," Kelly wrote, "the best I could muster up, as a response to their warm greeting, was: 'And to think that Sister De Padua and I expected most of you to end up in jail.'"[22] After finishing his book we understood Monsignor Kelly's humorous hyperbole as a way of capturing all the time and effort that once went into forming the character of the young in a typical New York Catholic parish.

The idea of human dignity as an arduous achievement, the result of receptivity and exhortation, is not exclusively Catholic. Consider a short story by mystery writer Agatha Christie entitled "Wasps' Nest." It seems to be about the poisoning of wasps with potassium cyanide but is really about how one man exhorts another to value life.

John Harrison discovers that he is terminally ill and devises a plan to poison himself in such a way that another man, Claude Langton, will surely be blamed for his death and hanged. The terminally ill man is overcome with a desire for revenge against Monsieur Langton who has won the heart of Harrison's former fiancée. Hercule Poirot, Christie's super sleuth, realizes what is happening and tries to make Harrison, his old friend, come to his senses and give up his plan to commit murder.

Poirot "advanced to his friend and laid a hand on his shoulder. So agitated was he that he almost shook the big man, and as he did so, he hissed into his ear: 'Rouse yourself, my friend, rouse yourself. And look—look where I am pointing. There on the bank, close by that tree root. See you, the wasps returning home, placid at the end of the day? In a little hour, there will be destruction and they know it not. There is no one to tell them. They have not, it seems, a Hercule Poirot.'"[23]

John Harrison resists the instruction and exhortation. Poirot then finds a way to substitute washing soda for the poison and confronts his friend after the failed suicide. Harrison moans when he realizes that Poirot has thwarted his suicide and saved Langton from being hanged for murder.

Harrison asks, "Why did you come? Why did you come?"

Poirot replies, of course, that he wanted to prevent a murder and then adds: "'Listen, *mon ami*, you are a dying man; you have lost the girl you loved, but there is one thing you are not: you are not a murderer. Tell me now: are you glad or sorry that I came?'

"There was a moment's pause and Harrison drew himself up. There was a *new dignity* in his face—the look of a man who had conquered his own baser self. He stretched out his hand across the table. 'Thank goodness you came,' he cried. 'Oh! Thank goodness you came.'"[24]

The story is a nice example of the transformation of one person's disordered desire by the prudent behavior and exhortation of his friend, and, of course, the preservation of his dignity. The receptivity of persons to instruction and exhortation is a most important element in the realization of their dignity. The ultimate end of a Christian community is both to educate the faithful to the love of God and neighbor with their whole heart and soul and to be a living witness to that love. If a person's dignity depends on growing in true love, then there should be no doubt that human dignity is both a quality bestowed at the beginning of life and a destiny.

Human Dignity and Rights

In order to further clarify the concept of human dignity, let us reflect on it as used in the United Nations Universal Declaration of Human Rights. Mary Ann Glendon, a professor of law and newly appointed President of the Pontifical Academy on Social Science, recently published a book on the origin and meaning of the Declaration. Glendon speaks of the intrinsic value and dignity of man as "the single most important reference point for cross-national discussions of how to order our future together on our increasingly conflict-ridden and interdependent planet."[25]

The Declaration proclaims "the dignity and worth of the human person and . . . the equal rights of men and women."[26] It also says that "recognition of the inherent dignity and of the equal and inalienable rights of all members of the human family is the foundation of freedom, justice and peace in the world."[27] In other words, there is no foundation for human rights if the dignity of the human person is not recognized.

At the end of the Preamble to the Declaration, the UN General Assembly "proclaims this Universal Declaration as a common standard of achievement for all peoples and all nations, to the end that every individual and every organ of society, keeping this Declaration constantly in mind, shall strive by teaching and education to promote respect for these rights and freedoms. . . ." The Declaration is implicitly saying that respect for rights is not a given but something to be achieved by individuals and nations. Education and teaching play an important role in generating respect for rights.

More specifically, Article One of the Declaration says that human beings "are endowed with reason and conscience and should act toward one another in a spirit of brotherhood." This means that a dignified person uses his reason and conscience and does some good for his fellow human beings in a heartfelt way. Article 29 says "that everyone has duties to the community in which alone the free and full development of his personality is possible." The Declaration doesn't give an explicit list of duties, but surely implies that all human beings have a duty to respect rights and to work for the rights of others. Articles 22-27 give a list of socio-economic and cultural rights that require strenuous, informed efforts to be undertaken by individuals, groups, and government for the benefit of others. These efforts will not be undertaken if people don't have a sense of obligation toward those in need. The willingness and ability to perform duties conscientiously and intelligently requires a person to have knowledge and good character or virtue. Education in the family, school, university, and church will, then, be crucial for inculcating the duty to respect and foster socio-economic and cultural rights.

Can we not, then, say that the recognition of dignity in others requires a sense of our own dignity as well as diligent efforts to realize it? People with ingrained vices will not be inclined to recognize the dignity of others. In other words, human beings have to achieve their own dignity by the acquisition of knowledge, and especially by the practice of virtue, before they will be ready both to recognize dignity in others and to respect their rights.

In commenting on articles 22-27, which deal with socio-economic and cultural rights, Glendon wonders whether the framers of the Declaration would have done better to speak of the duties of the public and private sector rather than the entitlements of individuals. "With hindsight," she writes, "it is perhaps regrettable that the framers, in dealing with these provisions, did not adopt the obligation model. To couch the social security and welfare principles in terms of a common responsibility might have resonated better than rights in most of world's cultures and would still have left room for experiments with different mixes of private and public approaches."[28] This kind of formulation would have made clear that people would have to prepare themselves to fulfill obligations toward others.

Otherwise stated, people may have been prompted to realize that they would have to achieve their own dignity as a preparation for recognizing the dignity of others.

Glendon knows that dignity "will remain a shaky foundation for human rights unless and until that concept can be fleshed out and made intelligible to all men and women of good will."[29] One way to do that is to ponder the foundation of human dignity and to think about dignity as an achievement of every single individual. Glendon comments, "From a Christian point of view, [it] may be that human rights are grounded in the obligation of [all men and women] to perfect their own dignity, which in turn obliges [them] to respect the 'given' spark of dignity of others whatever they may have done with it. In other words, it may be our own quest for dignity (individually and as a society) that requires us to refrain from inflicting cruel punishments on criminals, or from terminating the lives of the unborn."[30] People with a sense of their own dignity will not be inclined to trample on the rights of others, because they know that by so doing they will do harm to themselves and offend God as well.

Human Dignity and Bioethics

The Christian teaching that dignity is both a given and a high calling or a destiny can be appreciated by non-Christians and even by non-believers. Leon Kass, a Jewish physician, is Chair of the President's Council on Bioethics. Kass's thinking on human dignity, as expounded in his recent book, *Life, Liberty and the Defense of Dignity: the Challenge for Bioethics*, illustrates our point. The most common understanding of human dignity in the contemporary period, Kass rightly argues, is that inspired by Immanuel Kant. The German philosopher attempts to supply a foundation for universal human dignity by his doctrine of respect for persons. Kass explains Kant's approach: "Persons—all persons or rational beings—are deserving of respect not because of some realized excellence of achievement, but because of a universally shared participation in morality and the ability to live under the moral law."[31] This is the view that persons have dignity because they can reason and make choices.

While Kass applauds Kant's efforts and his influence in promoting the respect for persons in contemporary canons of ethics, he finally judges Kant's view of human dignity as *inhuman.*

> Precisely because it dualistically sets up the concept of "personhood" *in opposition* to nature and body, it fails to do justice to the concrete reality of our embodied lives—lives of begetting and belonging no less than willing and thinking. . . . Precisely, because "personhood" is distinct from our lives as embodied, rooted, connected, and aspiring beings, the dignity of rational choice pays no respect at all to the dignity we have through our loves and longings—central aspects of human life understood as grown togetherness of body and soul. Not all human dignity consists in reason or freedom.[32]

Under the influence of Kant, many Catholics look at human dignity simply as a quality bestowed at birth but not as "a realized excellence" of a person, for example, who avoids serious sin, loves his family, friends and neighbor, and seeks to realize communion with God. Catholics rightly look to God's creation of man in His image and likeness as the foundation of dignity, but then fail to see that living in accord with God's image is the way of realizing their dignity in everyday life. They fail to see what is obvious to Kass—that our loves and longings may increase or diminish our dignity.

Kass makes his most extensive comments on dignity in his chapter on "Death with Dignity and the Sanctity of Life." The roots of the English and Latin words for dignity are instructive, says Kass. "The central notion etymologically, both in English and in its Latin root (*dignitas*), is that of worthiness, elevation, honor, nobility, height—in excellence or virtue."[33] If dignity is understood as various kinds of excellence, then it cannot be provided, or claimed as a right. It makes as little sense to assert a right to dignity as to claim a right to wisdom or courage.

Realizing that this description may strike his readers as a denial of man's special dignity, Kass reaffirms his position that human beings have dignity because they are created in God's image and likeness, and that the sanctity of life at all stages is based on human dignity. "Yet," he adds, "on further examination this universal attribution of

dignity to human beings pays more tribute to human potentiality, to the *possibilities* for human excellence. *Full* dignity, or dignity proper-ly so-called, would depend on the *realization* of these possibilities."[34]
In what ways is dignity realized? The dignity of human beings is realized when they live a moral life, for one thing. Kass is right to say that full dignity depends on virtuous achievements. Why else would people say in ordinary speech, "That attitude or behavior is *beneath your dignity*"?

Kass further argues that "the *sanctity* of human life rests absolute-ly on the *dignity*—the God-likeness—of human beings."[35] Kass arrives at this conclusion after examining the Ten Commandments, the story of Cain and Abel, and especially the covenant with Noah subsequent to the flood. Kass observes that the first commandment on the second table, "Thou shalt not murder," does not make murder wrong simply because God says so. Echoing Saint Thomas's natural-law teaching, Kass says, "The entire second table of the Decalogue is said to pro-pound not so much divine law as natural law, law suitable for man as man, not only for Jew or Christian."[36] Cain's remark, "Am I my broth-er's keeper?" shows that he senses the wrongness of murder. Otherwise, he could have responded to God's question regarding the whereabouts of Abel with the straightforward answer, "I killed him." Kass explains, "If there was nothing wrong with murder, why hide one's responsibility? A 'proto-religious' dread accompanies the encounter with death, especially violent death."[37]

Kass finds the best evidence for his position in the story about the new order of things after the flood. God issues a prohibition enjoin-ing all mankind to refrain from murder and explains why. Genesis 9:6 reads, "Whoever sheds the blood of man, by man shall his blood be shed; for God made man in His own image." Kass comments, "The fun-damental reason that makes murder wrong—and that even justifies punishing it homicidally!—is man's divine-like status. Not the other fellow's unwillingness to be killed, not even (or only) our desire to avoid sharing his fate, but *his*—any man's—*very being* requires that we respect his life."[38] Kass goes to Genesis 1 to elucidate the meaning of God-like. It means that man speaks, reasons, contemplates, exercises freedom, makes judgments and distinguishes good from bad, and "lives a life freighted with moral self-consciousness." All these quali-ties give human beings a dignity that engenders and requires respect.

Kass believes the achievement of dignity is possible when people have the proper models to imitate and the right kind of education. He shows that this achievement is frequently noticed in the ordinary routine of life. "In truth, if we know how to look, we find evidence of human dignity all around us, in the valiant efforts ordinary people make to meet necessity, to combat adversity and disappointment, to provide for their children, to care for their parents, to help their neighbors, to serve their country."[39]

Of course, people need various virtues to make these kinds of valiant efforts, which is still another indication that we have to strive day in, day out to realize our dignity. The achievement of dignity is really the most ordinary occurrence, but not a common phrase in everyday modern speech. The absence of appropriate language keeps us from accurately perceiving all aspects of dignity.

What *does* get talked about is "death with dignity." By that term people mean both good and bad things.

The good side is the belief that people should not be dehumanized at the end of life by unnecessary or burdensome medical treatments, or subject to unnecessary institutionalization.

The chilling side of "death with dignity" is the argument that euthanasia or physician-assisted suicide will assure the dignity of a terminally ill patient whose quality of life has diminished. Kass calls euthanasia "undignified and dangerous." The assault on human dignity, he argues, comes not from the declining quality of life, but from improper treatment and care by hospital staff, relatives, and friends. "Withdrawal of contact, affection and care is probably the greatest single cause of the dehumanization of dying. Death with dignity requires absolutely that the survivors treat the human being at all times as if full God-likeness remains, up to the very end."[40] Encouragement by "many small speeches and deeds" will shore up the courage of the dying and help them to face their physical and emotional pain.[41] By bearing up in the face of suffering, the dying person maintains and increases his dignity as do his loving relatives and friends, argues Kass. There is no dignity in asking for lethal injections from relatives and friends. Placing such a burden on people is not dignified action at all.

Human Dignity, Grace, and Conversion of Heart

Kass's reflection on Kant, bioethics, and the events of daily life confirms Catholic teaching about human dignity. So does Glendon's analysis of the U.N. Declaration of Human Rights. What remains to be done, as Glendon suggests, is to flesh out and make intelligible the full meaning of human dignity through conversations in both private and public places. Otherwise, dignity will remain "a shaky foundation for human rights." Rights will be respected only when people *both* realize that it is beneath their dignity to violate them *and* acquire the virtues which enable them to live a dignified life.

Of course, this means that rights will frequently not be respected, since people will not always make the effort to live in a dignified way. Catholics, especially the hierarchy and intellectuals, could make even more of a contribution to the well-being of the United States if they are able to persuade American citizens that human dignity is not only something we possess as creatures of God but also an excellence born of our loves and longings.

The Church's teaching on human dignity is only one part of the Church's social teaching, but it is the most fundamental part. From that concept all other aspects of social doctrine flow. This paper shows how difficult it is to rightly explain the content of that teaching. It goes without saying that all other aspects of Catholic social teaching require the same explication.

For Catholic social teaching to take hold in the American Church, we also need a catechesis attuned to a complete understanding of human dignity. The *Catechism* sets the proper tone for such instruction: "It is necessary, then, to appeal to the spiritual and moral capacities of the human person and to the permanent need for his *inner conversion*, so as to obtain social changes that will really serve him."[42] Otherwise stated, conversion leading to love of God and neighbor is necessary for real social reform to take place. So that there is no misunderstanding, the *Catechism* adds: "The acknowledged priority of the conversion of heart in no way eliminates but on the contrary imposes the obligation of bringing the appropriate remedies to institutions and living conditions when they are an inducement to sin, so that they conform to the norms of justice and advance the good rather than hinder it."[43] In other words, reform of institutions and living conditions requires that people really know and love the right things. Finally, the *Catechism* links conversion, the theological virtue of charity, and social reform to grace:

> Without the help of grace, one would not know how "to discern the often narrow path between the cowardice which gives in to evil, and the violence which under the illusion of fighting evil only makes it worse" (CA 25). This is the path of charity, that is, of the love of God and neighbor. Charity is the greatest social commandment. It respects others and their rights. It requires the practice of justice, and it alone makes us capable of it. Charity inspires a life of self-giving.[44]

Put another way, the virtues and grace deserve a high place among the major themes of Catholic social teaching. It is not an accident that the *Catechism* places Catholic social teaching squarely in the context of the seventh commandment ("You shall not steal") and the tenth commandment ("You shall not covet anything that is your neighbor's"). Only those who properly understand human dignity, freedom, conscience, the theological and cardinal virtues, and the requirements to love God and neighbor as expressed in the commandments will be able to properly present the Christian response to injustice in the temporal order.

Social Justice and the Common Good

No discussion of Catholic social teaching would be complete without a reference to the concern for the common good. The term "social justice" more often than not means, even in sophisticated Catholic circles, a more equitable distribution of wealth through government intervention and/or a reconstruction of the social order through reform of institutions. Other meanings include progressive social and political opinions, volunteer work, say in a soup kitchen or helping tsunami victims, or recognition of a wide variety of rights, especially for the disadvantaged. While these descriptions are all part of social justice they fail to go to the heart of the concept. For that, one needs to go to the writings of Saint Thomas Aquinas.

Social justice in the twenty-first century means exactly what legal justice meant to Saint Thomas. He held that it is the virtue that "directs the acts of all the virtues to the common good."

Pius XI in *Divini Redemptoris* gives a Thomistic definition of social justice: "It is of the very essence of social justice to demand from each individual all that is necessary for the common good."[45]

In other words, social justice is the virtue that inclines individuals to work for the common good of each and every person or groups of persons such as the family, the neighborhood, the community, the school, the nation. In this understanding, "the duty of making oneself a neighbor to others and actively serving them becomes even more urgent when it involves the disadvantaged, in whatever areas this may be."[46]

This Catholic perspective opens up vistas of service for individuals of widely differing talents. It also implicitly raises the question about what types of knowledge and suitable dispositions are necessary for service. For example, what is really necessary to insure that Catholic high school and college students graduate with the ability to serve the common good well?

Father Lawler's friend Monsignor Kelly put it well: "The Church's social mission and her humanist aspirations or successes are irrelevant if her dogmatic claims are dubious or untrue. The human race does not need a Church to complement the state as an instrument of human betterment."[47] Furthermore, said Monsignor Kelly, "The Church will scandalize her faithful if she seems more interested in politics than in holiness or if she seeks to impose prudential judgments as moral norms or usurps the proper role of the laity in the reform of secular institutions."[48] To exhort the faithful to the simple practice of the whole faith is the most important contribution the Church can make to the common good of temporal society as well as to the salvation of the world. A laity well-informed about the principles of Catholic social teaching who live lives of moral rectitude will have much to contribute to the betterment of society.

Father Lawler was once quoted as saying, "One of the most important things in the world is homilies. They have to be good. They really have to teach the faith and how to live a Christian life."[49] What good will it do to renew the understanding of Catholic social teaching and not communicate that to the faithful? Bishops and priests who are well educated in Catholic social teaching will be able to offer helpful guidance and suggestions to the laity. Most importantly, they will be able to offer encouragement and instruction to lay Catholics whose responsibility it is to take the initiative to campaign against clear evils such as abortion, euthanasia, racism and other threats to life.

In *Guidelines for the Study and Teaching of the Church's Social Doctrine*, the Vatican Congregation for Education made clear what is necessary to implement Catholic social teaching. "The Church must have knowledge about local, national, and international situations, and about the cultural dignity of every community and people."[50] Furthermore, the Congregation argued, application of Catholic social teaching requires knowledge of philosophy, theology, and social sciences, not to mention a keen political sense and an ability to dialogue among many, and often hostile, political movements and major currents of thought.

If the need for knowledge is so great, then the labor of students at their studies is already a service and a contribution to the common good. In other words, the struggle to educate the minds and hearts of the young about faith, morality, justice, and the common good is already an act of social justice.

This little-admitted understanding of Catholic social teaching is a thought that would have piqued the curiosity of a Father Ronald Lawler. And in this great act of social justice Father Lawler was a giant. His efforts to teach the faith clearly and in the simplest of terms to Catholics and non-Catholics of all ages are a testimony to his own deep appreciation for the breadth and depth of the Church's social doctrine. "In particular, Father encouraged and challenged the laity to generously respond to the call of God. His message was very simple: 'Be great people. Love our Lord and love the Church, for there you will find joy.'"[51]

Notes

1 United States Catholic Bishops, *Sharing Catholic Social Teaching, Challenges and Directions* (Washington, D.C.: United States Catholic Conference, 1998), 3.

2 Ibid., 2.

3 Monsignor George A. Kelly, *Battle for the American Church Revisited* (San Francisco: Ignatius Press, 1995), 18.

4 Monsignor George A. Kelly, *Inside My Father's House* (New York: Doubleday, 1989), 273.

5 Quoted from F. X. Hogan and M. Rea-Luthin, "Exporting Death or Offering Compassion: Vignettes of the American Experience with Physician-assisted Suicide." in *The Dignity of the Dying Person: Proceedings of the Fifth Assembly of the Pontifical Academy for Life*, edited by J. Correa and E. Sgreccia (Vatican City: Libereia Editrice Vaticana, 2000), 378.

6 Pope John Paul II, *Evangelium Vitae* (March 25, 1995), no. 19.

7 Pope John Paul II, *Christifideles Laici* (December 30, 1988), no. 37.

8 Second Vatican Council, *Gaudium et Spes* (December 7, 1965), no. 19.

9 Pope John Paul II, *Veritatis Splendor* (August 6, 1993), no. 34.

10 Pope Leo XIII, *Rerum Novarum* (May 15, 1991), no. 37.

11 *Catechism of the Catholic Church*, no. 1691.

12 *Gaudium et Spes*, no. 17.

13 *Veritatis Splendor*, no. 34.

14 Pope John Paul II, *Dominum et Vivificantem*, (May 18th, 1968) no. 60.

15 Pope John Paul II, On the Hundredth Anniversary of Rerum Novarum *Centesimus Annus* (May 1, 1991), 11, quoting Vatican Council II, *Gaudium et Spes*, no. 24.

16 *Sharing Catholic Social Teaching, Challenges and Directions*, 4.

17 United States Catholic Conference of Bishops, *A Century of Social Teaching: A Common Heritage, A Continuing Challenge* (Washington, D.C., USCCB, 1990).

18 *Origins*, vol. 19, no. 1, 182, 174.

19 *Centesimus Annus*, no. 65.

20 Pope John Paul II, Homily in Baltimore, 1995.

21 Joseph Ratzinger, *Introduction to Christianity* (New York: The Crossroad Publishing Company, 1988), 202.

22 Kelly, *Inside My Father's House*, 18.
23 Agatha Christie, "Wasps' Nest," in *Hercule Poirot's Casebook* (New York: Dodd, Mead & Company, 1984), 814.
24 Ibid., 818, my emphasis.
25 Mary Ann Glendon, *A World Made New: Eleanor Roosevelt and the Universal Declaration of Human Rights* (New York: Random House, 2001), xvi-xvii.
26 *Universal Declaration of Human Rights*, Preamble, Clause 5.
27 *Declaration*, Preamble, Clause 1.
28 Glendon, *A World Made New*, 189.
29 Mary Ann Glendon, "The Deconstruction of Dignity: Contemporary Challenges to the Universality of Human Rights," unpublished address delivered at the University of Notre Dame, October 14, 1999, 3.
30 Ibid, 17.
31 Leon Kass, *Life, Liberty and the Defense of Dignity: the Challenge for Bioethics* (San Francisco: Encounter Books, 2002), 16.
32 Ibid., 17.
33 Ibid., 246.
34 Ibid., 247.
35 Ibid., 242.
36 Ibid., 239.
37 Ibid.
38 Ibid., 241.
39 Ibid., 248.
40 Ibid., 249.
41 Ibid., 253.
42 *Catechism of the Catholic Church*, 1888.
43 Ibid.
44 Ibid., 1889, quoting Pope John Paul II, *Centesimus annus* 25.
45 Pope Pius XI, *Divini Redemptoris* (March 19, 1937), 51.
46 *Catechism of the Catholic Church*, 1932.
47 Kelly, *Battle for the American Church Revisited*, 17.
48 Ibid., 33.
49 Molly Mulqueen, *Good Shepherds*, Catholics United for the Faith website (www.cuf.org).
50 *Origins*, Vol 19, no 1.
51 "In Memoriam: Rev. Ronald Lawler, O.F.M. Cap.," Catholics United for the Faith website (www.cuf.org).

Moral Issues, Political Candidates, and the Vocation of Public Service

ROBERT P. GEORGE

The Catholic Church proclaims the principle that every human being—without regard to race, sex, or ethnicity, and equally without regard to age, size, stage of development, or condition of dependency—is entitled to the protection of the laws. The Church teaches that human beings at every stage of development—including those at the embryonic and fetal stages—and those in every condition—including those who are mentally retarded or physically disabled, and those who are suffering from severe dementias or other memory and mind impairing afflictions—possess fundamental human rights. Above all, each of us possesses the right to life.

Now this teaching is disputed by some. There are those who deny that human embryos are human beings. They assert that an embryo is merely "potential" human life, not nascent human life. The trouble with this position is not theological but scientific. It flies in the face of the established facts of human embryology and developmental biology. A human embryo is not something distinct in kind from a human being—like a rock or potato or alligator. A human embryo is a human being at a particular, very early stage of development. An embryo, even prior to implantation, is a whole, distinct, living member of the species *Homo sapiens*. The embryonic human being requires only what any human being at any stage of development requires, namely, adequate nutrition and an environment hospitable to survival.

From the beginning, human beings possess—actually and not merely potentially—the genetic constitution and epigenetic primor-

Robert P. George is McCormick Professor of Jurisprudence and director of the James Madison Institute at Princeton University.

dia for self-directed development from the embryonic into and through the fetal, infant, child, and adolescent stages and into adulthood with its unity, determinateness, and identity intact. In this crucial respect, the embryo is quite unlike the gametes—that is, the sperm and ovum—whose union brought a new human being into existence. You and I were never sperm or ova; those were genetically and functionally parts of other human beings. But each of us was once an embryo, just as each of us was once an adolescent, and before that a child, an infant, a fetus. Of course, in the embryonic, fetal, and infant stages we were highly vulnerable and dependent creatures, but we were nevertheless complete, distinct human beings. As the leading textbooks in human embryology and developmental biology unanimously attest, we were not unintegrated "clumps of cells." The basic rights people possess simply by virtue of their humanity—including above all the right to life—we possessed even then.

Another school of thought concedes that human embryos are human beings and that the life of a human being begins at conception; however, it denies that all human beings are persons. There are, according to this school of thought, pre-personal and post-personal human beings, as well as severely retarded or damaged human beings who never will be, and never were, persons. Proponents of this view insist that human beings in the embryonic and fetal stages are not yet persons. Indeed, logically consistent and unsentimental proponents say that even human infants are not yet persons, and therefore do not possess a right to life; hence, the willingness of Peter Singer, Michael Tooley, and others to countenance infanticide as well as abortion. Permanently comatose or severely retarded or demented human beings are also denied the status of persons. So euthanasia is said to be justified for human beings in these conditions. Although some who think along these lines will allow that human individuals whom they regard as "not yet persons" deserve a certain limited respect by virtue of the purely biological fact that they are living members of the human species, they nevertheless insist that "pre-personal" humans do not possess a right to life that precludes them from being killed to benefit others or to advance the interests of society at large. Only those human beings who have achieved and retain what are regarded as the defining attributes of personhood—whether those are considered to be detectable brain function, self-awareness, or immediately exercisable capacities for characteristically human mental functioning—possess a right to life. The trouble with this position is that it makes nonsense of our political, philosophical, and, for many Americans, theological commitment to the principle that all human beings are equal in fundamental worth and dignity. It generates puzzles that simply cannot be resolved, such as the puzzle as to why this or that accidental quality which most human beings eventually acquire in the course of normal development but others do not, and which some retain and others lose, and which some have to a greater degree than others, should count as the criterion of "personhood." The superior position, surely, is that human beings possess equally an intrinsic dignity that is the moral ground of the equal right to life of all. This is a right possessed by every human being simply by virtue of his or her humanity. It does not depend on an individual's age, or size, or stage of development; nor can it be erased by an individual's physical or mental infirmity or condition of dependency. It is what makes the life of even a severely retarded child equal in fundamental worth to the life of a Nobel prize-winning scientist. It explains why we may not licitly extract transplantable organs from such a child even to save the life of a brilliant physicist who is afflicted with a life-threatening heart, liver, or kidney ailment.

In any event, the position that all human beings equally possess fundamental human rights, including the right to life, is the definitively settled teaching of the Catholic Church. It is on this basis that the Church proclaims that the taking of human life in abortion, infanticide, embryo-destructive research, euthanasia, and terrorism are always and everywhere gravely wrong.

And there is more. For the Church also teaches that it is the solemn obligation of legislators and other public officials to honor and protect the rights of all. The principle of equality demands as a matter of strict justice that protection against lethal violence be extended by every political community to all who are within its jurisdiction. Those to whom the care of the community is entrusted— above all those who participate in making the community's laws—

have primary responsibility for ensuring that the right to life is embodied in the laws and effectively protected in practice. Notice, by the way, that the obligation of the public official is not to "enforce the teaching of the Catholic Church"; it is, rather, to fulfill the demands of justice in light of the principle of the inherent and equal dignity of every member of the human family.

Yet today many Catholic politicians are staunch supporters of the "right to abortion." Many now support the creation and government funding of an industry that would produce tens of thousands of human embryos by cloning for use in biomedical research in which these embryonic human beings would be destroyed. And it is not just Democrats. Although the Republican Party is officially pro-life, more than a few important Republican figures support legal abortion and publicly funded embryo-destructive research. It is probably safe to say that the most prominent of these figures happen to be Catholics.

Catholic politicians of both parties who support legal abortion and its public funding typically claim to be "personally opposed" to abortion but respectful of the rights of others who disagree to act on their own judgments of conscience without legal interference. Former New York Governor Mario Cuomo famously articulated and defended this view in a speech at the University of Notre Dame in 1984. A couple of years ago, Cuomo revisited the issue, speaking in Washington at a Pew Forum on Politics and Faith in America. He offered an argument which, if successful, not only justifies Catholic politicians in supporting legal abortion and embryo-destructive research, but requires them to respect a right of people to engage in these practices despite their admitted moral wrongfulness.

Cuomo asserted that holders of public office—including Catholic office-holders—have a responsibility "to create conditions under which all citizens are reasonably free to act according to their own religious beliefs, even when those acts conflict with Roman Catholic dogma regarding divorce, birth control, abortion, stem cell research, and even the existence of God." According to Cuomo, Catholics should support legalized abortion and embryo-destructive research, as he himself does, because in guaranteeing these rights to others, they guarantee their own right "to reject abortions, and to refuse to

participate in or contribute to removing stem cells from embryos."
But Cuomo's idea that the right "to reject" abortion and embryo-
destructive experimentation entails a right of others, as a matter of
religious liberty, to engage in these practices is simply fallacious.
The fallacy comes into focus immediately if one considers whether
the right of a Catholic (or Baptist, or Jew, or member of any other
faith) to reject infanticide, slavery, and the exploitation of labor
entails a right of others who happen not to share these "religious"
convictions to kill, enslave, and exploit.

By the expedient of classifying pro-life convictions about abortion and embryo-destructive experimentation as "Roman Catholic
dogmas," Cuomo smuggles into the premises of his argument the
controversial conclusion he is trying to prove. If pro-life principles
were indeed merely dogmatic teachings—such as the teaching that
Jesus of Nazareth is the only begotten Son of God—then according
to the Church herself (not to mention American constitutional law)
they could not legitimately be enforced by the coercive power of the
State. The trouble for Cuomo is that pro-life principles are not mere
matters of "dogma," nor are they understood as such by the Catholic
Church, whose beliefs Cuomo claims to affirm, or by pro-life citizens, whether they happen to be Catholics, Protestants, Jews,
Muslims, Hindus, Buddhists, agnostics, or atheists. Rather, pro-life
citizens understand these principles and propose them to their fellow citizens as fundamental norms of justice and human rights
that can be understood and affirmed even apart from claims of
revelation and religious authority.

If Cuomo would like to persuade us to adopt his view that people have a right to destroy nascent human life by abortion or in
embryo-destructive research despite the wrongfulness of these practices, it is incumbent upon him to provide a rational argument in
defense of his position. It will not do to suggest, as Cuomo seems to
suggest, that the sheer fact that the Catholic Church (or some other
religious body) has a teaching against these practices, and that some
or even many people reject this teaching, means that laws prohibit-
ing the killing of human beings in the embryonic and fetal stages
violate the right to freedom of religion of those who do not accept
the teaching. If that were anything other than a fallacy, then laws

against killing infants, owning slaves, exploiting workers, and many other grave forms of injustice really would be violations of religious freedom. Surely Cuomo would not wish to endorse that conclusion. Yet he provides no reason to distinguish those acts and practices putatively falling within the category of religious freedom from those falling outside it. So we must ask: If abortion is immunized against legal restriction on the ground that it is a matter of religious belief, how can it be that slavery is not similarly immunized? If today abortion cannot be prohibited without violating the right to religious freedom of people whose religions do not object to abortion, how can Cuomo say that the Thirteenth Amendment's prohibition of slavery did not violate the right to religious freedom of those in the nineteenth century whose religions did not condemn slaveholding?

Cuomo cannot respond to this challenge by asserting that, religious teachings aside, slaveholding really is an unjust practice and abortion is not. Cuomo takes pains to assure us that he believes what the Catholic Church teaches about abortion: that is to say, that it is nothing less than the unjust taking of innocent human life. Nor, I hope, would Cuomo wish to retreat to the position that those nineteenth century politicians who recognized the profound injustice of slavery should have supported a "right" to own slaves, on the "prudential" ground that no social consensus existed at the time on the question of slaveholding. Surely this is not what Cuomo means in mentioning "an American Catholic tradition of political realism" in connection with the slavery question "in the late nineteenth century." Cuomo says that the Catholic Church "understands that our public morality depends on a consensus view of right and wrong," but it would be scandalous to argue that Catholics should have opposed a constitutional amendment abolishing slavery in the nineteenth century, or legislation protecting the civil rights of the oppressed descendants of slaves in the mid-twentieth century, on the ground that "prudence" or "realism" requires respect for "moral pluralism" where there is no "consensus" on questions of right and wrong.

At one point at the forum on Politics and Faith, Cuomo suggested that laws against abortion and embryo-destructive research would force people who do not object to such things to practice the religion of people who do. But this is another fallacy. No one imagines that the constitutional prohibition of slavery forced those who believed in slaveholding to practice the religion of those who did not. Would Cuomo have us suppose that laws protecting workers against what he, in line with the solemn teaching of every pope since Leo XIII, considers to be exploitation and abuse have the effect of forcing non-Catholic factory owners to practice Catholicism?

At another point, in denying that there was any inconsistency between his willingness as governor to act on his anti-death penalty views but not on his antiabortion views, Cuomo denied ever having spoken against the death penalty as "a moral issue." He claimed, in fact, that he "seldom talk[s] in terms of moral issues" and that, when he speaks of the death penalty, he never suggests that he considers it a moral issue. Then, in the very next sentence, he condemned the death penalty in the most explicitly, indeed flamboyantly, moralistic terms: "I am against the death penalty because I think it is bad and unfair. It is debasing. It is degenerate. It kills innocent people." He did not pause to consider that these are precisely the claims made by pro-life citizens against the policy of legal abortion and its public funding—a policy that Cuomo defends in the name of religious liberty.

After more than two decades of bobbing and weaving on the subject of prenatal homicide, it is time for Mario Cuomo and those who follow his lead to face up to the fact that people who oppose abortion and embryo-destructive research oppose these practices for the same reason they oppose postnatal homicide. Catholics and other pro-life citizens oppose these practices because they involve the deliberate killing of innocent human beings. Their ground for supporting the legal prohibition of abortion and embryo-destructive research is the same ground on which they support the legal prohibition of infanticide, for example, or the principle of noncombatant immunity even in justified wars. They subscribe to the proposition that all human beings are equal in worth and dignity and cannot be denied the right to protection against killing on the basis of age, size, stage of development, or condition of dependency.

If Cuomo is indeed the faithful Catholic he claims to be, then he too believes this. But if he does believe it, then he has no rational warrant for denying that the unborn, like the newly born, are entitled to the equal protection of the laws—above all, the laws against homicide. His claim that one can be "personally opposed" to abortion yet support its legal permission, and even its public funding, collapses. But things are worse for Cuomo, for by supporting the right to abortion and embryo-destructive research he is implicating himself in the injustice of these practices.

As governor of New York and as an influential figure in national Democratic Party politics, Cuomo has actively defended legal abortion and its public funding. From his own perspective, he was protecting not abortion as such but, rather, a woman's right to choose an abortion. The resulting abortions, he no doubt told himself, were in no way his responsibility. If they were wrong, unjust, even homicidal (as the Catholic Church teaches, and as Cuomo presumably believes—after all, why otherwise would he profess to be opposed to abortion and to believe what the Church teaches about its wrongfulness?), they were not burdens on his conscience. While defending others' right to choose what he himself "personally opposed," he did not encourage them to exercise that right. Indeed, Cuomo might contend that he actually reduced the number of abortions by advancing social and economic policies that helped women to avoid unwanted pregnancy and enabled women who did become pregnant to afford to carry their babies to term. In any event, I assume that Cuomo's sincere hope was that fewer, rather than more, women would choose abortion, despite his belief that the choice was their right.

Of course, it is possible for a person wielding public power to use that power to establish or preserve a legal right to abortion while at the same time *hoping* that no one will exercise the right. But this does not get Cuomo off the hook. For someone who acts to protect legal abortion necessarily *wills* that abortion's unborn victims be denied the elementary legal protections against deliberate homicide that one favors for oneself and those whom one considers to be worthy of the law's protection. Thus one violates the most basic precept of normative social and political theory, the Golden Rule. One divides humanity into two classes: those whom one is willing to admit to the community of the commonly protected and those whom one wills to be excluded from it. By exposing members of the disfavored class to lethal violence, one deeply implicates oneself in the injustice of killing them—even if one sincerely hopes that no woman will act on her right to choose abortion. The goodness of what one *hopes* for does not redeem the evil—the grave injustice—of what one *wills*. To suppose otherwise is to commit yet another fallacy.

If my analysis so far is correct, the question arises: What should the leaders of the Church do about people like Cuomo and his successor as New York's Governor, Republican George Pataki, who evidently takes the same position? What should they do about those who claim to be in full communion with the Church yet promote gravely unjust and scandalous policies that expose the unborn to the violence and injustice of abortion?

Saint Louis Archbishop Raymond Burke offers an answer. He has declared that public officials who support abortion and other unjust attacks against innocent human life may not be admitted to Holy Communion, the preeminent sacrament of unity.

Pro-life citizens of every religious persuasion applauded the archbishop's stand. Many commented that it is long past time for religious leaders to show that they are serious about their commitment to the sanctity of human life. Critics, however, were quick to condemn Archbishop Burke. They denounced him for "crossing the line" separating church and state. Indeed, one pro-abortion partisan went so far as to brand the mild-mannered Archbishop a "fanatic."

The "crossing the line" charge is silly. In acting on his authority as a bishop to discipline members of his flock who commit what the Church teaches are grave injustices against innocent human beings, Archbishop Burke is exercising his own constitutional right to the free exercise of religion; he is not depriving others of their rights. No one is compelled by law to accept his authority. But Archbishop Burke—and anyone else in the United States of America—has every right to exercise spiritual authority over anyone who chooses to accept it. There is a name for people who do accept the authority of Catholic bishops. They are called "Catholics." (And, again, please notice that Archbishop Burke is denying Communion to supporters of abortion *not* because "they are in violation of church teaching," but because they are committing grave injustices against innocent human beings. The norm to which they are being held as Catholics is not a norm properly stated as "do what the Church says"; rather it is the norm demanding respect for the inherent and equal dignity of all.)

By demanding that Catholic legislators honor the rights of all whose lives their laws touch, the unborn not excluded, Archbishop Burke may stimulate second thoughts in them about implicating themselves in the injustice of abortion. (Surely he hopes to do that.) But not even his harshest critics charge that the Archbishop said or implied that the law of the state should be used to compel anyone to accept his authority. Catholic legislators remain legally free to vote as they please. Archbishop Burke, in turn, enjoys the legal right to exercise his spiritual authority as a bishop to order them to refrain from receiving Communion so long as they persist in what the Church teaches are acts of profound injustice against their fellow human beings. Freedom is a two-way street.

In many cases, the charge that Archbishop Burke and other bishops who adopt the policy of excluding pro-abortion politicians from Communion "are crossing the line separating church and state" is also hypocritical. A good example of this hypocrisy comes from the *Bergen Record*, a prominent newspaper in my home state of New Jersey. John Smith, the Bishop of Trenton, did not go as far as Raymond Burke had gone in forbidding pro-abortion Catholic politicians from receiving Communion. Bishop Smith did, however, in the words of the *Bergen Record*, "publicly lash" Governor James McGreevey, a pro-abortion Catholic, for his support of abortion and embryo-destructive research. For criticizing the governor on these grounds, the *Record* lashed the bishop in an editorial. The paper accused him of jeopardizing the delicate "balance" of our constitutional structure, contrasting Bishop Smith's position unfavorably with President John F. Kennedy's assurance to a group of Protestant ministers in Houston in 1960 that he, as a Catholic, would not govern the nation by appeal to his Catholic religious beliefs. Since the *Record* had seen fit to take us back to 1960 for guidance, I thought I would invite its editors to consider a case that had arisen only a few years earlier than that. In a letter to the editor, I proposed a question that would enable readers to determine immediately whether the editors of the *Bergen Record* were persons of strict principle or mere hypocrites.

I reminded readers that in the 1950s, in the midst of the political conflict over segregation, Archbishop Joseph Rummel of New Orleans publicly informed Catholics that support for racial segregation was incompatible with Catholic teaching on the inherent dignity and equal rights of all human beings. Rummel said that "racial segregation is morally wrong and sinful because it is a denial of the unity and solidarity of the human race as conceived by God in the creation of Adam and Eve." He warned Catholic public officials that support for segregation placed their souls in peril. Indeed, Rummel took the step of publicly excommunicating Leander Perez, one of the most powerful political bosses in Louisiana, and two others who promoted legislation designed to impede desegregation of diocesan schools. So I asked the editors of the *Bergen Record*: Was Archbishop Rummel wrong? Or do Catholic bishops "cross the line" and jeopardize the delicate constitutional balance, only when their rebukes to politicians contradict the views of the editors of the *Record*? To their credit, the editors published my letter. I am still waiting for an answer to my question.

Now back to Archbishop Burke. What about the allegation that his exclusion of pro-abortion Catholic politicians from Communion makes him a fanatic?

The archbishop said that he acted for two reasons. One was to warn Catholic legislators that their unjust acts were spiritually harmful to *them*—"grave sins." The other was to prevent "scandal": that is, weakening the faith and moral resolution of *others* by one's bad example. Having made every effort to persuade pro-abortion Catholic legislators to fulfill their obligations in justice to the unborn, Archbishop Burke articulated the obvious: any Catholic who exercises political power to expose a disfavored class of human beings to unjust killing sets himself against the very faith he claims to share. The Church cannot permit such a person to pretend to a sharing in the faith he publicly defies. By receiving Communion— the sacrament of unity—Catholics who support embryo-killing by abortion or in biomedical research are pretending exactly that. The archbishop has called a halt to the pretense.

To see that this is true, all one need do is imagine that the disfavored class is not the unborn, but some other category of individuals. Would Burke's critics condemn a bishop who excluded from Communion politicians who favored removing all legal protection from persons of Hungarian extraction, or who proposed to fund deadly research on Hungarians with taxpayer dollars? To this, the only possible answer is: Well, there is a difference. Hungarians are persons with a right to life; human beings prior to birth are not. But that is not an answer that any faithful Catholic can give. Catholics, like others who believe that human dignity is intrinsic and is fully shared by every member of the human family, reject the idea that the unborn or newly born or retarded or demented or frail elderly, or any other class of human beings, are anything other than persons with human rights. To believe that some human beings are human non-persons is to reject a core teaching of Catholicism. It is quite literally to break communion with the Church. For someone who has broken communion by denying the inherent and equal dignity of all to present himself at the Communion table is, as Archbishop Rummel saw in the 1950s and as Archbishop Burke sees today, to make of Holy Communion a sham. And it is truly to bring scandal to the larger Catholic community.

Scandal is not a peculiarly Catholic or even religious concern. Business executives who wink at accounting shenanigans or racist humor permit a corrupt or racist corporate culture to flourish. We have all heard of cases where male employees' sexual bantering was tolerated, despite a firm's pretence of wholesomeness and sexual equality. Actions speak louder than words. Where leaders do not act to uphold stated principles, everyone concludes that the principles are nothing more than cynical propaganda. No one need take them too seriously.

Scandal occurs in religious communities in the same way, and has the same effect. When some bishops did nothing about priests who abused children, those who knew the facts had to wonder: Do church authorities not *really* mean it when they say these acts are wicked? Are such acts *really* so gravely wrong, if nothing happens to those known to perform them? If they are wrong, wouldn't the bishops act decisively against those who commit them?

The same concern underlies the discussion of what Church leaders did and failed to do during the Holocaust. No serious person suggests that the German bishops or Vatican officials actively supported the Nazis' murderous policies. The suggestion, rather, is that by their (alleged) failure to denounce those policies and to excommunicate those Nazi leaders who had Catholic backgrounds, Church officials signaled that Catholics could legitimately support Nazi policies without peril to their souls or to their standing in the Church. Critics of those Church leaders suppose precisely what Archbishops Rummel and Burke suppose: If the Church is to be in solidarity with victims of injustice, bishops *must* not permit those Catholics who commit or abet the injustices to pretend to be Catholics fully in communion with the Church.

What Archbishop Burke's critics have failed to see is that he is not acting as a lobbyist or political partisan. He knows perfectly well that his actions might, in fact, redound to the political advantage of the legislators to whom his order is directed. They might successfully generate a backlash by claiming to stand up against the intrusion of religious leaders into politics. Burke's aim is not to win specific legislative battles about abortion (however much he would agree that these battles should be fought and won); his purpose, rather, is to defend the integrity of Catholic teaching on human equality and the sanctity of human life, and to confirm in the minds and hearts of the Catholic faithful their solemn moral obligation to oppose the killing of the innocent.

Yet some good and sincere people have expressed concern that Archbishop Burke and bishops of similar mind are guilty of a double standard when it comes to demanding of politicians' fidelity to Catholic teaching on morality and the common good. They point out that the bishops who would deny Communion to those who publicly support abortion and embryo-destructive research do not take the same stand against politicians who support the death penalty, which Pope John Paul II condemned in all but the rarest of circumstances, and the war in Iraq, which the same pope and many other Vatican officials opposed.

Pope John Paul II indeed taught that the death penalty should not be used, except in circumstances so rare these days as to be, in his words, "practically non-existent." His teaching has been incorporated into the *Catechism of the Catholic Church*, and represents, according to Pope Benedict XVI, a development of Catholic doctrine on the subject. However, two points must be borne in mind in considering the obligations of Catholics and the question whether Catholic politicians who support the death penalty have in fact broken faith and communion with the Church. First, neither Pope John Paul II nor the *Catechism* places the death penalty on a par with abortion and other forms of direct killing of the innocent. (Indeed, the Church will probably never equate the death penalty with these forms of homicide, even if it eventually issues a definitive condemnation of the practice, as I personally believe it someday will.) Second, the status of the teaching differs from the status of the teaching on abortion. As *Evangelium Vitae* makes clear, the teaching on abortion (as well as on euthanasia and all forms of direct killing of the innocent) is infallibly proposed by the ordinary and universal magisterium of the Church pursuant to the criteria of *Lumen Gentium* 25. The same is plainly not true of the developing teaching on the death penalty. Moreover, Cardinal Avery Dulles and others have interpreted the teaching against the death penalty as essentially a prudential judgment about its advisability, not a moral prohibition following from the application of a strict principle. As it happens, I don't agree with their analysis, but no one will be able to say with confidence from a Catholic point of view which side in this debate is right until the *magisterium* clarifies the teaching. So, despite my belief that the Church is moving in the direction of a definitive condemnation of the death penalty, it cannot be said that supporters of the death penalty are "obstinately persisting in manifest grave sin," and may or should be denied Holy Communion pursuant to Canon 915 of the *Code of Canon Law*. No one can legitimately claim for opposition to the death penalty the status of a definitively settled moral teaching of the Church. (Nor can one claim that the Church teaches or will ever teach that the death penalty—except in cases where it is *applied* unjustly—involves the grave intrinsic injustice attaching to any act involving the direct killing of the innocent.)

Regarding the question of the war in Iraq, it is important to understand the precise terms of Catholic teaching on just and unjust warfare. These terms are set forth with admirable clarity in the *Catechism*. In line with the Church's historic teaching on the subject, Pope John Paul II did not claim, and would not claim, that his opposition to the war was binding on the consciences of Catholics. His statements opposing the use of force in the run up to both the first Gulf War and the second war plainly questioned the *prudential judgments* of political leaders who, in the end, had and have the right and responsibility (according to the *Catechism* and the entire tradition of Catholic teaching on war and peace) to make judgments as to whether force is in fact necessary. That is why the Pope and the bishops have not said, and will not say, that Catholic soldiers may not participate in the war. This contrasts with their clear teaching that Catholics may not participate in abortions or other forms of embryo-killing or support the use of taxpayer monies for activities involving the deliberate killing of innocent human beings. (By the same token, Catholics may not participate in terrorism, even to advance causes that are in themselves just or even noble. Nor may Catholics participate in direct attacks on non-combatants, even in just wars.)

I wish to close with a word to liberals who have expressed anger, even outrage, at those bishops, such as Archbishop Burke, who teach that Catholics must never implicate themselves in unjust killing by supporting legal abortion and embryo-destructive research. Many liberals these days insist that "separation of church and state" means that *no* religious leader may presume to tell public officials what their positions may and may not be on matters of public policy. But if we shift the focus from abortion to, say, genocide, slavery, or segregation we see how implausible such a view is. When Archbishop Rummel excommunicated the segregationist politicians in the 1950s, liberals rightly applauded. They were right then; they are wrong now.

The Choice to Homeschool

GERARD V. BRADLEY

In less than fifteen years homeschooling has entered the mainstream of Catholic life in America. Before 1990 homeschooling was almost exclusively a feature of the Protestant fringe; now it is unremarkable to hear faithful Catholic parents say that they educate their children at home. In 1990 no bishop (to my knowledge) had explicitly condoned homeschooling. Many have done so since then, and their statements range from acceptance to what sounds like praise. It is almost inconceivable that an American bishop would now question, in principle, the choice of Catholic parents to homeschool even where a Catholic school is available.

Some say that the choice should, in principle, be questioned. One reason why has been offered by Father Peter Stravinskas in *The Catholic Answer*: parents have an "eminently clear" duty to patronize Catholic schools. He cites *Gravissimum Educationis* (GE), Vatican II's Declaration on Christian Education, which says (in section 8) that parents have a "duty of entrusting their children to Catholic schools wherever and whenever it is possible." Father Stravinskas said that this means that "Catholic schools are to be used by Catholic parents whenever and wherever such schools are available."

Father Clarence Hettinger, in a subsequent piece in *The Catholic Answer*, advanced two more reasons for the illegitimacy of homeschooling. He asserted, first, that the relevant provision of Canon Law—Canon 798—does *not* "authorize" parents to make a judgment "on the suitability of a school to . . . provide a fully Catholic education." "The Church presumes that [a Catholic school]

Gerard V. Bradley *is a professor of constitutional law at Notre Dame Law School.*

presents orthodox Catholic teaching." Father Hettinger evidently means that parents should presume it, too.

Just in case the presumption is defeated, Father Hettinger asserts that the parents' duty remains intact. "If one thinks that the school is not orthodox," he said, "the remedy is not to remove the children from school. It's your school, fight for it."

The full reply which these arguments deserve is beyond the limits of this paper, which is aimed at helping parents to think through the decision to homeschool. Though the net effect of this clarification is to caution against homeschooling past the first few grades, the paper supposes that the objections just described miss the mark, and that homeschooling *is* a legitimate option for Catholic parents.

Well, not quite "supposes." Here I take up and rebut the three points raised in the *Catholic Answer* exchange, as they are described above: GE 8, parental incompetence to judge Catholicity, and the "duty to stay and fight." My response to these points constitutes Part II of this paper.

In Part III I look at some considerations affecting the decision to homeschool. The force of these considerations partly depends upon emphasizing two of the main purposes or ends of education, which emphasis I provide mostly in Part IV. The first of these two ends is the culturally specific point of Christian education, that its purposes prominently include preparing youngsters to contribute productively to the society in which they live—here, the USA of the twenty-first century. In this case, to "contribute productively" means to bring Gospel values to bear upon our secularized culture, to evangelize it. The second end is discernment of personal vocation, the life of good works envisioned by God in which the Christian assists Jesus in building up His Kingdom. These two ends, I shall argue, are *generally* better served by going to school, at least after the first few grades.

The results of my analysis are paradoxical. Though I mean to paint no idealized portrait of Catholic schools, the argument generally in favor of sending older children to school depends upon characteristic features of Catholic schools which many may fail to exhibit. The argument depends, in other words, upon criteria by which one might judge available Catholic schools to be inferior to what parents can offer at home. Though these considerations may therefore lead some parents to homeschool, I think that they should, in the first instance, be reasons for conscientious parents to strive to improve the schools their children attend, or to found new ones.

Part I

No one denies that sometimes parents justifiably determine that this or that child is ill-served by a particular Catholic school, or that a certain child (one with a grave learning disability, for example) really must attend public school because of the resources uniquely available there. No one denies that in locales with no Catholic schools, parents may legitimately choose to homeschool rather than take their chances with what the state has on offer. Thus the question we are asking is whether homeschooling is *generally* legitimate; that is, whether parents may homeschool children when those kids do not have special needs or unusual characteristics, and where a Catholic school is available.

I also put aside the question of how *much* education parents are required to provide to their children. There is no categorical answer. Our Lord received systematic instruction from His parents in a trade and sufficient otherwise to become a practicing adult Jewish man. More than that we cannot say He received; more than that his parents probably were neither required nor able to provide. In most times and places in human history such a rudimentary education as Jesus received would be enough, too.

But not now. Not now because for American children their vocational responsibilities—the need to work for a living in a complex service economy, and to be able to provide for the education of *their* children someday—require much more than basic literacy. So do the responsibilities of American citizenship. How much more those responsibilities require depends upon a range of factors, many of them unique to the child, his or her vocation, and the child's family. These matters will often be the most difficult for parents (and children) to sort through. In the following discussion, however, I assume that parents have already decided to provide *in some way* an education similar (in ambition and aim) to that obtained by one who graduates from a decent high school. The question is, in which way: at home or at school?

I assume in this paper that homeschooling does not put seriously at risk a child's opportunity to participate as an adult in the cultural and economic life of society. I take it for granted that a child's opportunities to go to college (if the child is otherwise able and inclined), to function in the contemporary job market, and to perform basic civic functions (jury service and the like) are *not* put at risk by his or her parents' choice to homeschool. I assume that we are not talking about Catholic parents who want to go primitive.

I leave aside, too, higher education—college and beyond. No one supposes that college education can be provided at home. Everyone understands that even the most accomplished autodidact or home-schooler has to have a diploma if he or she wants to be considered a college graduate. There are no equivalency exams for college.

Finally, I follow the definition of "homeschooling" provided by Joshua Kibler in his fine (though yet unpublished) paper on the choice to homeschool. According to Kibler, homeschooling "primarily consists in a one-to-one parent-tutorial or parent-directed educational environment that is based in the home." Field trips and a limited exposure to classes with other children and with tutors outside the family are consistent with this definition. But the more that education moves away from the home and parents only, the more it tends to blend into an informal *school* setting.

Part II

Is there a duty to send one's children to Catholic school? As we already mentioned, there are several arguments that there is such a duty.

A. Gravissimum Educationis 8

Gravissimum Educationis 8 "reminds" parents of their "duty" to send children to Catholic schools wherever "possible." The "duty" is not explained nor is "possible" elaborated. I do not deny that the strict reading of "possible" offered by Father Stravinskas is, well, possible. The language *bears* the interpretation "where not impossible," or "unless special circumstances obtain; there is no general exemption from this duty." But the language bears other, less rigorous, interpretations, such as: "where the parents judge that their obligation to educate their children *may* be discharged" by sending their children to Catholic school.

My judgment is that GE 8 should be interpreted less rigorously. The reason why I think so arises from the axiom of sound interpretation which prefers that reading that makes coherent sense of *all* the relevant texts. The fact is, parents are told unequivocally and repeatedly by authoritative Church teachings that *they* are responsible before God for educating their children. This grave responsibility *entails* the liberty to make the choices which the parents deem necessary to perform their duty. This is clear from GE 6:

> Parents, who have a primary and inalienable duty and right in regard to the education of their children, should enjoy the fullest liberty in their choice of school.

If this parental liberty is to be strictly specified as a duty to attend Catholic schools, the specification would have to be argued for, or at least imposed by authority in clear terms. But it has not been: the proffered strict reading is said to be the "clear" meaning of an authoritative norm.

Is the meaning plain? Does GE 8 *clearly* state that Catholic parents must send their children to an available Catholic school? No. GE 8 is at least ambiguous, and it may be vague. Looking solely at its terse language does not allow us to confidently prefer one reading—either the more or less rigorous, as they are indicated above. Given that the overwhelming evidence is in favor of parental liberty (corresponding to their duty) as the default reading, context would have to supply powerful evidence indeed for that in favor of the more rigorous interpretation. But the context instead supports parental liberty.

Let me explain.

The terseness of GE may owe to its being only a "reminder": the Council Fathers evidently understood themselves as referring to a preexisting obligation, either a natural moral obligation (further understood to have been authoritatively articulated previously), or a more specific positive duty previously declared by competent authority.

I take up these two possibilities in turn.

1. *Natural Duty*

The only natural moral duty in the vicinity is that repeated often in GE (and elsewhere in authoritative Church texts): *parents*—not the Church and surely not the state—are inalienably responsible for the Christian education of their children. The primordial and finally controlling moral obligation is, again, plainly parental. Mothers and fathers will be judged by God according to how they provide for their children's Catholic formation. *This* is what mother and father vow to do at the child's Baptism. *This* the relevant Church documents derive from the marital act itself:

> Since parents have given children their life, they are bound by the most serious obligation to educate their offspring and therefore must be recognized as the primary and principal educators (GE 3).

> *Parents* are *the first and most important educators* of their own children, and they also possess a *fundamental competence* in this area: they are *educators because they are parents.* (John Paul II, *Letter to Families*, 16, emphasis in the original).

The most natural reading of GE 8 *in light of these texts* would seem to place the Church (i.e., its schools) in a subsidiary role to help parents fulfill their sacred obligation to educate their children. The most natural reading would be that parents have a right, corresponding to the aforementioned duty, to *choose* which persons and institutions shall assist them in educating their children. Parents who choose Catholic schools, parents who choose to homeschool, parents who choose public school—*all* would be responsible before God for the reasonableness of their choices, for the diligence with which they considered the question, and for the criteria which they relied upon in deciding. And, though the reasonableness of parents' choices could be objectively gauged (and "objectively" could include the special and unique circumstances of children and families), there would be no *duty* to send children to Catholic schools.

The more natural reading is attested in other authoritative documents.

Catholic parents also have the duty and right of choosing those means and institutions through which they can provide more suitably for the Catholic education of their children according to local circumstance (*Code of Canon Law*, Can. 793).

Parents "share their educational mission with other individuals such as the Church or the state," Pope John Paul II said in his *Letter to Families* (no. 16). But this "sharing" must abide by the principle of "subsidiarity," which "implies the legitimacy and indeed the need of giving assistance to the parents, but finds its intrinsic limits in *their* prevailing right and *their actual capabilities*" (no. 16, emphasis added). The Pope here actually seems to *assert* the legitimacy of homeschooling: capable parents have the "right" to decline the aid of Church and state in educating their children.

We might better understand the place of Church schools in the overall scheme of parental responsibility for education, by comparing it to the place of the medical doctor in the scheme of an individual's health. Adults of sound mind bear an inalienable responsibility to take care of their own health. Medical professionals can offer vital expert assistance to such persons, and reasonable people commonly trust the judgment of doctors. Reasonable people usually follow doctors' orders. Often enough, however, people irresponsibly disregard the advice of doctors and other health-care professionals. Often enough these people get sick and die from avoidable causes. (Just think of what we have been told about smoking for the last forty years, and think about how many people still smoke.) These people bear moral responsibility for their bad—lazy, self-indulgent, unfair—decisions. Their bad decisions are subject to moral criticism; while the decisions include individual factors and perhaps even non-cognitive (emotional) considerations almost impossible for anyone else to gauge, these decisions are usually amenable to objective ethical evaluation. We can justly criticize someone who ignorantly (or stubbornly or arrogantly) turns down the assistance of competent professionals.

Even so, health-care decisions are left to individuals. Even if doctors almost always know best and that it is foolish to ignore their prescriptions, it does not follow that the basic moral responsibility has shifted to *doctors*. It would not follow that the basic moral duty is, or should be, that persons are *duty-bound* to do what doctors say. No: individuals are responsible for deciding whose help, and how much of it, they wish to accept for the benefit of their own health. Their performance of their duty to be good stewards of their bodies and health can be measured more or less objectively, but it is always, in the end, their call.

2. Positive Duty

Is there a *positive* duty—other than the contentious reading of GE 8 just investigated—to send children to Catholic schools where "possible?" The Council Fathers cited in support of their "reminder" one source, the papal *Allocution* of January 4, 1954 to an assembly of Italian teachers. In this *Allocution* Pope Pius XII said nothing what-soever about a putative duty to send children to Catholic schools. The *Allocution* instead affirmed parents' inalienable obligation to educate their children properly. The Pope described the Catholic school-teacher as "first of all a delegate of the family." Teachers are called, the Pope said, to "collaborate" with parents, as are parents with teachers. The relevant portions of the *Allocution* support, then, not a duty to send children to Catholic schools, but the proposition that (in the words of GE 8) parents "cooperate with [teachers] in their work for the good of their children."

Families should not be allowed to believe (as many do) that they have satisfied their duties toward their children when they have sent them off to school, giving no thought to working hand in hand with the teachers, on whom they wrongly think they can com-pletely unload a part of their own responsibilities

Is there another positive norm in Church law which asserts or implies the general illegitimacy of homeschooling? In the *Baltimore Catechism* (no. 3, 1941) we find: "The Church forbids parents to send their children to schools in which the Catholic religion is not taught and which are frequented by non-Catholics, except in cases in which the bishop decides that because of the particular circum-stances it may be permitted." This norm against enrolling children in non-Catholic schools—even if it is still in force—does not imply the illegitimacy of homeschooling. The choice to send a child to public school is not like the choice to educate the child at home. In one case the parents decline to delegate their own responsibilities and personally assume the duty of teaching their own children. They do not choose state employees over diocesan employees as their substitutes or delegates. Homeschooling parents do not delegate their duty to persons who give no assurances that they will form the child in the Catholic faith. They do not hire people who might scandalize their children, as parents who send their children to public or to a non-Catholic private school risk doing.

The pastoral judgment reflected in the *Baltimore Catechism* is radically different from any which might be reflected in a pastoral directive that parents *must* send their children to Catholic school, or that homeschooling is generally wrong. The difference is that pastors *should* warn the faithful against practices, places, institutions which present a danger to faith. That was evidently the judgment of the American hierarchy for many years of non-Catholic schools. Whether that judgment was prudent is now beside the point. The judgment was made, it rested upon abundant experience and sound reasoning, and Catholics were obliged to treat it as authoritative. But it would have been entirely another matter for bishops to have said—and for bishops today to say—that parents must *not* personally discharge their moral duty to educate their children. It would have been another matter entirely for bishops to have told parents— and to tell today's parents—that it would be sinful *not* to delegate their responsibility to persons outside the family.

A further word on the *Baltimore Catechism*. Given the often aggressive Protestantism characteristic of the nineteenth-century (and, to a lesser degree, twentieth-century) American public schools, it is easy to see what the bishops were worried about. They worried over scandalous schools, not the home. To read any adverse judgment upon homeschooling into the *Baltimore Catechism* is simply ahistorical. For during the course of the long struggle in America over Protestantism in public schools and the constitutional liberties of Catholic parents, the bishops based their case for public subsidies of parochial schools, not on the rights of the Church, but upon the right of parents to choose the schools they trusted to impart Catholic faith to their children.

In any event, the norm in the *Baltimore Catechism* has been superseded by the 1983 *Code of Canon Law*.

B. Parental Judgments of Catholicity

Is it true, as Father Hettinger asserts, that parents are incompetent to judge that a Catholic school is not Catholic enough for their children? He says that the Church "presumes" the school's orthodoxy. He implies that parents should as well. Is he right about parents?

No. There are a number of problems with the "parental incompetence" position.

First, Father Hettinger makes a mistaken textual argument in support of his "parental incompetence" thesis. He says that Canon 798 does not "authorize" parents to judge whether a school offers a fully Catholic education. Maybe so; but that canonical provision does *not* say that parents must send their children to Catholic school no matter what. And what it "authorizes" parents to do is not dispositive; the source of the overarching parental rights and responsibilities, upon which Father Hettinger's position founders, are *not*, by anyone's estimation, exclusively to be found in Canon 798. Attestations to those parental prerogatives are strewn about authoritative Church teachings, as this paper has already established.

Second, the objection has force only where the parents homeschool due to perceived heterodoxy. This is sometimes the case. Very often it is not: homeschooling parents commonly judge the pace of learning in school to be glacially slow, the social milieu to be unwholesome, and the curriculum weak. Often the decision to homeschool has *nothing* to do with perceived deficiencies in the available Catholic schools. For many parents the attractions of homeschooling are entirely positive, and have to do not just with superior educational achievement but with the great benefits to family solidarity which the joint venture in Christian education promises. (More on this later.) So far considered, Father Hettinger's argument does not undermine the legitimacy of homeschooling. He simply rejects one *reason* for it.

Third, no *general* or *definitive* judgment about a school's Catholicity need be involved where parents homeschool, *even where the reason has to do with the faith formation on offer in the Catholic school*. Father Hettinger seems to suppose otherwise. He seems to think that parents would usurp the bishop's prerogative should they decide to homeschool because of faith-formation concerns at the school. Not so. A particular child may be ill-served by a religion teacher whom most parents think is fine—and who *is* fine. Even good teachers fail to connect with some students, and almost every one of us has had difficulty with at least one teacher who is effective with most other students. It could be the case that parents of twenty-nine children in third grade at Saint Albert's School choose rightly by leaving their children in the school. And it could also be the case that the thirtieth set of parents chooses rightly by keeping their child at home. If you are the parents of that thirtieth child and you choose to homeschool him or her, your choice simply does not imply any disrespect of or even disagreement with the bishop.

Now, "orthodoxy" in the case of teachers denotes correct belief and, probably, personal rectitude. But it is possible for religion teachers who possess sound doctrine and good morals to be poor *teachers*. Children who have sound doctrine presented to them by an incompetent teacher are not being effectively formed in the faith. Sometimes a teacher's incompetence—say, a lack of apparent interest in the children themselves—*undermines* the sound doctrine being proposed. Where this occurs, parents should consider (among other options) homeschooling, even though the school *and* the particular teacher are solidly Catholic.

Fourth, Father Hettinger seems to *presume* that parents must send their children to Catholic schools. He casts upon parents a high (if not impassable) burden of proving any possible exceptional case for their children. But homeschooling parents tend to presume the opposite: primary education *should* occur in the home, not outside of it. Their view is this: why should parents send their children to any school? Why shouldn't children be educated in the family *unless* the faith formation in the school is clearly superior to what the family can provide at home? In this view, the "parental incompetence" objection is essentially question-begging: it assumes that the burden of proof is on the parents to prove their superiority over the Catholic school.

Fifth, the local Ordinary's designation of a school as "Catholic" is a matter of positive Church law. Being a positive law, and not a moral truth or a definitive teaching pertaining to faith, the Ordinary's designation cannot be the end of the matter for conscientious parents: Church law (like the civil law) is (only) *presumptively* binding in conscience. The Ordinary's designation cannot *satisfy* by itself the parents' duty before God to form their children in the Catholic faith.

Sixth, Catholic parents are called to be constantly vigilant of the Catholic schools' faith formation, even where parents enroll their children in Catholic school. Parents are called to be involved with their formation, to go over what the children learn in school, to work with teachers on sacramental preparation, special feast day projects and the like. Pope Pius XII called for precisely this kind of parental vigilance in his 1954 *Allocution,* upon which the authors of GE 8 relied.

Parents are obliged, in other words, to investigate and critically evaluate the faith formation on offer in the parish school. Called to learn about the school and to monitor the work of their delegates (the teachers), parents must learn what the school is about. They must know if the school is off the rails. Parents should not *try* to forestall the judgment that a "Catholic" school education is actually harming their children's faith formation, if that is what the evidence shows.

C. *"Stay and Fight"*

Father Hettinger says that parents are not excused from their duty to send their children to a Catholic school even where the school is not orthodox. Leaving aside the simple oddness of considering a heterodox school to be "Catholic," the question is: *are* parents obliged to "stay and fight" for school reform?

No.

Parents are not bound by natural moral duty or by their baptismal vows to "fight" for the improvement of Catholic schools. To the extent parents have any such duty at all, it is subordinate to their primordial duty to educate their children and provide for their faith formation. While the prospects for a school's immediate improvement should be a factor in parents' deliberations about withdrawing a child from a heterodox environment, they can be no more than that: *one factor.* Otherwise, parents would be reasoning in the following way: "I'll leave my son (or daughter) in the nearby Catholic school, knowing that the school is undermining their faith, hoping that someday the school will turn around and other people's children's faith will not suffer as mine no doubt will." I think this way of reasoning is wrong.

I can think of another argument in favor of Father Hettinger's position, and my response to it sheds some light on why I think there is no duty to "stay and fight." Someone might say that parents ought to be concerned about the parish community, other parents' children, and sound education generally—and not just about their own children. Yes, they should. And if it were a close call as to what is best for one's own children, and if there were good reasons to think that one's children's involvement in the school would really benefit the other children, that could tip the balance in favor of school over home education. Given the inexact quality of the relevant considerations and that many times the balance might well be teetering, solidarity with and charity towards other families could well be the deciding factors. But parents are far more responsible for their own children than for others' children. They cannot rightly do anything beyond what is strictly required in justice to benefit others if that will involve or entail any cost to their own children's welfare. And so, communal concerns are no more than a tipping factor.

In any event, one can "fight" for the parish school without having their children "stay" in it.

It is worth observing, too, that apostolate-minded people without children in a Catholic school might be called to get involved in that school for the sake of the children who go to it. Homeschooling parents are not relieved of this duty, if their other responsibilities permit involvement. If they are members of the parish then the school is *their* school, too, whether their children attend it or not. And if it could be shown that homeschooling parents tend to see the school as someone else's business, then that would be one more reason to discourage homeschooling as a general matter.

Part III

Homeschooling is a legitimate option for Catholic parents, even where their children are not "special" cases and even where a Catholic school is available. This option amounts to a parental *right* to homeschool. Partly due to the contemporary association of the term "right" with raw subjectivity—as if "right" indicated a decision unhinged from objective standards—some readers will have trouble accepting this conclusion. But to say that parents have a "right" to homeschool is not to suggest that they may do so without good reason. To affirm a "right" to homeschool is not *per se* to endorse or presuppose any kind of subjectivism in moral decision-making. As we have seen, affirmation of this "right" within the Catholic tradition is little more than the corollary of the parents' moral *duty* to educate their children in the faith and according to their state in life. To affirm such a "right" is not to say or imply that pastors should not speak plainly, and even forcefully, in favor of Church schools, so long as parents' "rights" are respected.

To affirm a "right" to homeschool is to affirm, first, the locus of final decision—mother and father. It is *their* call. It is to affirm, second, that the parents' call is to be respected so long as it is made conscientiously. Third, it is to affirm that home schooling parents are not to be criticized *just* because they homeschool. Finally, it is to say that there is no violation of Church law in homeschooling normal children where good Catholic schools are available.

There is one large exception to, or limitation of, the parental right to homeschool which we have yet to mention: sacramental preparation. Nothing in what I say about parental authority over education implies any diminution in the Church's responsibility for administration of the sacraments. *All* children presented for reception of the school-age sacraments—Penance, First Holy Communion, Confirmation—should be held to the same standards for faithful and valid reception. Diocesan and parish staff have the *right*, corresponding to *their* duties, to insist that all children possess the requisite mastery of the faith and disposition of character. What parents think of these matters is unimportant, and homeschooling parents have no more to say than any other parents. What the minister of the sacrament thinks is all that counts. Sacramental preparation thus provides parish (and school) authorities a very important check upon the progress and success of homeschooled children.

Now note well: any effort to clarify or guide parents' choice to homeschool (including this one) must be introduced with a strong caveat. All aspects of human flourishing are at stake in educating children. It is really a matter of raising and forming them with respect to all aspects of their well-being: psychological, intellectual, emotional, spiritual. Thus the criteria for deciding whether to home-school include the ability (and predicted success) of parents at home compared to that of the available schools to do the job in respect to all of them. It is therefore a very delicate thing to attempt (as I do, now) to prioritize or narrow down the pertinent considerations.

Also, the vocational responsibilities of parents are dramatically involved in the decision to homeschool. This is especially true for mothers who in most families will end up doing the bulk of the teaching. We know that raising children generally requires the constant presence of at least one parent in the home; again, usually the mother. Engaged couples should be made to understand this fact better than they are now. But homeschooling would add significantly to parents' and especially to mothers' responsibilities. A young mother's opportunities to pursue friendship, healthy recreation, remunerative work, and apostolate outside would all be diminished by choosing to homeschool. But moms are called to do apostolate, and sometimes have to make money, outside the home.

Now the question: *should* Catholic parents homeschool? If so, under what circumstances? According to which considerations? Below are some generally relevant considerations which parents inclined to homeschool might undervalue.

Parents considering homeschooling should consider very, very carefully their child's social development. Unless care is taken to promote social skills in other ways, homeschooled children can fail to gain needed experience in dealing with a variety of other children, making friends, and fending off bullies or harassers. Socialization in many Catholic schools may be less than ideal. Nevertheless the need for genuine socialization—for experience with diverse persons in different settings; for learning to cooperate with and treat fairly others, especially strangers or persons we dislike; for accepting rules which stem from the needs of a large group, ranging well beyond the ties of family and friendship; of learning the moral importance of coming to accept authority which is not rooted in the family—may still be overlooked by many parents inclined to homeschool.

GE points to these types of considerations. The Council Fathers said, for example, that children should be "open to discourse with others and willing to do their best to promote the common good" (GE 1). "Between pupils of different talents and backgrounds it promotes friendly relations and fosters a spirit of mutual understanding" (GE 5).

One aspect of school-based socialization is entirely unavailable at home. That aspect is legitimate non-parental authority. All children (homeschooled or not) receive an education in parental cooperation and authority. All children see how their parents handle problems. All children learn from their parents' example how to deal with life. All children learn by observing their parents about loving commitment and fair dealing within the home.

But the homeschooled child encounters only parents and siblings; discipline and authority are inescapably familial. In the home school the "pupil" sees much the same as what he or she sees as a family member. At an institutional school, children see how adults unrelated to them can be committed to their well-being. At school children see other adults act out of equal commitment to the well-being of each and every student. Children at school see how non-familial authority figures can treat each child as a unique individual and yet as members of a class with a common identity. These immensely valuable lessons are unavailable in homeschool, and they have almost nothing to do with the curriculum. Again, just as (in my opinion) the most valuable lessons children learn from parents are not didactic, but rather come in observing the parents deal with life's decisions and challenges, so too in school the most valuable lessons are learned from non-curricular activities, episodes, problems, and challenges.

I said earlier that many parents choose homeschooling because of the benefits to family life which homeschooling promises. These benefits are no doubt considerable. But I doubt that these benefits should be given the high value they are given by many homeschooling parents. Plainly put, family solidarity is not a purpose of education. Mistakenly thinking that it is tends to impede the proper development of adolescents and young adults. In fact, parents are called to accept and to promote a certain *loss* of family solidarity in and through education and to do so at a rather early age, no later than Confirmation and probably earlier.

The *Allocution* of Pope Pius XII cautioned parents to stay abreast of their children's education in schools. The picture he paints of adolescents and teens seems as true today as it was fifty years ago:

> For at this period growing adolescents begin to set themselves
> free from subjection to their parents and it often happens

that they set up an opposition between the teacher and the father, the school and the home. Many parents find themselves at such a time almost deprived of all authority before the bizarre humor of their children, and some errors that are committed in these years can eventually turn out to be unfortunate for the equilibrium of the adolescent.

The picture is painful as it is familiar. The adolescent and teenage child fitfully strives to acquire an identity apart from the family, and apart from what the parents have in mind for them. Any parent knows how difficult these years can be, for child and parent. Any parent knows, too, that these are mistake prone years, for child and parent alike.

In my experience and observation, many dedicated parents are guilty of over-determining their children's futures. They do not give their children the space they need to grow into adulthood. Formal schooling, no matter why exactly it is chosen, fosters the necessary independence: several hours a day free of parental supervision; a curriculum not of the parents' choosing but rather the result of collaboration among a range of adults with vast accumulated experience; more adult role models; access to the stories of other parents and their jobs, activities, habits through the stories of school chums. In short, school forces the child to confront a world not of his parents' design, and to make his or her way (largely) without his parents help. I guess I am saying that going to school generally helps children to grow up.

All parents need to be reminded that their children are not theirs. Catholic parents need to be reminded that their children's lives have already been laid out for them by God. Conscientious parents who are serious Catholics and who are worried about the wiles of the secularized and sexualized culture all about them (and I am one such parent) need to be reminded to value their children's freedom and independence. They—we—need to be reminded to stand close by—but not too close—while their children acquire an adult faith, a grown-up identity. We need to stand close by while they discern their vocations *in* a culture most such parents detest and *for* a culture—that of tomorrow—they would probably like even less. But our children are called to be leaven in that culture, to bring Gospel values to the world, to engage the great society as evangelists.

I think that attendance at a good Catholic school is generally the best preparation for answering that call, and my reflection on the two main purposes of education which follows will, I hope, say much about why.

Part IV

Christian education is education for productive citizenship. Productive citizenship is, for the Christian, a lot more than voting and pulling one's weight in the economy. Productive citizenship is not, for the Christian, much about civics lessons, American history class, or field trips to Washington. It is not even mainly about the classroom curriculum, or about mastering a body of knowledge. It is, rather, primarily about becoming a young adult within a diverse society, having accepted and prepared for the mission of evangelizing that society. The mission of education is to get young people ready to *engage* the culture for Christ.

The Vatican II Fathers stressed this end of education repeatedly: "For a true education aims at the formation of the human person in the pursuit of his ultimate end and of the good of the societies of which, as man, he is a member, and in whose obligations, as an adult, he will share" (GE 1). The school "is designed not only to develop with special care the intellectual faculties but also to form the ability to judge rightly, to hand on the cultural legacy of previous generations" (GE 5). School "establishes as it were a center whose work and progress must be shared together by families, teachers, associations of various types that foster cultural, civic, and religious life, as well as by civil society and the entire human community " (GE 5). "So indeed the Catholic school, while it is open, as it must be, to the situation of the contemporary world, leads its students to promote efficaciously the good of the earthly city and also prepares them for service in the spread of the Kingdom of God, so that by leading an exemplary apostolic life they become, as it were, a saving leaven in the human community" (GE 8).

Here, in the Council document on education, we see that the school is an important (though not invariably indispensable) way station to engagement with the culture. If properly constituted and managed, the Catholic school supplies the middle ground between home and secular society, shaping the Christian conscience and character of young people even as it propels them into the de-Christianized world around us.

Being leaven in society is the heart of the lay apostolate. I have just argued that going to school generally is the better preparation for evangelizing the culture. Within this broad evangelical calling, each one of us has a more distinctive "personal vocation," a unique life of good works chosen by God. Getting young people shaped up to discern their "personal vocation" is another great aim of education. I think it, too, is generally better accomplished by going to school.

Throughout his pontificate John Paul II mined the Second Vatican Council's development of the concept of personal vocation. Vocation means, most simply, calling. For centuries before the Council, standard usage of "vocation" almost always referred to the religious life. Laypersons evidently had no "vocation." Married life was sometimes said to be a calling but rarely a vocation; "vocation" in reference to the family meant the possibility that one of the children might become a priest, brother, or a nun.

But Catholic faith teaches, and has always taught, that we and everything we do are envisioned by God from before time, that we are all called to be God's adopted children, that we all may be saved. The faith has always taught that nothing happens save according to God's will, or at least by God's permission; everything we do is encompassed by God's providence. The implication of these truths must be that each of us is somehow involved, in all that we do, in carrying out the work initiated by Jesus Christ, the work of sanctifying the world. Recent Catholic Church teaching confirms explicitly that there is such an organizing principle of the life of each Christian: personal vocation.

What is a personal vocation? Christians have a common calling to lives of faith, hope, and charity. All are required to observe the moral law. The Ten Commandments are not variables according to our vocation; they are universally binding. These common obligations are, one might say, the foundational elements, the infrastructure, of one's Christian life. They are parts of one's vocation, one might also say, but they are not distinguishing features of each one's personal vocation. Beyond the common obligations of Christians, we must choose from among alternatives, often many, that are equally consistent with the moral law and theological virtues. What is God's will for me? Which option has my name written on it?

The concept of personal vocation presupposes justification by grace through faith. But justification transforms a person—God's gracious work makes one a new "creature," a new "human being," a member of Christ's gloriously risen Body. Living now in Christ, one has one's own part or function to perform, just as each bodily organ has its own work to do. Being a member of Christ does not make one do one's part automatically. Persons still are free human beings; they contribute to the building up of the one Body by cooperating with Jesus in completing God's overall plan. Each one has a unique life of good works, planned by God beforehand, to "walk in." This unique life of good works is not always easy or pleasant: as Jesus' disciple, a person must take up his or her cross each day and follow Christ.

There is a simulacrum of personal vocation abroad in today's culture. This counterfeit would have one ask oneself: What do I really want out of life? What is my dream? This phony "vocation" or "calling" is a matter of identifying one's objectives or goals (as guidance counselors might phrase it), of setting one's priorities and persevering despite obstacles with an optimistic expectation of success.

This counterfeit can be very hard to distinguish from the real item. Consider the boast of disgraced Enron corporate executive, Ken Lay: "The Bible is very clear that we each need to be the best we can be to realize our God-given potential. I use these words quite freely within Enron." But "realizing our God-given potential" is, at least, ambiguous. It could mean (and probably does mean on Ken Lay's lips) the proficient exercise of human cognitive and physical faculties, such as we would recognize in, say, Michael Jordan or a Nobel Laureate—human greatness as such. But "human greatness" is not a moral criterion; developing one's "God-given potential" is not an answer to the question: are you doing

something right, or wrong? All human acts, including those undertaken with the motive or aim to develop one's abilities, are to be
judged according to moral norms. The development of one's
"potential" is just as likely as any other undertaking to involve
unfairness to others or the immoral indifference to other moral
responsibilities. For example, it is wrong to try to develop one's
potential as a doctor by experimenting on aborted children, and it
is wrong for a mother of, say, five to undertake an exercise regimen
which takes her away from parental responsibilities.

"I basically try to create an environment at Enron where
everybody has the opportunity to realize his or her God-given
potential," Ken Lay says. But did he create an environment in
which God's moral law was strictly observed? Did he create an environment in which people cultivated their abilities in order to put
them at service of building Jesus' Kingdom? No.

Personal vocation can be expressed in *some* of the same ways: "be
all you can be"; "live life to the fullest." But, no matter how it is
expressed, the connotation is quite different, for "personal vocation"
refers to putting oneself entirely at the service of God, and of others,
after clearheaded, protracted discernment. It is not, like the counterfeit, a thing of imaginative fancy, of emulating the well-known, of
pursuing enlightened self-interest. "Personal vocation" is *God's* plan
for using, with our cooperation, His special gifts to us ("our God-
given potential") in serving others, and thereby building up the
heavenly *communio*. The Church was born of and for discipleship.
The Eucharist was given to the Twelve. The Paraclete descended upon
the gathered believers. From that moment the Church was to make
disciples of all nations.

Now, the Church in America struggles to make disciples of men
and women immersed in a culture which discredits heteronomy,
inauthenticity, and inequality, and which declares discipleship to be
bound up with all that the culture discredits. The culture—as we
find it in law, in popular entertainment, in serious academic
endeavors—says: "Reject servility and hypocrisy! Here is the alternative—a life of genuine freedom and joy. Be whatever you wish!
Realize your dream!" But the "joy" is so much pleasure. The
"dream" is to do what one pleases. "Freedom" is a rootless search for

new experiences and feelings. The culture celebrates an autonomy and individuality which is, in truth, antithetical to discipleship. Indeed, as Pope John Paul II made clear in *Veritatis Splendor*, this individuality is antithetical to truth.

It seems to me that the single greatest contribution Christians can make today to our culture is to show that there is equality and individuality and freedom in the Way of the Lord. As Pope John Paul II wrote on the Fortieth World Day of Prayer for Vocations:

> How can one not read in the story of the "servant Jesus" the story of every vocation: the story that the Creator has planned for every human being, the story that inevitably passes through the call to serve and culminates in the discovery of the new name, designed by God for each individual? In these "names," people can grasp their own identity, directing themselves to that self-fulfillment which makes them free and happy.

Here is the great adventure of Christian life! Not to do as we please, to "realize our dreams." We are instead invited by Christ to go where no one has gone before—or will, ever again. We are given the chance to help build the house which lasts forever, and to do so precisely as a worker of inestimable value in the vineyard. Each one of us is called by name to be a servant in the only way that matters, to the unique set of tasks God has saved for us to do. It is equally important—to God's plan, to our salvation—that each of us performs that distinctive and irreplaceable set of tasks.

Discerning personal vocation is prodigious, prayerful work. But it is not contemplative or private. Discernment involves taking candid stock of one's talents and interests and cultivated abilities—what *can* one do. One needs to be exposed (sometimes against one's inclinations) to opportunities to test for the presence or absence of latent talents, interests, skills, capacities. Schools can supply the opportunity.

Discernment is also a matter of seeing other peoples' needs and what needs to be done. It is to ask: what is it that I *can* do which, by doing it, would help others with respect to human goods and at the same time build up the heavenly *communio*? What are the signs from the environment and other persons' actions that confirm my provisional judgments about these matters? Often enough personal vocation hinges upon the consent of another. Feeling himself called to marriage, perhaps a young man does not meet a suitable spouse. In that case he is called (surprisingly enough) to the single life. The same young man might wonder if he is called to the priesthood. But he finds that no bishop or superior will admit him to seminary. He is called, then, to the single lay life.

The point is that discernment involves a great deal of to-and-fro with one's environment, reading off the signs and signals "out there," not so much "in here"—in the heart and mind. This proactive-reactive combination of operations requires a great deal of contact with diverse people and different environments. Schools can supply the feedback in a relatively controlled setting. Schools can also supply sympathetic and committed helpers in the discernment process. In addition to parents and pastors, teachers and coaches and counselors can help young people get their view of reality clear and right.

Conclusion

Genuinely Catholic schools are vitally important to the maturation of children into adults who can witness to the truth in the modern world. A few of our children are called to withdraw and pray for others' success, and those called to religious life are generally to concern themselves with sacraments and the life of the Church. The vast majority of our children, however, are called by God to help Jesus redeem the society in which they are going to spend their lifetimes. Getting ready to do that is the unifying purpose of education. Homeschooling is a legitimate choice for parents and, where the Catholic schools miss their mark, may be the best choice. But the inherent limitations of homeschooling, considered in light of the purposes of education, make it a second-best choice for children past the first few grades.

"Male and Female He Created Them": Catechesis on Human Sexuality and Sexual Ethics

WILLIAM E. MAY

Introduction

In some ways the teaching of the Catholic Church on human sexuality and sexual ethics is well known. Many people and most Catholics know *what* the Church teaches. Her basic teaching is this: men and women are complementary in their sexuality, and one can rightly choose to exercise one's genital sexual powers only when one, as a spouse, freely chooses to engage in the conjugal act and, in that act, chooses to respect fully the goods of mutual self-giving and of human procreation. From this it follows that it is never morally good to unite sexually outside of marriage (i.e., to fornicate or commit adultery), or to masturbate or commit sodomy (i.e., have oral or anal intercourse whether with a person of the opposite or same sex), nor ought one intentionally bring about or maintain sexual arousal unless in preparation for the conjugal act.

Unfortunately, a great many people, including large numbers of Catholics, have no idea of the reasons *why* the Church teaches this. Many believe that her teaching is anti-sex, rigoristic and repressive, completely unrealistic, and indeed inhuman. They think that this teaching is a set of arbitrarily imposed rules, a series of "don'ts" intended to prevent people from enjoying themselves and doing what comes naturally and spontaneously. Some persons, including influential Catholic theologians, charge that "official" Catholic teaching on human sexuality and sexual ethics is based on an untenable "physicalistic" view of natural law that makes persons

William E. May *is Michael J. McGivney Professor of Moral Theology at the John Paul II Institute for Studies on Marriage and Family, Catholic University of America.*

slaves to their own biology and is completely irreconcilable with a "personalistic" understanding of the moral order.

I want to show that the Church's teaching on human sexuality and sexual ethics, far from enslaving persons, liberates them and enables them to become fully themselves, to become the men and women a loving God wants them to be, to become happy. It does so because it is rooted in a profound reverence for human persons, male and female, as bodily, sexual beings, summoned from their depths to self-giving love.

The Church's teaching is rooted in the revealed Word of God. But this teaching is also fully reasonable, and is so precisely because it is true. I have therefore divided this paper into two parts. In the first I offer a summary of the teaching of Holy Scripture on human sexuality and sexual morality as understood by the Church and as presented by Pope John Paul II in his remarkable addresses on the "theology of the body."[1] In the second I consider fundamental moral principles and their relevance to making choices concerning sexual behavior.

Part One:
The Scriptures, Human Sexuality and Sexual Morality, and the "Theology of The Body"

The "Beatifying Beginning" of Human Existence

It is fitting to begin with the first two chapters of Genesis because these chapters, which contain the stories of what Pope John Paul II called the "beatifying beginning of human existence,"[2] set forth precious truths of utmost importance to our topic.

In the first chapter of Genesis, we read:

So God created man [*ha 'adam*] in his own image; in the image of God he created him; male and female he created them. And God blessed them, saying, "Be fruitful and multiply, and fill the earth and subdue it; and have dominion over the fish of the sea and over the birds of the air and over every living thing that moves upon the earth" (Gen. 1:27-28).

The second chapter of Genesis declares:

The LORD God formed man [*ha 'adam*] of dust from the ground, and breathed into his nostrils the breath of life; and man became a living being. . . . Then the LORD God said, "It is not good that the man [*ha 'adam*] should be alone; I will make him a helper fit for him." . . . So the LORD God caused a deep sleep to fall upon the man, and while he slept took one of his ribs and closed up its place with flesh; and the rib which the LORD God had taken from the man [*ha 'adam*] he made into a woman [*ishshah*] and brought her to the man [*ha 'adam*]. Then the man [*ha 'adam*] said,

> "This at last is bone of my bones
> and flesh of my flesh;
> She shall be called 'woman' [*ishshah*],
> because she was taken out of Man [*ish*]."

Therefore a man [*ish*] leaves his father and mother and cleaves to his wife [*ishshah*], and they become one flesh. And the man [*ish*] and his wife [*ishshah*] were both naked, and were not ashamed (Gen. 2:7, 18, 21-25).

Reflecting on these chapters, Pope John Paul II develops two ideas central to the "theology of the body:"

1. That the human body is the expression or revelation of the human person
2. That the human body, because it exists as masculine and feminine, is the means and sign of the gift of the man-person to the female-person and vice versa, or what the pope calls the "nuptial meaning" of the human body.

The Human Body Expresses the Person

John Paul II introduces this idea in commenting on Genesis 2:18, which speaks of the man being "alone." The solitude in question is that of "'man' (male and female) and not just of the solitude of man the male, caused by the lack of woman. . . . [T]his solitude has two meanings: one derived from man's very nature, that is, from his humanity . . . and the other derived from the male-female relation-ship" (5.2). The solitude deriving from man's very nature, John Paul II says, "enables us to *link man's original solitude with consciousness of the body*, through which man is distinguished from all the *animalia* and is 'separated' from them, and also *through which he is a person*. It can be affirmed with certainty that that man, thus formed, has at the same time consciousness and awareness of the meaning of his own body, on the basis of the experience of original solitude" (6.3).

In short, man's awareness of his body as different from the bodies of other animals enables him to grasp the truth that he, alone among visible creatures, is a *person*, gifted with self-consciousness and self-determination.

Pope John Paul II perhaps most dramatically shows that the human body reveals the human person when he considers the second meaning of man's "solitude" and reflects on the text (Gen. 2:18-24) describing in poetic terms the "creation" of woman. "When the man first exclaims at the sight of the woman, 'This is bone of my bones and flesh of my flesh' (Gen. 2:23), he merely affirms," the pope says, "the human identity of both. Exclaiming in this way, he seems to say: here is *a body that expresses the 'person'!* " (14.4).

Since the body expresses the person, and since persons are to be loved, an ethical consequence is that we must never express with our bodies anything unworthy of the person. The body is a beautiful manifestation of a human person in all his or her God-given dignity.

The Nuptial Meaning of the Body

Reflecting once again on the first man's cry of joy, "This at last is bone of my bones and flesh of my flesh," the pope declares that these words in a way express "the subjectively beatifying beginning of man's existence in the world" (14.3). "That beatifying 'beginning' of man's being and existing, as male and female," John Paul II continues,

is connected with the revelation and discovery of the meaning of the body, which can be called "nuptial.". . . [T]he man's words of joy, "this at last . . ." are followed by the verse which establishes their conjugal unity (Gen. 2:24), and then by the one which testifies to the nakedness of both, without mutual shame (Gen. 2:25). Precisely this significant confrontation enables us to speak of the revelation and at the same time the discovery of the "nuptial" meaning of the body in the very mystery of creation (14.5).

In short, the male person's body is a sign of the gift of the male person to the female person and vice versa.

To put this another way, because of the nuptial meaning of the body, man, male and female, realizes that he can fulfill himself as a person only by giving himself to another in love, in the sincere gift of self. He realizes that his vocation is to love.

In a memorable passage, in which he links the original nuptial meaning of the body to the absence of shame in the state of original innocence prior to the "fall" (see Gen. 2:25), John Paul then says:

> Happiness is being rooted in love. Original happiness speaks to us of the "beginning" of man, who emerged from Love and initiated love. That happened in an irrevocable way, despite the subsequent sin and death. In his time, Christ will be a witness to this irreversible love of the Creator and Father, which had already been expressed in the mystery of creation and in the grace of original innocence. And therefore also the common "beginning" of man and woman, that is, the original truth of their body in masculinity and femininity, to which Genesis 2:25 draws our attention, does not know shame. *This "beginning" can also be defined as the original and beatifying immunity from shame as a result of love* (16.2, emphasis added).

This immunity from shame directs us to the mystery of man's original innocence, which is the mystery of his existence, prior to the knowledge of good and evil and almost "outside" it. The fact that man exists in this way, before the breaking of the first covenant with his Creator, belongs to the fullness of the mystery of creation. Why is this so? John Paul II explains as follows:

If . . . creation is a gift to man, then his fullness and deepest dimension is determined by grace, that is, by participation in the interior life of God himself, in his holiness. This is . . . , in man, the interior foundation and source of his original innocence. It is with this concept—and more precisely with that of "original justice"—that theology defines the state of man before original sin (16.3).

Of crucial importance is the fact that it is "the very awareness of the body—or, rather, awareness of the meaning of the body [its nuptial meaning]" that "reveals the peculiarity of original innocence" (16.3). In fact,

the body itself is, in a way, an "eye" witness of this characteristic. It is significant that the affirmation contained in Genesis 2:25—about nakedness mutually free from shame—is a statement unique in its kind in the whole Bible, so that it will never be repeated. On the contrary, we can quote many texts in which nakedness will be connected with shame or even, in a stronger sense, with "ignominy" (16.3; in footnote 1 John Paul II refers to Hosea 1:2 and Ezekiel 23:26, 29 as texts to illustrate this).

Original innocence "is what 'radically' . . . excludes shame of the body in the man-woman relationship, eliminates its necessity in man, in his heart, that is, in his conscience" and it refers above all to "the interior state of the human 'heart,' of the human will" (16.4). This original innocence is a "particular 'purity of heart' which preserves an interior faithfulness to the gift according to the nuptial meaning of the body" (16.4).

Concupiscence "Veils" the "Nuptial Meaning" of the Body

This is a third idea central to the "theology of the body," and the pope develops it both in his reflections on the third chapter of Genesis, which tells us of the sin of the first man and its dreadful consequences for human existence, and on the New Testament's teaching on "concupiscence." In reflecting on the Genesis text he likewise highlights the contrast between the lack of shame over their nakedness, as experienced by Adam and Eve in the state of original innocence, and the shame over their nakedness that they experience after their fall from grace.

Commenting on Genesis 3, John Paul II writes, "The man who gathers the fruit of the 'tree of the knowledge of good and evil' makes . . . a fundamental choice and carries it out against the will of the Creator. . . . Man turns his back on God-Love, on 'the Father'. . . . He detaches his heart and almost cuts it off from what 'is of the Father:' thus there remains in him what is 'of the world'" (26.4). "It was then that 'the eyes of both were opened, and they knew that they were naked' (Gen. 3:7). . . . Genesis 3:6 speaks explicitly of shame in connection with sin. That shame is almost the first source of the manifestation in man—in both, man and woman—of what 'is not of the Father, but of the world'" (26.5).

Because of their shame man and woman find it necessary to hide from God. This "indicates that in the depths of the shame they both feel before each other. . . . there has matured a sense of fear before God, a fear previously unknown" (27.1).

A certain fear always belongs to the very essence of shame: nevertheless original shame reveals its character in a particular way: "I was afraid, because I was naked." We realize that something deeper than physical shame . . . is in action here. Man tries to cover with the shame of his own nakedness the real origin of fear, indicating rather its effect, in order not to call its cause by name. . . . Actually, *through "nakedness"* there is manifested *man deprived of participation in the Gift,* man alienated from that Love which had been the source of the original gift, the source of the fullness of the good intended for the creature. This man . . . was deprived of the supernatural and preternatural gifts which were part of his "endowment" before sin. Furthermore, he suffered a loss in what belongs to his nature itself, to humanity in the original fullness "of the image of God" (27.2).

Shame is the sign that a radical change has come over man. In the state of original innocence, nakedness did not express a lack, but rather a full acceptance of the body in all its human and personal truth. It was "a faithful witness and a tangible verification of man's original 'solitude' in the world, becoming at the same time, by means of his masculinity and femininity, a limpid element of mutual donation in the communion of persons" (27.3). But now, as a result of original sin and of the concupiscence that has entered his "heart," man has lost, in a way, "the original certainty of the 'image of God,' expressed in his body" (27.4). This, John Paul II says, can be called "cosmic shame" that man experienced with regard to his Creator.

This "cosmic" shame "makes way in the biblical text for another form of shame . . . the shame produced in humanity itself."

> This is the woman's shame "with regard to" the man and also the man's "with regard to" the woman: mutual shame. . . . The Yahwist text seems to indicate explicitly the "sexual" character of this shame: "they sewed fig leaves together and made themselves aprons." However, we may wonder if the "sexual" aspect has only a "relative" character . . . i.e., if it is a question of shame of one's own sexuality only in reference to a person of the other sex (28.1).

The pope clarifies the "immanent" and "relative" meanings of sexual shame. He maintains that although the text of Genesis 3:7 ("the eyes of both were opened") seems to support the relative character of original shame, nonetheless deeper reflection

> makes it possible to discover its more immanent background. That shame, which is certainly manifested in the "sexual" order, reveals *a specific difficulty in perceiving the human essentiality of one's own body:* a difficulty which man had not experienced in the state of original innocence. Through these words there is revealed a *certain constitutive break* within the human person, almost a rupture of man's original spiritual and somatic unity (28.2).

John Paul II writes,

Immanent shame contains such a cognitive acuteness as to create a fundamental disquiet in the whole of human existence. . . . *[T]he body, which is not subordinated to the spirit as in the state of original innocence, bears within itself a constant center of resistance to the spirit and threatens . . . the unity of the man-person.* Lust, and in particular the lust of the body, is a specific threat to the structure of self-control and self-mastery through which the human person is formed (28.3; emphasis added).

Shame has a double meaning: "it indicates the threat to the value and at the same time preserves this value interiorly" (28.6). Shame is experienced because one fears that the sexual values of his body will be consumed by the lust of others, and one thus seeks to protect those values because they are *personal*.

Lust menaces the "communion of persons" and distorts the nuptial meaning of the body. John Paul II stresses that since the body, after the fall, no longer expresses the person adequately, "the capacity of communicating themselves to each other, of which Genesis 2:25 speaks, has been shattered" (29.2). It is as if the body, "in its masculinity and femininity, no longer constituted the 'trustworthy' substratum of the communion of persons" (29.2). Because of lust the man will want to "dominate" the woman, and the woman, who will desire her husband (cf. Gen. 3:16), will feel a lack of full unity. Thus the "original beatifying conjugal union of persons will be distorted in man's heart by lust" (30.4). An adequate analysis of Genesis 3, he maintains, "leads to the conclusion that the three forms of lust [referred to in John 2:16-17, namely, the lust of the flesh, the lust of the eyes, and pride of life] bring with them a limitation of the nuptial meaning of the body itself, in which man and woman participated in the state of original innocence" (31.5). Nonetheless, the human body, independently of our states of consciousness and our experiences, retains its nuptial meaning (cf. 30.5). It is simply that, as a result of sin and the entrance of the threefold concupiscence into the human heart, *"the nuptial meaning of the body, which in the situation of original innocence constituted the measure of the heart of both, of the man and of the woman, must have undergone a distortion"* (30.6; emphasis in original).

Through Union with Christ Man, Male and Female, Can Recover the "Nuptial Meaning" of the Body
This is the fourth concept central to the "theology of the body," and the pope develops this in his reflections on our Lord's Sermon on the Mount (Matthew 5) and also on the teaching of Saint Paul. Here I will summarize the relevant part of his reflections on the Sermon on the Mount.

The pope first cites Christ's words in Matthew 5:27-28: "You have heard that it was said, 'You shall not commit adultery.' But I say to you, everyone who looks at a woman with lust has already committed adultery with her in his heart." He declares:

> [These words] do not allow us to stop at the accusation of the human heart and to regard it continually with suspicion, but must be understood and interpreted above all as an appeal to the heart. . . . Redemption is a truth . . . in the name of which man must feel called. . . . He must realize this call also through Christ's words . . . reread in the context of the revelation of the body. Man must feel called to rediscover, nay more, to realize the nuptial meaning of the body and to express in this way the interior freedom of the gift, that is, of that spiritual state and that spiritual power which are derived from mastery of the lust of the flesh (46.4).

Christ's words "bear witness that the original power (therefore also the grace) of the mystery of creation becomes for each of them [man and woman] power (that is, grace) of the mystery of redemption. That concerns the very 'nature,' the very substratum of the humanity of the person, the deepest impulses of the 'heart'" (46.5). Christ's redemptive call is to "the rediscovery of the meaning of the whole of existence, the meaning of life, in which there is contained also that meaning of the body which here we call 'nuptial.'" Christ appeals to man's "heart" to the "supreme value that is love," called "as a person in the truth of his humanity, therefore also in the truth of his masculinity and femininity, in the truth of his body" (46.6).

"Eros," the Holy Father insists, must not be confused with lust. For Plato it "represents the interior force that drags man toward everything good, true, and beautiful" (47.2). It refers also to the natural and hence "good" desire experienced in the attraction of men for women and vice versa. However "erotic" desire is often identified with lust (47.3). A proper interpretation of the Sermon on the Mount, taking into account the multiple meanings of "eros," allows room "for that ethos, for those ethical and indirectly even theological contents which, in the course of our analyses, have been seen from Christ's appeal to the human "heart" (47.4). Christ's appeal is "the ethos of redemption. The call to what is true, good, and beautiful ["eros" in the Platonic sense] means, at the same time, in the ethos of redemption, the necessity of overcoming what is derived from lust in its three forms. . . . If the words of Matthew 5:27-28 represent this call, then they mean that, in the erotic sphere, 'eros' and 'ethos' do not differ from each other, are not opposed to each other, but are called to meet in the human heart, and in this meeting to bear fruit" (47.5).

Ethos, the pope continues, must become the "constituent form" of eros. Ethos is in no way hostile to "spontaneity." The person who accepts the ethos of Matthew 5:27-28 "must know that he is called *to full and mature spontaneity* of the relations that spring from the perennial attraction of masculinity and femininity. This very spontaneity is the gradual fruit of the discernment of the impulses of one's own heart" (48.2). "This discernment . . . has an essential relationship with spontaneity. . . . [A] noble gratification is one thing, while sexual desire is another; when sexual desire is linked with a noble gratification, it differs from desire pure and simple" (48.4). Only through self-control can man attain "that deeper and more mature spontaneity with which his 'heart,' mastering his instincts, rediscovers the spiritual beauty of the signs constituted by the human body in its masculinity and femininity" (48.5).

To put this another way, I think we could say that "self-control," an essential ingredient of purity of heart, enables us to *take possession* of our desires and not *be possessed* by them precisely so that we can give ourselves away in love.

John Paul emphasizes that Christ's words in Matthew 5:27-28 must be seen in the perspective of "the redemption of man and of the world (and, therefore, precisely of the 'redemption of the body').

This, in fact, is the perspective of the . . . whole mission of Christ"
(49.3). In His Sermon Jesus does not invite man to return to the state
of original innocence, because this has been irretrievably lost, "but he
calls him to rediscover—on the foundations of the perennial and . . .
indestructible meanings of what is 'human'—the living forms of the
'new man.'" He thus establishes continuity between the "beginning"
and the perspective of redemption, for "in the ethos of the redemption of the body the original ethos of creation will have to be taken
up again" (49.4). To achieve this redemption the man to whom
Christ appeals must, with His help, be pure of heart, for "purity is
a requirement of love" (49.7).

Christ makes it clear, when he affirms (Matt. 15:18-20) that what
defiles a man comes from his "heart," from within himself, that "the
concept of 'purity' and 'impurity' in the moral sense is in the first
place a general concept, not a specific one: so that all moral good is
a manifestation of purity" (50.4). The man, male and female, who is
"pure of heart" is the one who has taken possession of his or her
desires; he or she is the one who has, through union with Christ,
"redeemed" his or her body, has rediscovered its "nuptial meaning"
and is now able, thanks to Christ's redemptive work, to "give" himself or herself away in love and to become fully one flesh in the
beautiful reality of marriage.

Summary of Part One
An attentive reading of God's revealed Word shows us that the triune God of love made man, male and female, to image Him fully in
their communion of persons, a communion made possible precisely
because of their sexual complementarity as revealed in the nuptial
meaning of their bodies, which signifies that the male person is
intended by God as a "gift" to the female person and vice versa.
Male and female are to give themselves away to each other in love
and to become one flesh and in doing so open themselves up to the
gift of fertility and in so doing to image even more fully the God
who made them. In the state of original innocence the nuptial meaning of their bodies was manifest, and as a result the man and the
woman did not experience shame over their nakedness because they
did not fear that the other would view them, not as a person to be

loved but as an object to be consumed. But as a result of their fall from innocence, concupiscence entered into the human heart and "veiled" the nuptial meaning of the body, with the result that man and woman experience shame over their nakedness, a shame experienced because the person, male or female, fears that the sexual values of his or her body will be consumed by the lust of others and thus the person, male or female, seeks to protect those values because they are *personal.*

But God so loves man, male and female, that He comes in the Person of Jesus Christ to "redeem" His created image and to enable man, male and female, to become pure of heart, to come into possession of his desires and not to be possessed by them, so that man, male and female, can rediscover the nuptial meaning of the body and give himself and herself away in marital love.[3]

Part Two: Basic Moral Principles and Sexual Morality[4]

After first emphasizing the existential and religious significance of human acts as freely chosen, I will identify the true moral norms needed if we are to choose well and then consider how to make good moral choices in living our lives as sexual persons.

The Existential, Religious Significance of Human Acts as Freely Chosen

Human acts are *not* physical events that come and go, like the falling of rain and the turning of leaves, nor do they "happen" to a person. They are, rather, the outward expression of a person's choices, for at the core of a human act is a free, self-determining choice, which as such is something spiritual which abides within the person, determining the very *being* of the person.

The Scriptures, particularly the New Testament, are very clear about this. Jesus taught that it was not what enters a person that defiles him or her; rather, it is what flows from the person, from his or her heart, from the core of his or her being, from his or her choice (cf. Matt. 15:10-2; Mk. 7:14-23).

Although many human acts have physical, observable components, what is central to them is that they embody and carry out
human choices; because they do, they abide within the person as
dispositions to further choices and actions of the same kind, until a
contradictory kind of choice is made. Thus I become an adulterer
and remain an adulterer when, by choice, I freely adopt the proposal to have sex with someone other than my wife. I commit adultery
in the heart even before I engage in the outward, observable act.
And I remain an adulterer, disposed to commit adultery again, until
I make a contradictory choice, i.e., until I sincerely repent of my
adultery, do penance, and commit myself to amending my life and
being faithful to my wife. Even then, in a sense, I remain an adulterer because I freely gave myself that identity, but now I am a
repentant adulterer, resolved to be a faithful, loving husband, and I
am a repentant adulterer because I have given myself this identity
by my freely chosen act (made, of course, with the help of God's
grace) of repentance.

As freely chosen, human acts have an existential, religious significance. John Paul II emphasized this truth in his 1993 Encyclical
Veritatis Splendor. Reflecting on the question the rich young man
asked of Christ, "Teacher, what good must I do to have eternal life?"
(Matt. 19:16), the Holy Father says, "For the young man the question
is not so much about rules to be followed, but *about the meaning of
life*" (VS 7). The rich young man's question has existential and
religious significance precisely because it is in and through the
actions we freely choose to do that *we determine ourselves* and establish our identity as moral beings. "It is precisely through his acts,"
the Pope writes, "that man attains perfection as man, as one who is
called to seek his Creator on his own accord and freely to arrive at
full and blessed perfection by cleaving to him." Our freely chosen
deeds, he continues, "do not produce a change merely in the state of
affairs outside of man, but, to the extent that they are deliberate
choices, they give moral definition to the very person who performs
them, *determining his most profound spiritual traits*" (VS 71). Each
choice involves a "*decision about oneself* and a setting of one's own
life for or against the Good, for or against the Truth, and ultimately
for or against God" (VS 65).

We are free to choose what we are to do and, through our choices, make ourselves to be the kind of persons we are. But we are *not* free to make what we choose to do to be good or bad, right or wrong. We know this from our own experience, for we know that at times we have freely chosen to do things that we knew, at the very moment we chose to do them, were *morally wrong*. We can, in short, choose badly or well; and, if we are to be fully the beings we are meant to be, we need to choose well, i.e., in accordance with the truth. To this issue I now turn.

Norms for Making True Moral Judgments and Good Moral Choices
All human choices and actions, whether morally good or morally bad, are done for a purpose, an end. All are intelligible or rational, although immoral choices are unreasonable because they are not fully compatible with reason.

The very first principle of natural law is that good is to be done and pursued and its opposite is to be avoided.[5] It is the starting point for intelligent, purposeful human action. This principle, moreover, is not empty; it can be specified by identifying the real goods, perfective of human persons, that are to be done and pursued. And these goods, as grasped by human practical reason, serve as the "principles" or starting points of practical reasoning or natural law. These are goods such as human life itself, including bodily life and integrity and the handing on of life, knowledge of the truth and appreciation of beauty, living in fellowship and friendship with others, marrying and raising children, personal integrity and authenticity.[6] None of these goods is the highest good—only God is—but each is a real good perfective of human persons and constituents of their flourishing or "full being." Thus the principles or starting points of practical reasoning are principles such as "good is to be done and pursued and its opposite avoided"; "life is a good to be pursued and protected"; "friendship, knowledge of the truth, appreciation of beauty, etc. are goods to be pursued and done."

These principles of practical reasoning are, as such, not yet moral principles, since they do not enable us to distinguish between morally good and morally bad options of choice (evil-doers appeal to principles of this kind to rationalize their behavior).

But if these principles do not help us determine, prior to choice, which alternatives of choice are *morally good* and which are *morally bad*, then what principles enable us to do so?

Let us see what Thomas Aquinas teaches here. In showing that all of the moral precepts of the Old Law can be reduced to the ten precepts of the Decalogue, Saint Thomas taught that the commandments that we are to love God above all things and our neighbor as ourselves, while not listed among the precepts of the Decalogue, nonetheless pertain to it as the "first and common precepts of natural law." Consequently, all the precepts of the Decalogue must, he concluded, be referred to these two love commandments as to their "common principles." Thus the first *normative* principle of natural law is the principle that we are to love God above all things and our neighbor as ourselves. This is hardly surprising for Christians. After all, did not our Lord, in answering the question, "Teacher, which is the greatest commandment in the law?" say, "You shall love the Lord your God with all your heart, and with all your soul, and with all your mind. This is the great and first commandment. And the second is like it. You shall love your neighbor as yourself. On these two commandments depend all the law and the prophets" (Mt. 22:32-40).

Moreover, and this is most important, there is an inseparable bond uniting this first moral principle to the first practical principles that direct us to the goods perfective of us as human persons. For these goods are gifts of a loving God that we are to welcome and cherish both in ourselves and in others. It is obvious that we can love our neighbor as ourselves only if we are willing to respect the goods perfective of him and by being unwilling intentionally to damage, destroy or impede these goods, to ignore them, to slight them, or to put them aside because their continued flourishing keeps us from doing what we please to do here and now. Thomas taught that we offend God only by acting contrary to *our own good*[7] and John Paul II in *Veritatis Splendor* 13 reminds us that the negative precepts of the Decalogue (having to do with our neighbor), although formulated negatively, are positive in their thrust because they protect the *inviolable dignity of the human person*, and they do so by protecting his *good*, i.e., the different goods perfective of him at the different levels of his being, goods such as life itself, etc.

This fundamental normative truth is further clarified, I think, in the formula proposed by Germain Grisez, namely, that "in voluntarily acting for human goods and avoiding what is opposed to them, one ought to choose and otherwise will those and only those possibilities whose willing is compatible with integral human fulfillment," i.e., with a heart open to every real good meant to flourish in human persons.[8]

Making Good Choices in Matters of Sex

Like all choices, sexual choices must conform to the truth if they are to be morally good, if they are to enable men and women to give themselves the identity of persons who want to shape their lives in accordance with the truth and who want to become fully the persons they are meant to be. This means that sexual choices must respect the inviolable dignity of human persons made in God's image, and to do this they must respect the *goods* of human persons.

But what goods are at stake in making sexual choices? What goods come into focus (or ought to come into focus) when one is thinking about exercising his or her genital sexuality? They are the following: (1) the good of life itself in its transmission or the procreative good; (2) the good of intimate human friendship; (3) the good of marriage itself; (4) the good of personal integrity, a good intimately related to what Pope John Paul II calls the "nuptial meaning of the body."

The first two of these goods are obviously at stake when one considers engaging in genital sex. The act of sexual coition is the sort or kind of act intrinsically apt for generating new human life; it is indeed the only bodily act apt for doing so. The practice of contraception makes this evident, for one would not contracept did one not believe reasonably that one was about to engage in the sort of act through which new life can be given and, for some reason, one did not *want* that life to begin.

That the good of intimate personal friendship is also at stake in genital coition is evident from the fact that such coition is possible only between two persons, one male, the other female.

In short, when one chooses to engage in genital coition two of the goods at stake are those identified as the "unitive" and "procreative"

goods of human sexuality. Even if one chooses to exercise his or her
genital powers solitarily, as in masturbation, or in sodomitical or
non-coital acts (anally or orally or what have you), one realizes that
one is exercising a personal sexual power that is inherently life-
giving (procreative) and person-uniting (unitive).

Also at stake is the good of marriage itself. Marriage is truly a
basic human good, complex in nature, but grasped as something
good in itself and not merely instrumentally.

Another good at stake in choosing to have sex is the good of "personal integrity." This good, as John Finnis notes, "requires that one
be reaching out with one's will, i.e., freely choosing real goods, and
that one's efforts to realize these goods involves, where appropriate,
one's bodily activity, so that that activity is as much the constitutive
subject of what one does as one's act of choice is."[9] This good
entails one's own bodily integrity, for one's own body is integral to
one's being as an acting person. This good is basically an aspect of
what John Paul II calls the "nuptial meaning of the body," the
body as a sign of the gift of the male person to the female person and
vice versa.

Since these are the goods at stake in genital choices, such choices are morally good—that is, they enable persons, male and female,
to give themselves the identity to which they are summoned, from
the depths of their being, as persons called to give themselves away
in love—only if all the goods at stake are fully respected, for the
goods at stake are not abstractions but are rather aspects of the full-
being or flourishing of the persons whose goods they are. But it is
only in marriage and in the marital act, one open to the goods of
human sexuality and made possible only because of the nuptial
meaning of the body, that all these goods can be rightly respected
and honored. Contraception is opposed to the good of human life in
its transmission, because the whole point of contraception is to
"close" a freely chosen genital act to the gift of human life. Extra-
marital sex is opposed to the good of friendship and to the good of
marriage; such sex in no way unites two irreplaceable, nonsubsti-
tutable, and non-disposable persons but rather merely joins two
replaceable, substitutable, and disposable individuals. Similarly,
masturbation and sodomy instrumentalize the body and damage its

nuptial significance. All such sexual choices, far from liberating persons, harm them to the depths, insofar as, in making such choices persons, become possessed by their desires and less capable of self-giving love.

Appendix: Titles of the First Fifty Addresses in Pope John Paul II's Theology of the Body

Cycle One: Original Unity of Man and Woman (Addresses 1-23)
Here I provide a translation of the titles of the addresses as given in the original Italian edition, not the English translation, because the Italian titles, on the whole, more clearly indicate the scope of the individual addresses than do the English titles, although, in places, the English titles seem more fitting. The division of the twenty-three addresses into sections is my own.

Introduction: 1. A dialogue with Christ on the foundations of the family (Sept. 5, 1979); 2. The objective definition of man in the first creation account (Sept. 12, 1979); 3. The subjective definition of man in the second creation account (Sept. 19, 1979); 4. The bond between original innocence and the redemption wrought by Christ (Sept. 26, 1979).

Original experiences: 5. Meaning of man's original solitude (Oct. 10, 1979); 6. In his original solitude man's awareness of being a person (Oct. 24, 1979); 7. In the very definition of man the alternative between death and immortality (October 31, 1979); 8. The original unity of man and woman in their humanity (Nov. 7, 1979); 9. Through the communion of persons man becomes the image of God (Nov. 14, 1979); 10. [summary] The value of marriage, one and indissoluble, in light of the first chapters of Genesis (Nov. 21, 1979).

Nakedness: 11. The meaning of original experiences of man (Dec. 12, 1979); 12. The fullness of interpersonal communion of the original innocence (Dec. 19, 1979); 13 Creation as a fundamental and original gift (Jan. 2, 1980).

Nuptial meaning of the body: 14.The revelation and discovery of the body [English: Nuptial meaning of the body] (Jan. 9, 1980); 15.The man-person becomes a gift in the freedom of love (Jan. 16,

1980); 16. [summary] Knowledge and meaning of the body and original innocence [English: Mystery of man's original innocence] (Jan. 30, 1980).

Nakedness and shame: 17. The exchange of the gift of the body creates an authentic communion [English: Man and woman: a mutual gift for each other] (Feb. 6, 1980); 18. Original innocence and man's historical state (Feb. 13, 1980); 19. With the sacrament of the body man feels himself as a subject of holiness [English: Man enters the world a subject of truth and holiness] (Feb. 20, 1980).

Knowledge and procreation: 20. The biblical meaning of "knowledge" in marital life together (March 5, 1980); 21. The mystery of woman is revealed in motherhood (March 12, 1980); 22. The knowledge-generation cycle and the perspective of death (March 26, 1980).

Summary of cycle one: 23. The question of marriage in the integral vision of man (April 2, 1980).

Cycle Two: Part One: Catechesis on the Sermon on the Mount (Addresses 24-50)

I will use English titles and put translations of Italian titles in parentheses where I think the Italian is more accurate. If both are the same, there is no need to make any parenthetical observation. The suggested subdivisions of material are my own:

Introduction: 24. Christ appeals to man's heart; 25. Ethical and anthropological content of the commandment, "Do not commit adultery."

Reflections on the meaning of "lust" or "concupiscence": 26. Lust is the fruit of the breach of the covenant with God; 27. Real significance of original nakedness; (Italian: Radical change of the meaning of original nakedness); 28. A fundamental disquiet in all human existence (Italian: The body not subordinated to the spirit threatens the unity of the man-person; 29. Relationship of lust to communion of persons (Italian: meaning of the original shame in the interpersonal relationship of the man and the woman); 30. Dominion over the other in the interpersonal relation; 31. Lust limits nuptial meaning of the body (Italian: The threefold concupiscence limits the spousal meaning of the body); 32. The "heart"—a battlefield between love and lust (Italian: Concupiscence of the body deforms the man-woman relationship); 33. Opposition in the human heart between the spirit and the body (Italian: The communion of persons is in the will of the reciprocal gift).

Summary reflection: 34. The Sermon on the Mount to the men of our day.

Christ's deepening of the commandment, "You shall not commit adultery"; 35. Content of the commandment, "You shall not commit adultery"; 36. Adultery according to the law and as spoken by the prophets; 37. Adultery: a breakdown of the personal covenant (Italian: Adultery according to Christ: a falsification of the sign and a breach of the personal covenant); 38. Meaning of adultery transferred from the body to the heart.

"Looking lustfully": 39. Concupiscence as a separation from the matrimonial significance of the body; 40. Mutual attraction differs from lust (Italian: Desire and the intentional reduction of the horizon of the mind and heart); 41. Depersonalizing effect of concupiscence.

Summarizing reflection: 42. Establishing the ethical sense (Italian: Constructing a new ethical sense by means of the rediscovery of values); 43. Interpreting the concept of concupiscence (Italian: Psychological and theological interpretations of the concept of concupiscence).

Reaffirming the goodness of the body; 44. Gospel values and duties of the human heart; 45. Realization of the value of the body according to the plan of the Creator.

Redeeming the body: 46; The power of redeeming completes the power of creation; 47. "Eros" and "Ethos" meet and bear fruit in the human heart; 48. Spontaneity: the mature result of conscience (Italian: Spontaneity is truly human when it is the mature fruit of conscience); 49. Christ calls us to rediscover the living forms of the new man; 50. Purity of heart (Italian: The Old Testament tradition of "purity of heart" and the new meaning of "purity").

Notes

1 Pope John Paul II presented his "theology of the body" in a series of Wednesday audiences from September 5, 1979 through November 28, 1984. These Wednesday audiences comprised six "cycles" of addresses. The first cycle, entitled "The Beginning,"

includes the first 23 addresses, given from September 5, 1979 through April 2, 1980; the second, called "The Redemption of the Heart," includes addresses 24-63, given from April 16, 1980 through May 6, 1981; the third, "The Resurrection of the Flesh," numbers 64-72, given from November 11, 1981 through February 10, 1982; the fourth, "Christian Virginity," numbers 73-86, from March 10, 1982 through July 21,1982; the fifth, "Christian Marriage," numbers 87-117, given from July 28, 1982 through July 4, 1984; and the sixth, "Love and Fecundity," numbers 118-133, given from July 11, 1984 through November 28, 1984.

All these addresses have been gathered together in a one-volume definitive Italian edition, Giovanni Paolo II, *Uomo e Donna lo creò* (Città Nuova Editrice: Libreria Editrice Vaticana, 1987). The Daughters of St. Paul published cycle one under the title *Original Unity of Man and Woman: Catechesis on the Book of Genesis* in 1981; cycle two under the title *Blessed Are the Pure in Heart: Catechesis on the Sermon on the Mount and the Teaching of St. Paul* in 1983; cycles three, four, and five under the title *The Theology of Marriage and Celibacy* in 1986; and cycle six under the title *Reflections on Humanae Vitae* in 1985 (Boston: St. Paul Editions). In 1998 the Daughters published the entire series in one volume, Pope John Paul II, *Theology of the Body: Human Love in the Divine Plan* (Boston: Pauline Books and Media), with an introduction by John Grabowski. In my opinion the one-volume English edition grants concessions to "politically correct" language (e.g., use of "human being" or "person" in place of "man"), with the result that I think it preferable to use the four-volume edition. In addition, both the Italian text and the four-volume English edition provide paragraph numbers for the different sections of each of the addresses, whereas the one-volume edition fails to provide them. Their use facilitates finding the location of given texts within the addresses. Thus, in this paper, I will refer to the number of the address followed by a reference to the appropriate paragraph number within the address. For example, 4.2 refers to the fourth address, paragraph 2. John Paul developed the concepts central to the "theology of the body" in the first two cycles, "The Beginning," i.e., the addresses found in *Original Unity of Man and*

Woman, and "The Redemption of the Heart," i.e., the addresses contained in *Blessed Are the Pure of Heart.* In an appendix I will list all the addresses in the first two cycles since it is from these that citations will be made in the text, followed by the number of the address and the appropriate paragraph number. Christopher West provides a comprehensive presentation and analysis of all these addresses in his *The Theology of the Body Explained* (Boston: Pauline Books and Media, 2003).

2 See Pope John Paul II, "Nuptial Meaning of the Body," 14.2. In this text Pope John Paul II is explicitly concerned with the account in Genesis 2, but the expression "beatifying beginning" can also be applied to the narrative in Genesis 1.

3 On the biblical teaching on human sexuality and sexual ethics see also Ronald Lawler, O.F.M. Cap., Joseph Boyle, and William E. May, *Catholic Sexual Ethics: A Summary, Explanation, and Defense,* second edition (Huntington, IN: Our Sunday Visitor, 1998), p. 32-45.

4 A fuller presentation of basic moral principles and sexual morality is found in Lawler, et al. *Catholic Sexual Ethics,* pp. 68-95, 140-198. See also William E. May, *Catholic Sexual Ethics,* a pamphlet in the Veritas Series, published by the Knights of Columbus (New Haven, CT: Catholic Information Service of the Knights of Columbus, 2001). In this part of my essay I have abridged several pages of this pamphlet.

5 See St. Thomas, *Summa theologiae,* 1-2, 94, 2.

6 See William E. May, *Introduction to Moral Theology,* second edition (Huntington, IN: Our Sunday Visitor, 2003), pp. 49-68.

7 See his *Summa Contra Gentiles,* 3.122.

8 See Germain Grisez, *Christian Moral Principles* (Chicago: Franciscan Herald Press, 1983), p. 184.

9 John Finnis, "Personal Integrity, Sexual Morality, and Responsible Parenthood," *Anthropos: Rivista di studi sulla persona e la famiglia* 1 (1985), 46.

The Biological Justification for *Humanae Vitae*

EVELYN AND JOHN BILLINGS

In the encyclical letter *Humanae Vitae* (Of Human Life), His Holiness Pope Paul VI made a call to men of science to explain more thoroughly the various conditions favoring a proper regulation of births. He quoted a wish already expressed by Pope Pius XII that medical science succeed in providing a sufficiently secure basis for a regulation of birth, founded on the observation of natural rhythms.

By 1968, when *Humanae Vitae* was published, there was already a large body of such scientific research on the regulation of births. In 1953, we began the research that led to the Billings Ovulation Method of natural family planning.

Our attention was soon directed to the behavior of the cervix of the uterus during the menstrual cycles.

All the fertile women in our study described a vaginal discharge over three to six days, or perhaps only one to three. When the women were questioned about the discharge, they were asked whether it remained the same day after day, and they quickly answered that it did not. Whatever the length of the time for which the discharge was present, women always described a change which was felt and seen from day to day. The sequence of the descriptions was clearly reflecting a chemical control of the mucus effecting a change in its chemical and physical characteristics.

Smith in England, Sims and Huhner in the United States, Knaus in Australia, Ogino in Japan, and more recently Seguy and Vimeux in

Evelyn and John Billings *are Australian physicians who developed the Billings Ovulation Method of natural family planning.*

France gradually built up an increasing body of knowledge, later augmented by two modern giants, James Brown of New Zealand and Erik Odeblad of Sweden. Among other important discoveries, the endocrinologist James Brown found an interval of eleven to sixteen days between ovulation and menstruation. Erik Odeblad was—and continues to be—involved in classifying the various types of mucus and their functions by a reference to their physical structure and their specific contribution to a full understanding of the menstrual cycle.

In this way knowledge had been increasing steadily from 1953 to 1968. In 1967, the year before *Humanae Vitae,* Pope Paul VI gave John a Papal Knighthood in recognition of our work.

In 1968 we made a teaching visit to New Zealand, and in 1969 we traveled to Singapore, Malaysia, and Hong Kong to give lectures on natural family planning. In Hong Kong a missionary priest who had served in the United States Army during the war listened to our talk and asked whether we would be visiting countries on the other side of the Pacific Ocean. If so, he recommended that we write in advance to a wonderful priest in Los Angeles, namely Monsignor Robert E. Deegan.

A Richer and More Human Life

It happened that we were invited to visit Guatemala and also to make studies in all the countries of Central America. We were able to meet Monsignor Deegan in Los Angeles on our way to Guatemala and Central America. He asked us to stop for a time on our return journey to Australia to speak to a group of doctors and nurses he would enlist to listen to what we had to say.

Monsignor Deegan was at that time the director of the Department of Health and Hospitals in Los Angeles and was also the parish priest in the Church of the American Martyrs in Manhattan Beach. He had quickly become convinced of the value of our discoveries and established what he referred to as "Institutes." These meetings drew attendees from all around the world, especially doctors, who would come to Los Angeles for about two weeks a year over the course of several years. Their goal was to establish teachers in the various foreign countries.

These Institutes continued for many years, and in January 1980 Father Ronald Lawler was invited to present a paper on the whole subject of regulation of birth based on sound evidence obtained from nature.

This was not our first encounter with Father Lawler, as he had been a speaker at a *Humanae Vitae* conference organized at the University of Melbourne in 1978 by the Ovulation Method Research and Reference Center of Australia. He entitled that talk "Toward a Richer and More Human Life."

In the beginning of that talk, echoing a call by God to each man and woman to a rich flourishing of life, he referred to the call by the Second Vatican Council to holiness. The Church, he said, is defending the dignity of man and wife. "The teaching of faith and morality can be understood only in the light of the total vision of man which faith proclaims. Man is called to a human life, a life which even on this earth is enriched with supernatural gifts and depths, but which finds its entire fulfillment only in eternal life." He chose also to quote a statement from the Dogmatic Constitution on the Church (*Lumen Gentium*) of the Second Vatican Council: "All Christians in any state of life are called to the fullness of Christian life and to the perfection of love." The marriage state itself is to be based on conjugal love as a special kind of love, making possible the profoundly human but divinely ordered friendship which the marriage union is to create. One must not do evil that good may come of it; and it is evil to act directly against any good.

Defending Catholic Truth

It is only gradually being understood that chemicals can be used in evil actions, particularly to attack those natural processes which maintain a healthy fertility in both the wife and the husband. Chemicals are used especially to suppress the fertility of the woman. If the woman accepts these substances to destroy natural hormones, she is then acting to withdraw the most important gift that she brought to the marriage, which is the divine gift of fertility. If the woman withdraws this gift, and perhaps also the husband rejects the gift of his wife's fertility, the marriage will be severely damaged as long as that situation prevails.

The strength of the adversaries of life and the family comes from their success in persuading people that what they are doing is for a good purpose and therefore to be encouraged. What the World Health Organization and the United Nations Family Planning Association recommend is a new cultural revolution, a change of hearts and minds; Christians who accept such programs must understand the severity of the damage that husbands and wives may be accepting for themselves and for one another.

Father Lawler recognized the disregard for the truth and its acceleration by the lack of courage. He perceived that Pope Paul agreed with those scholars who supported immemorial Church traditions. As Pope Paul wrote in *Humanae Vitae*: "One could not accept the teaching [of the opponents of Catholic ethics] on contraception without undermining principles essentially guarding all those values which Catholic sexual teaching defends. The married people especially and the clergy should be confident that God is able and willing to give men and women the strength to carry out what the good of human life and love requires. This discipline, which is proper to the purity of married couples, far from harming conjugal love, rather confers on it a high human value. . . . Such discipline bestows upon family life fruits of serenity and peace, and facilitates the solution of other problems; it favors attention for one's partner to help both husband and wife to drive out selfishness, the enemy of true love; and deepens their sense of responsibility."

A Call to Greatness

Monsignor Deegan and Father Lawler were present at two conferences, one in Los Angeles and the other in Melbourne. They were most agreeable individuals and undoubtedly great friends, with a clear vision of what must be done. Regrettably, Monsignor Deegan died suddenly in 1983 as the result of a heart seizure. His gentle wisdom can be perceived in the story we heard about him, that he had composed the songs—words and music—for a school play, and had himself provided the musical support with great success. These two men were greatly loved by a very large number of people who had enjoyed the virtue of their friendship.

Father Lawler told us on a number of occasions that the promotion of the welfare of the family was probably the most important theme to be addressed by the various groups of Catholic laity. He believed that *Humanae Vitae* could lead Catholic families "Toward a Richer and More Human Life."

In 1980, at the Sixth International Ovulation Method Institute in Los Angeles, Father Lawler strengthened his appeal to the laity by giving his presentation the title "Marriage, A Call to Greatness."

His first paragraph in that paper stated that "One of the constant objections to natural family planning is that it asks too much of people. Many will acknowledge its positive features as a form of a family planning: it reverences life, is never abortifacient, it has no deadly side effects; it demands only a moderate amount of abstinence, still—it requires self-denial and self-discipline of a kind that ordinary people will not put up with. At the bottom line, it won't work."

He went on to say that this objection, in his view, is "un-Christian and anti-human." It fails to appreciate what an "ordinary person" can and will do, given a motive and given loving help. If we do not think that the ordinary person is transcendentally important and essentially capable of greatness, we cannot talk of Christian morality at all.

He ended his presentation with a message of love: "The cruelest people in the Church, I think, are those who, hoping to be kind to suffering people today, destroy or neglect (or fail to insist on) the sacred values that are needed to brace ordinary lives." Christ is making demands on the hearts of men and women: to faithful love and forgiveness, and generosity. Father Lawler understood that the new law is established through "the grace of the Holy Spirit." This is the grace that gives men and women power to do with generosity what is necessary for them to do to be good persons at all. He quoted the words of Pope Paul VI in *Humanae Vitae:* "It is an excellent work of Divine Love to lessen in no way the saving law of Christ" (HV 29).

Ordinary people come to happiness and greatness and are called to these virtues. Marriage is the sign of love between Christ crucified and His Church.

Father Lawler observed countless examples of couples who chose what seemed to be beyond their capabilities, but who found that the love that is given requires and gives them strength to persevere.

Teaching Love

We have made teaching visits to more than ninety countries around the world, and everywhere we have found many couples in distress because they still believe that the Catholic inspiration is too hard for them. But when they discover and try the Billings Method of natural family planning, many of them tell us, "This method is love." In faith they learn to do what is right and recognize that this is the best thing any human person can do.

Father Lawler believed and preached that "The arguments of theologians to justify moral revolution have all been based on very weak arguments. All these arguments are in fact forms of a claim that 'We may do evil that good may come of it.'" He recognized the danger of falling into the trap of false compassion—of invoking the trials of our times to justify the acceptance of evil.

Many of the countries that we visited most often, such as India, Mexico, and China, had very large populations and widespread poverty. In South America we saw the pernicious results of Depo-Provera injections (Medroxyprogesterone Acetate). Some of the women were complaining of their infertility, others of the fact that they had been bleeding for several months without interruption and they were pale. We learned the horrors of "chemical birth control," often organized from the United States of America. Our teaching offered an option, and we saw good results in every country we visited.

In El Salvador there were couples who were living together without marriage and without baptism of the children. When they learned that there was a form of regulating birth without harm and with approval of the Catholic Church, the missionaries visiting their homes were able to teach them the Billings Method. The result was that not long afterwards the couples began coming to the Church and would arrange that, on the same day, the children would be baptized and the parents would be married. All of this was very

rewarding and, as a result of the activities of the visiting missionaries, the local bishops reported that there were many vocations to
the priesthood from these families.

The Gospel of Love in China

In February 2004 Evelyn read a report about our work in China
at a meeting of the Pontifical Academy for Life at Vatican City. In
that presentation she reported on our work in China. There, accompanied by two of our best Australian teachers, we had trained 1,871
core teachers who were, in turn, responsible for training 48,449
Chinese teachers to work in their local provinces. During this time
important refinements were made to the teaching techniques, and
comprehensive teaching materials were developed and translated
into Chinese.

By December 2003 the method was being used by more than
3,645,600 fertile couples for avoiding pregnancy. The overall success rate was estimated at more than 99%. Of 48,267 sub-fertile
couples 15,640 had already conceived in a short time by using the
Billings Method. (The Chinese government wishes every couple to
have a child, and more than one in certain circumstances.) These
figures come from complete records of the Chinese centers of
teaching, but many more Chinese couples are using the Billings
Method without centralized records, as the Billings Method is now
one of the principal choices of fertility regulation in China.

The Chinese conducted a randomized one-year comparison of
the efficacy of the BOM (Billings Ovulation Method) and the
CopperT intra-uterine. The CopperT has been the most commonly
used birth-control method in China, but the Chinese study showed
marked superiority of the BOM compared with the CopperT device.

The Chinese statistics reveal another very interesting result.
Recent surveys of all areas where the BOM is taught have shown an
encouraging sevenfold decline to 0.61 percet in artificial abortion
rate, as compared with 4.06 percent rate where the BOM has not
been introduced. So, in a province where the BOM had been taught,
there would be only one artificial abortion for every seven in a similar adjacent province where the BOM had not been taught at all.

Another interesting revelation has been the wonderful result in the protection against HIV/AIDS by the increased use of the BOM method. In these poor countries, there has developed a common practice of the husband and wife separating after the birth of a child. This is designed to prevent another pregnancy within a short interval. The result is that the husband finds another woman for sexual intercourse. When the BOM is taught to a couple, preferably before the child is born, the husband is instructed to stay at home with his wife; then intercourse can occur during the infertile periods of the menstrual cycle without the risk of pregnancy. With this new understanding, it is less likely that the husband will visit any other woman, and so will escape any possibility of HIV/AIDS infection.

The Truth about Condoms

Condoms are often touted as an effective means of preventing pregnancy and disease, but it is important to understand that condoms are not a reliable method of avoiding either.

On July 20, 2001 a report was issued by the United States Department of Health and Human Services. The scientific panel reporting had been co-sponsored by the National Institutes of Health (NIH), the Food and Drug Administration (FDA), the Centers for Disease Control and Prevention (CDCP), and the USA Agency for International Development. The report was based on a year-long study in which 28 researchers reviewed 138 peer studies on the heterosexual transmission of sexually transmitted diseases (STD).

The panel studied condom effectiveness in preventing the eight most prevalent sexually transmitted diseases: HIV, Gonorrhea, Chlamydia, Syphilis, Cancroids, Trichomoniasis, Genital Herpes, and Human Papilloma Virus (HPV). None of these diseases were effectively excluded.

Even when used correctly and consistently, condoms were still found to be associated with a 15% HIV infection rate in heterosexual activity.

At a conference in Melbourne in February 2003, Pope John Paul II referred to support for these biological findings, and he conferred Papal Knighthood on Evelyn, just as John had received years earlier from Pope Paul.

"Clearing a Little Space, and Time, and Light"

At the end of his talk in Melbourne, Father Lawler quoted a poetic statement of Jean Baptiste Lacordaire, O.P.:

> *A Priest Forever*
> To live in the midst of the world without craving its pleasures; to be a member of every family yet confined to none; to share all sufferings; to be trusted custodian of all secrets; to heal all wounds; to go from men to God and offer Him their prayers; to return from God to men and bring pardon and hope; to have a heart of fire for charity and a will of bronze for loyalty to vows; to teach and pardon, to console and bless always!
>
> —Jean Baptiste Lacordaire, O.P.

In return, we Australians offered a comparable contribution from a famous Australian poet, James McAuley:

> Do not offend your souls with bitterness:
> Think rather that I never shrank in fear
> But fought the monsters of the lower world,
> Clearing a little space, and time, and light,
> For men to live in peace.

The Logic of Doctrine and the Logic of Catechesis: The Relationship between the *Catechism of the Catholic Church* and the *General Directory for Catechesis*

FATHER J. AUGUSTINE DiNoiA, O.P.

Introduction: the *Catechism* and the *General Directory* as Complementary

Through his seminal work, *The Teaching of Christ*, Father Ronald Lawler, O.F.M. Cap., mentored a generation of American catechists. Father Ronald taught us to appreciate the critical connections between doctrine and catechesis—how our teaching of the faith must draw not only its "content" but also its "logic" from the Biblical and doctrinal sources of the faith.

I hope this article on the relationship between the *Catechism of the Catholic Church* and the *General Directory for Catechesis* would have pleased him. To my mind, the relationship between these two documents of the Magisterium demonstrates the truth and pedagogical potential of Father Lawler's fundamental insight.

The essence of this relationship can be stated in this way: the logic of doctrine gives structure to the logic of catechesis. Thus, while the *Catechism* provides the doctrinal content to be imparted in catechetical formation, the *Directory* outlines the manner in which that catechesis should proceed. With the *Catechism* as a fundamental source of Catholic doctrine, the *Directory* draws out the

Rev. J. Augustine DiNoia, O.P., *is under-secretary of the Vatican Congregation for the Doctrine of the Faith.*

implications for effective catechesis and in this way advances the purpose of the Magisterium in the preparation and publication of the *Catechism* by facilitating the adaptation of its contents in the many catechetical programs throughout the world. If the principal thrust of the *Catechism* is to furnish a synthesis of Catholic teaching, then that of the *Directory* is to assist local churches in developing effective methods for transmitting essential Catholic doctrine in diverse cultural and social settings.

The *Directory* itself describes the relationship between the two documents by speaking of their "mutual complementarity:"

> The complementary nature of both of these instruments justi-fies the fact, as already mentioned in the Preface, that this *General Directory for Catechesis* does not devote a chapter to the presentation of the contents of the faith, as was the case in the 1971 *General Catechetical Directory* under the title: "The more outstanding elements of the Christian message." Such is explained by the fact that this *Directory*, as far as the content of the Christian message is concerned, simply refers to the *Catechism of the Catholic Church*, which is intended as a methodological norm for its concrete application (120).

This presentation takes its point of departure from Part Two, Chapter II of the *Directory* (119-130), which charts the "mutual complementarity" of the *Catechism* and the *Directory* under the following headings: the organization of the *Catechism*, the doctri-nal structure of the *Catechism*, the genre of the *Catechism*, the relationship of the *Catechism* to the deposit of faith, the role of Sacred Scripture in the *Catechism* and in catechesis, and the *Catechism* in the perspective of patristic catechetical traditions.

1. Significance of the Organization of the *Catechism of the Catholic Church*

How, precisely, do the contents of the *Catechism* and the content of the faith furnish the rule or measure for the methodology of the pastoral ministry of catechesis? The *Directory* offers the basic principles of pastoral theology drawn from Scripture, Tradition, and the Magisterium of the Church, and in a special way from the Second Vatican Council, as it shapes and directs pastoral action and the ministry of the Word in catechesis. The *Catechism* thus supplies a kind of norm for the pastoral theology which the *Directory* is itself concerned to present.

The *Directory* (122) first addresses the significance of the organization or structure of the *Catechism*. This organization is familiar to all of us. The four major parts of the *Catechism*, its "four pillars" (CCC 13), are Creed, Sacraments, Commandments, and Our Father. This ordering of material is telling: it provides an interpretative key for construing the content of catechesis and for the structuring of catechetical programs. The *Catechism*, in fact, reflects a particular order of presentation chosen over against other possible organizational plans. It is worthwhile asking about the rationale for the *Catechism's* organization and about its bearing on proper doctrinal formation.

Creed

The Creed is presented to us first for the simple reason that there would be nothing to say, there would be nothing for the Church to communicate to anyone, if God had not spoken to us in the first place. What God announces to us is, most fundamentally, the divine desire at the source of everything that exists in the entire created universe: angels, human beings, the world, the Church. This divine desire at the root of everything that exists is the desire of the Father, the Son, and the Holy Spirit to invite created persons—angels and human beings—into communion with themselves. Nothing would exist apart from this divine desire.

The *Catechism* clearly embraces this perspective. We have nothing to say if we do not begin with the articulation of the fundamental truth about this divine desire. This desire, on the part of the Triune God, to share His own life with creaturely persons, is the foundational mystery of Christianity, for from this desire flows the entirety of creation and salvation. God, whose perfection and happiness can be neither enhanced nor diminished, nonetheless expresses His mysterious desire to share a participation in His own interior life with creatures by the act of creation. As Saint Irenaeus said, "God, who has no need for anyone, gave communion with Himself to those who need Him." This amazing truth must therefore be accounted of primary importance. And, indeed, the *Catechism* stresses the gratuity of the divine initiative as one of its principal themes throughout, and particularly in the early sections of part one (cf. 26-141). The Creed is nothing other than the unfolding in each of its articles—the articulation—of this very simple truth. For this reason, the confession of Trinitarian faith is, in a sense, all that needs to be said; and, conversely, if this confession is not made, nothing else is worth saying and nothing else makes sense.

Sacraments

The sacraments are treated next, constituting the second pillar of the *Catechism*. Although this sequence is not in itself controversial, one could easily overlook the didactic importance of placing a treatment on the sacraments just here. For it might be supposed that the treatment of the commandments should follow the creed, according to the logic that our response follows God's invitation. After all, the commandments tell us what we must do to respond to the divine invitation to communion.

Our response does, of course, follow God's invitation, but not immediately. Why not? Because there is no possibility of responding to God's initiative without divine grace. The second part of the *Catechism* establishes the possibility of human persons' engagement with the Father, Son, and Holy Spirit—something which transcends not only our merits and our capacities, but our very nature itself. The *Catechism*'s section on the sacraments concerns not only the celebration of our faith, but also, and more importantly, the primacy of grace in the Christian life. By His grace God is acting in us, enabling creaturely persons to be at home in the uncreated communion of Trinitarian life.

Commandments

Only after our nature is empowered by God's grace to share this communion is it possible for us to observe the Commandments. Thus, in the *Catechism*, the explanation of the sacraments provides the indispensable context for the teaching of the Commandments. It is in part three of the *Catechism* that readers and teachers are likely to encounter new material, in terms of moral formation and catechetical methodology. There is much here to challenge contemporary notions of the moral life. This part must be read in light of Pope John Paul II's encyclical letter *Veritatis Splendor*. It frames the whole issue of the Christian moral life, not principally in terms of observing commandments, but of sharing the life of God Himself by being transformed by His grace. The moral life, in other words, is supposed to change us in our very being so that we seek the Good above all else. The breathtaking vision of the moral life given us by *Veritatis Splendor* and the *Catechism*'s third part by placing such needed emphasis on the following of Christ, grace, virtue, the beatitudes, and the Gifts of the Holy Spirit is a great challenge to many of us who perhaps have been trained to place the moral life in a more legalistic and duty-centered perspective.

Our Father

Finally, in part four, the *Catechism* takes up the Our Father. In the human heart attuned to the Triune God in prayer, we have the very culmination of the Christian life. It has been rightly observed that the *Catechism* could have begun with the Our Father. For, by concluding with the communion of the Christian in prayer with the Holy Trinity, the *Catechism* has come full circle: it could have begun with prayer because, in a sense, it begins in the Trinity only to return to the Trinity in the end.

In summary, then, by drawing attention to the *Catechism*'s organization, the *Directory* points us to a first principle of pastoral theology in catechesis: discern and respect the inner order or logic of the faith. Sound catechetical methodology must strive to exploit this inner logic and allow it to shape doctrinal, sacramental, moral, and spiritual formation at all levels. The logic of catechesis follows the logic of doctrine.

2. Doctrinal Structure of the *Catechism*: the Trinitarian-Christological-Ecclesial Core

It is precisely to this inner logic of the faith that the *Directory* (123) turns when it moves from a consideration of the organization of the *Catechism* to its deeper theological structure. The organization of the *Catechism* teaches us that, in communicating the faith at whatever level, priority must be given first to the divine invitation to

Trinitarian communion, then to the grace-filled sacramental enablement which makes such communion possible to creaturely persons, and then to the pattern of life which leads free persons to embrace this communion, and finally to the consummation of this communion in prayer and adoration. In the next section of the *Directory's* treatment of the bearing of the *Catechism* on catechetical methodology, our attention is drawn to the doctrinal structure of the *Catechism* and thus to the central mysteries of the Christian faith: the dogmatic or doctrinal core of Catholic teaching. This "Trinitarian-Christological-Ecclesial core" locates the focal mysteries of the faith at the heart of all other doctrines, and provides a divine perspective on the nature and dignity of the human person.

As we have already seen, the *Catechism* emphatically states that the ultimate destiny of all personal life—the meaning of personal life, communal and private—is to be found in ultimate communion with the Triune God. God's plan for us is to draw us into the family that God is, in Himself. This truth of our faith—so much taken for granted and therefore hardly understood—is that God is Triune. The ultimate, transcendent source of all things is not a self-possessed, isolated, silent, inactive Superbeing. God is, rather, a conversation whose inner life can best be characterized, as the Greeks have said, as a perichoresis, what one theologian has called the "harmonious life" of the Triune God which He wants to share with us. God wants us to become partners in this conversation, this round dance, this harmonious life. The meaning of our life lies here.

One point made clear in the *Catechism*, and which must be made clear in our teaching as well, is that God Himself could not provide us with a more intimate participation in His life than the one He has in fact already begun in us by Baptism and which He will consummate in the life to come. The idea bears repeating: there is no greater intimacy to which God could draw us short of making us, impossibly, other gods than the one which He has already begun in us by Baptism and will consummate in the life to come. Having said that, we must also say that God does in fact make us "other gods," properly understood. The Fathers of the Church (both East and West) often speak of man's transformation by grace and participation in Trinitarian life as a theosis or "divinization." We are, in a very real sense, made like God, partakers in the divine nature, in order to share the communion of Trinitarian life in God.

One cannot presume that such an understanding of the Trinity is widely appreciated or grasped these days. The doctrine of the Trinity has come to be regarded as a metaphysical puzzle. To be sure, the articulation of the doctrine of the Trinity throughout the history of Christian thought has posed a considerable conceptual challenge to the bishops and theologians of the Church. The theology of the Trinity is, in the end, an inexhaustible mystery that cannot be fully comprehended by anyone, however learned. But the conceptual challenges which the articulation of the doctrine poses cannot be allowed to obscure the fundamental marvel—or, as Pope John Paul II said, the "stunning novelty"—of the truth that the life that God enjoys is a life of communion and that He desires to share this communion with creatures who are not God. The doctrine of the Trinity is not a puzzle that requires solution, but itself the solution to all puzzles.

The principal reason why the *Catechism* is so important is that it emphatically makes the Trinity central, not only to theology but to basic doctrinal instruction and, indeed, to the Christian life itself. A frequently noted characteristic of theology in the twentieth century has been the endeavor by both Protestant and Catholic theologians to recover the primacy of the doctrine of the Trinity. Everything taught in the Church must be related to this Trinitarian mystery. If we fail to communicate the mystery of the Trinity, we fail in our teaching of the Christian faith.

Inseparable from the doctrine of the Trinity, and flowing from it, are the doctrines of Christ and the Church: Christ is the Way through which we enter into the communion of Trinitarian life which is the Church.

Tradition speaks of our sharing in this life as an adoptive participation through Christ. The theme of adoptive participation draws together elements from the letters of Saint Paul and the Gospel and letters of Saint John. Thus, according to Scripture and Tradition, Christ, who is Son of God by nature, makes it possible for us to become members of the family of the Trinity by adoption.

Perhaps a down-to-earth analogy may make the force of this truth more vivid. Imagine, if you will, your young son bringing a friend home with him, and asking you: "Mom, can you feed him tonight? Can he stay for dinner?" Imagine, furthermore, that your son's friend never leaves and suppose that every day your son brings home a new friend. In a very limited way, this comparison helps make more clear our place in God's plan through adopted participation. Christ is continually bringing home to the family of the Trinity, as it were, new mouths to feed.

The *Catechism's* emphasis on the Church signals that the doctrines of Trinitarian communion and adoptive participation in Christ do not in any sense entail a privatized view of the human person and of human destiny. Life with God is not a private affair, but a radically communal and social one. Participation in the Trinitarian life is something that is shared by many persons. It is a communion we share in the Father, the Son, and the Holy Spirit, and with one another in them. The Church, in a sense, is nothing less than the extended and extending adopted family of the Trinity. Through the Holy Spirit, we become bound to the Trinity and to one another in them. In its essence, the Church is this communion.

At its core, then, the Christian faith is Trinitarian in affirming the reality of ultimate communion with the Triune God, Christological in affirming the reality of adoptive participation in Trinitarian life through Christ, and ecclesial in affirming the reality of communion of created persons rooted in the Holy Spirit.

With its emphasis on the community of divine Persons and their desire to share their own life with created persons, and with its insistence on the dignity of the human person and the universal call to holiness and communion with God, there is in the *Catechism* what we may call a vigorous "personalist realism." What this term means is that education in the faith is not simply a matter of communicating a body of knowledge, in the manner of learning a science from a textbook. By studying a biology textbook (and performing experiments, etc.) one can come to know a fair amount about biology. In teaching the Christian faith, on the other hand, the aim is not merely to impart a body of knowledge—important though that is—but to help people to be established in a relationship with the Father, the Son, and the Holy Spirit and with one another in them.

This vocation, which Pope John Paul II termed "the universal call to holiness," bestows upon the human person an exalted dignity. In fact, it is so high an understanding of the human person that many regard it as absurd. It is absurd, many say, to think that God, who no doubt has many things to do, should pay attention to every person one by one. Such skeptics see this Christian vision of human nature as a ludicrously inflated view of the human person. These skeptics help remind us that what we confess is indeed remarkable. Human persons, invited to enjoy life in God, must be seen within the perspective of this divine vocation, and never simply according to any this-worldly purposes, objectives, or ends.

A "methodological" remark might be in order at this point. Adoptive participation in the life of the Trinity is, to be sure, a deeply mystical doctrine, but it has a nonetheless obvious and momentous point to it. As educators of the young, as preachers to the faithful, and as teachers of theology, we must find ways of bringing the force of this awesome teaching home to our audiences. The doctrines of Trinitarian communion and adoptive participation in Christ cannot be seen as the preserve of theological or spiritual elites, but must be central to instruction in the faith at all levels. The logic of catechesis must be true to the logic of doctrine.

3. Creeds, Catechisms, and the Rule of Faith: the Functions and Timeliness of the *Catechism*

The *Directory* (124) next takes up what it calls the "literary genre" of the *Catechism of the Catholic Church*. The *Directory* here asserts that the *Catechism* provides a rule or measure of the Christian faith, both in specifying the substance of baptismal affirmation and, more generally, in supplying criteria for theological reflection. This description of the genre of the *Catechism* invites comparison with another genre, namely, that of the creed. When viewed in the light of the functions of creeds and confessions throughout Christian history, the functions and timeliness of the *Catechism* moves into sharper focus. Let us consider these in turn.

The two basic functions of the *Catechism* correspond to two basic functions of creeds. In the first place, at the moment of initiation, when a person comes forward for baptism, the issue immediately arises: what beliefs and pattern of life are entailed in the embrace of the life of faith?

Creeds have traditionally supplied the answer to this question by expressing the substance of baptismal confession as it is drawn from Sacred Scripture. Secondly, in addition to expressing the substance of baptismal confession, creeds also serve as the norm of orthodox teaching in the history of the Church. The Nicene-Constantinopolitan Creed, for example, is clearly more than a baptismal confession. As a doctrinally ramified expression of the faith, this creed was to serve as the norm for theological affirmation and inquiry.

Thus, creeds provide both a measure for instructing people in the faith, and a rule for the more extended reflection on the faith that theological research and writing have always involved. We look to creeds to see how matters are expressed in order to have a clear idea of the content of divine revelation and Church teaching in these areas.

Like other major catechisms in the history of the Church, the *Catechism of the Catholic Church* serves a twofold role that closely parallels the basic functions of creeds. We might note the second function in passing before moving to a consideration of the first, which has a more direct bearing on our topic. Like the great creeds of the Church, catechisms provide a test of the orthodoxy or authenticity of theological positions. The *Catechism of the Catholic Church* has already been recognized as functioning in this fashion.

More directly relevant to our topic here, however, we want to underscore the role of the *Catechism* as supplying criteria for the composition of catechetical and educational materials. As highly compressed summaries of the content of Christian faith, creeds furnish the basis for the education or formation that precedes baptism. Creeds that were originally drafted to serve a role in baptismal confession came to fulfill an educational or catechetical role as well. Viewed in this light, major catechisms constitute the development or unfolding of the more formulaic and stylized expression of the faith in the creed (the *symbolum fidei*). Just as creeds provide the basis for extended catechetical instruction of neophytes preparing for baptism, so major catechisms become the basis for the development of local catechisms and other educational tools for initial and ongoing formation in the Catholic faith. The work of the Bishops' Committee to Oversee the Use of the *Catechism* demonstrates how providential and significant this function of the *Catechism* can be for the Church in the United States.

The parallel between the creedal and catechetical genres throws light also on the timeliness of the *Catechism of the Catholic Church*. Like the creeds, the *Catechism* meets the need, first, for a unified expression of the faith across time and culture, and secondly, the need for clear doctrinal formulation in response to the related phenomena of what might be termed "creedless Christianity" and "contentless catechesis."

As the history of Christianity (as well as the history and sociology of other major world religions) shows, there is a crucial need for an expressible trans-cultural unity in the faith. Creeds strive to articulate a universally communicable and followable statement of the Christian faith.

This point helps us to see why the *Catechism* possesses such a monumental significance for the Church at this moment in its history. There were those who objected to the drafting of the *Catechism* on the grounds that it is impossible to formulate a "universal catechism" (as it was called initially) when the faith exists in so many different cultures. But, in fact, just the reverse is true. The very rationale for a "universal catechism" is the fact that the faith exists in so many different cultures. It is a muddle to object to a universal formulation of the faith by saying that a faith held throughout a diversity of cultures cannot itself come to expression except in the language and idiom of those cultures. Precisely what the *Catechism* sought to achieve was an expression of a universally shared faith. The need for a diversely inculturated faith presupposes an expressible unity in faith, especially in a world that is fast becoming a global village.

A second aspect of the *Catechism*'s timeliness is in meeting the challenge of what might be called "creedless Christianity." The notion that authentic Christianity must be creedless traces its origins chiefly to some of the more radical movements within sixteenth-century Protestantism in which the trilogy of foundational Reformation principles—namely, *sola fide, sola scriptura*, and *solus Christus*—was exaggerated to such an extent that it led to a progressively greater simplification of the articulation of the faith. The notion was somewhat new in the history of Christianity, which, in all of its branches, had stressed the importance of the articulation and communication of a "saving" body of knowledge. In some forms of radical Protestantism, however, the only permissible creed was that there could be no creed. Creedlessness, or at least doctrinal minimalism, received added support with the emergence of philosophical religiosity (especially in deism) during the Enlightenment.

While it is beyond the scope of this presentation to trace the history of this phenomenon, it is important to note that creedlessness and doctrinal minimalism are now firmly entrenched in western popular culture, especially where Reformation and Enlightenment conceptions of religiosity have been influential. This phenomenon poses a considerable challenge to catechetical instruction for many communities within the Christian ambit. In the Catholic Church, the emergence of a kind of "contentless" catechesis is one form which this challenge has taken. The *Catechism of the Catholic Church* has already begun to confront the "contentless" catechesis to which creedless Christianity has in part given rise. In the next section of this presentation, we will see what is at stake in meeting this challenge.

4. The *Catechism* and the "Deposit of Faith": Divine Truth as Personal and Intelligible

The drift toward creedless Christianity and contentless catechesis was in part inspired by the wholly admirable desire to recover the personal character of faith as a relationship to Christ. The confusion here lay in thinking of objective content and personal encounter as opposed rather than strictly complementary. The sources of this confusion run deep and are beyond our scope in this presentation. Partly in reaction to an over-dogmatizing of the nature of faith, some theologians and religious educators seemed to suggest that doctrine as such is an obstacle or hindrance to a personally interiorized faith.

In fact, however, this is no more true of our relationship with God than it is of our relationship with creaturely persons. Our ability to know the truth about our friends and, if necessary, to affirm it, is not an obstacle to friendship but both its precondition and its consequence. Similarly, our ability to know and affirm truths about God is no obstacle to our friendship with Him. Christ wants to be Lord not only of our hearts, but of our minds as well. He is calling us to an affective union with Him that must embrace our intellects. Being true to Him is essential to our being related with Him.

The challenge for catechesis at all levels is to communicate the content of the Catholic faith in such a way that its personal focus is always maintained. The logic of doctrine turns out in the end to be a logic of relationship.

Faith as Ordered to a Personal Truth

The *Directory* (125) describes the content in terms of the ancient metaphor of the "deposit of faith." This metaphor properly suggests that the Church has received from Christ a treasury of truth which is to be preserved in perpetuity as a trust and from the riches of which it is always possible to draw. But the deep significance of this highly suggestive metaphor is that we have been entrusted with the living Truth Himself. The deposit of faith is a living deposit: Christ Himself is the treasury. Our faith in Christ is not a faith in some-one now departed. We cannot speak the full truth about Jesus Christ if we speak only in the past tense. Rather, it is a faith in the One who taught, who suffered and died, who rose from the dead, who now reigns in glory and is here present among us. It must be made clear in speaking of the deposit of faith that we refer to the living person of Christ who is the Way, the Truth, and the Life.

In catechesis, fidelity to the deposit of faith—or doctrinal ortho-doxy—for all its obvious importance in the Church, is not an end in itself. Orthodoxy has for its objective fidelity to the One who loves us: Jesus Christ, the Lord of our hearts and minds. This personal fidelity is the reason why Christians must be orthodox. We promote doctrinal orthodoxy in the Church, not simply to ensure that our life as a well-ordered religious community will have common doc-trinal norms, but more importantly so that our communal life will be ordered to the truth about the One who loves us and whom we strive to love in return. The content of catechetical formation draws upon the deposit of faith in order to bring to life in the hearts and

minds of Christian disciples the fullness of the truth about Jesus of
Nazareth, delivered to us as Christ and Lord.

Catholic tradition has striven to preserve the intrinsic connection between the subjective relationship and the objective content
of faith by affirming that faith is nothing less than a participation
in the divine knowledge itself. Faith is the human form of knowing
divine things. God knows Himself without having to compose propositions, as we do. His knowledge of Himself is simple. Human beings
do not possess the capacity to see God as He is, in a single intuitive
vision. Only God knows Himself in that way. Rather, we know the
fullness of the truth about God line by line, doctrine by doctrine.
This prolixity on our part is necessary, not because God is compli-
cated, but because our knowledge of God takes a human form. In
this way, faith is a participation in a divine knowledge: there is a
doctrinal content surely, a "deposit of faith." But our faith does not
end in doctrines: it leads us to the Father, Son, and Holy Spirit

Faith as Ordered to an Intelligible Truth

If the metaphor of the deposit of faith can only be properly
understood as referring to the living treasury of the knowledge of
the Triune God, it follows that, because this truth is intelligible in
itself, it continually draws the human mind more deeply into its
mystery. Note this: in a properly Catholic understanding, "mystery"
does not mean "unintelligible" but "endlessly intelligible." The
truth about God is not, finally, an impenetrable opacity, but an
infinity of light. With regard to the mysteries of the deposit of faith,
there is no end of knowing them and seeking their intelligibility.
The intrinsic intelligibility and the personal character of faith are
closely linked: the deposit of faith contains and transmits the
infinitely intelligible truth of the Trinitarian communion of interpersonal life into which creaturely persons are drawn.

In this connection, it is significant that, in his encyclical *Fides
et Ratio*, Pope John Paul II spoke not about the reasonability of the
faith but of its intelligibility: "Reason . . . is not asked to pass judgment on the contents of faith, something of which it would be inca-
pable. . . . Its function is rather to find the meaning, to discover
explanations which might allow everyone to come to a certain

understanding of the contents of faith" (42). But seeking the intelligibility of the deposit of faith is not the same as seeking its reasonability. This means that the canons of reasonability are challenged by inner intelligibility and interconnectedness of the mysteries of faith. The faith is not shaped by what we think reasonably possible, but by what God has made possible for us.

The capital importance of the *Catechism*, as the *Directory* indicates, is that it presents the entire deposit of faith in a manner directed precisely to exhibiting its inner intelligibility. To quote *Fides et Ratio* again: "Divine truth . . . enjoys innate intelligibility, so logically consistent that it stands as an authentic body of knowledge. The *intellectus fidei* expands this truth, not only in grasping the logical and conceptual structure of the propositions in which the Church's teaching is framed, but also, indeed primarily, in bringing to light the salvific meaning of these propositions" (66).

An important key to the logic of doctrine, thus to the innate intelligibility of the deposit of faith, is the principle of the hierarchy of truth. The hierarchy of truth refers to the interconnection among the many "truths" in which the one Truth about the Triune God comes to be expressed in our human way of knowing and speaking. Seen in this light, the "hierarchy of truth" refers not to the authority or ranking of the different doctrines within the deposit of faith but to their interconnectedness and mutual intelligibility.

It is a mistake to understand the hierarchy of truth as a ranking of doctrines that allows us to distinguish so-called essential truths from accidental, and therefore less important truths. A simple analogy may help us to see this mistake. We are all made up of bodily parts—ears, eyes, nose, fingers, pinkies, heart, and so on. Naturally, if someone asks, "which is your most important part?" you would answer that it was the heart or the brain. If asked, "which is your least important part?" you might say the pinkie finger. But who would be prepared to part with one square inch of flesh unnecessarily? The idea simply makes no sense. Would someone give up his pinkie finger because it is not as important as the heart or brain?

This simple analogy throws light on the nature of the hierarchy of truth. It does not imply that certain doctrines are essential, and therefore indispensable, while others are accidental, and therefore inconsequential: as if, for example, the Trinity were important but the perpetual virginity of Mary were less so. Rather, the hierarchy of truth draws attention to the internal relationships among the doctrines of the faith: the perpetual virginity of Mary can only be understood properly with respect to the Trinity. To return to our analogy of bodily parts, the pinkie finger depends on the blood that flows from the heart. The point of the hierarchy of truth is to draw attention to the intrinsic connections among the doctrines within the deposit of faith: truths "farther removed" from the Trinitarian-Christological-Ecclesial core are nonetheless essential to the fullness of truth but rightly intelligible only with respect to that core.

Viewed in this perspective, the hierarchy of truth—or, the logic of doctrine—has direct implications for the logic of catechesis and, indeed, for all instruction in the Catholic faith. It demands that teachers strive to make the necessary connections that will locate Catholic teaching about sexuality, or the family, or fasting with respect to the truth about God. A correct understanding of the hierarchy of truth implies that, unless the subject matter can be formulated and communicated in such a way that its relationship to the Father, Son, and the Holy Spirit is made clear, it cannot be made properly intelligible as an element within the deposit of faith.

In summary, a properly Catholic catechetical methodology must understand itself to be a formation in faith that directs the Christian mind and heart to the personal and intelligible Truth who is God.

5. The Role of Scripture and the Fathers of the Church in the *Catechism* and Catechesis

"In the light of this relationship between the *Catechism of the Catholic Church* and the deposit of faith, it may be useful to clarify two questions of vital importance for catechesis: the relationship between Sacred Scripture and the *Catechism of the Catholic Church* as points of reference for the content of catechesis; [and] the relationship between the catechetical tradition of the Fathers of the Church, with its rich content and profound understanding of the catechetical process, and the *Catechism of the Catholic Church*"

(GDC 126). With this introduction, the *Directory* turns to a discussion of the role of the Scriptures and the patristic catechetical tradition in catechesis (127-130).

I will confine myself to two brief comments concerning the contribution which the *Catechism* makes to our understanding of the place of Scripture and the Fathers of the Church in catechetical formation and instruction.

First, the *Catechism* trains us to read the Scriptures with a company of readers: the liturgy, the popes, the great councils, the Fathers and doctors of the Church, and the saints. One could say that a properly Catholic "Bible study group" is composed not just of our neighbors and fellow-parishioners, but of Leo the Great, Augustine of Hippo, Thomas Aquinas, Catherine of Siena, Teresa of Avila, Pope John Paul II, and countless other saintly "readers" and teachers. Catechetical formation in the Catholic tradition teaches new Christians to read the holy Bible as the Church's book.

Secondly, the *Catechism* avails itself of the insights of the patristic catechetical tradition in which Christian formation is seen as a progressive but complete configuration to Christ. The Church Fathers called this process the *sequela Christi* or *imitatio Christi*: the following or imitation of Christ. The Fathers teach us about a mystagogical rather than a psychological *imitatio*. The proper question is not, "What would Christ do in this or that situation?" but rather "How do I become transformed by the paschal mystery, the mystery of Christ?" By pondering and celebrating the mysteries of Christ's life, we come to be shaped and transformed in His image. Christ is thus the pattern and principle of our transformation as we grow more and more "at home" in the life of Trinitarian communion. The *Catechism* and *Directory* thus converge on a central theme in the Scriptures and in the patristic tradition—the need for our proclamation and teaching of the faith to have as its goal the conversion and transformation of the individual in and through Christ.

We find this theme also running like a bright thread through Father Ronald Lawler's catechetical and theological writings. It is a fitting tribute to his influence that these core pastoral documents of the Church acknowledge this fundamental link between the logic of doctrine and the logic of catechesis.

The Challenge for Catechesis in the New Evangelization

FATHER KRIS STUBNA

In an address to the Bishops of Lithuania, Pope John Paul II spoke about the ministry of catechesis in the life of the Church. "Genuine catechesis is not limited to imparting a patrimony of truths, rather it *aims* at introducing people to a full and conscious life of faith."[1] This is a theme Pope John Paul II often addressed. In his exhortation following the Synod of the Americas, *The Church in America*, he said that catechesis must help people to "meet" Jesus Christ, to converse with him, "to lead all people to encounter Christ."[2] As he reminded the Lithuanian bishops, "Without the vibrancy of this living encounter, Christianity becomes soulless religious traditionalism which easily yields to the attacks of secularism or the enticements of alternative religious offerings."[3]

It is not at all surprising then that in speaking of the great task confronting the Church today, the Pope claimed that catechesis will play a significant role in the work of the new evangelization. In speaking to another group of catechists, Pope John Paul II told them: "We cannot hope that those who hear the message will grasp it and understand it if at the same time we are not opening their hearts to experience the saving love and mercy of God that comes only to those who live in Christ and His Church."[4]

Catechesis and evangelization go hand in hand; one succeeds only with the other. As Pope John Paul II made clear in his apostolic exhortation *Catechesi Trandendae*, "catechesis is a very remarkable moment in the whole process of evangelization."[5] This is the same point made in the *Catechism of the Catholic Church*: "Catechesis is

---

Rev. Kris Stubna *is secretary for education in the Diocese of Pittsburgh.*

an *education in the faith* which includes especially the teaching of Christine doctrine imparted, generally speaking, in an organic and systematic way, with a view to initiating the hearers into the fullness of Christian life" (5). In a summary, *catechesis must* lead people into a living encounter with Jesus Christ, whole and entire, and that is a life in Christ and a life in His Church.

Cultural Impact

We need to understand, however, the contemporary cultural impact on the ministry of catechesis in this new evangelization: the "American" mindset that affects the transmission and reception of the faith. There are three important issues to consider here.

Secularism

Our culture is aggressively secular, to such an extent that the environment is actually hostile to Christian faith. In examining our societal context today we can see social mores, along with the means of social communications that reach the entire country, have so changed in the past years as to produce a climate that is not only secular but almost entirely focused on the material world. Today commentators often speak of a generation that has lost its moral compass.

Author Robert Wilken noted that this secularization is nothing other than "practical atheism,"[6] while noted jurist Mary Ann Glendon, in a synopsis of four recent religious cases decided by the Supreme Court, said: "The continued reign of the growing separationism between Church and state means that the court remains a collaborator, unwitting, of the cultural forces bent on secularizing America."[7]

Nowhere is this more evident than in a number of our public schools. In Arkansas, a teacher ordered one fifth grader to turn his T-shirt inside out to hide the Bible verse on it. In another case, a school principal in Spokane told a student that, by praying silently before eating in the cafeteria, he violated the separation of Church and state. Finally, a certain social studies text instructs sixth-graders that the first Thanksgiving had nothing to do with the pilgrims thanking God; they were simply thanking the Indians for being good neighbors.

Commenting on a school prayer case in which he was writing for the minority, Chief Justice William Rehnquist said: "Even more disturbing than its holding [against prayer in public school] is the tone of the court's opinion; it bristles with hostility to all things religious in public life."[8] Many people share Justice Rehnquist's belief that these current court interpretations go too far, and we must fight against the "bleaching out" of God and religious expression from public life, resulting in a hostility to all things religious.[9]

Individualism
Concomitant with this is the disintegration of the community and social structures that once supported religious faith and encouraged family life. The heavy emphasis on the individual and his or her rights has greatly eroded the concept of the common good and its ability to call people to something beyond themselves. This impacts strongly on our capacity of calling people to accept revealed teaching that cannot be changed by democratic process and to follow an absolute moral imperative that is not the result of prior popular approbation.

Sometimes the damage to faith is done more by undermining than by direct assault. Too often the case is made that every opinion is as good as any other—that what really counts is freedom of choice rather than what is chosen—and that religious faith is so personal as to admit of no ecclesial guidance let alone the expectation that faith could impact our collective lives in a society. In a word faith, religion, and religious conviction are marginalized by this reduction to personal preference (choosing religion much as one chooses a long-distance phone service or credit card) without any serious consequence and subject to change as desired.

The context, then, of our proclamation of the Good News of Jesus Christ is what is increasingly described as "the American mindset," an understanding of life that is more *individual* than communal, more *competitive* than cooperative, and, generally, more *self-serving* than self-giving. It finds expression in the difficulty many of our faithful have in feeling comfortable with the Church that identifies itself as a community that exists before the decision of individual members to bring it into being, a Church that claims to bind conscience, and a Church that expects more from Sunday worship than a warm sense of being comfortable.

In the use of the word "community," for example, many Americans will automatically assume a community of like-minded individuals from the same economic group, political persuasion, or social class—what Robert Bellah refers to in *Habits of the Heart* as "lifestyle enclaves."[10] The community of Christ's Church, however, is a radically inclusive assembly made up of both friends and strangers, fellow citizens and "foreigners," all standing before the face of God in worship and mutual acceptance. As Saint Paul wrote centuries ago, "There is neither Jew nor Greek, there is neither slave nor free, there is neither male nor female; for you are all *one* in Christ Jesus" (Gal. 3:21, emphasis added).

There is today, as to some extent there has always been, a temptation for some of the faithful to treat the Church as if it were *incidental* to salvation. The *Catechism of the Catholic Church* has, perhaps, devoted such a large section to the function of bishops and priests precisely because the acceptance of the teaching authority of Christ exercised by bishops, and by priests in union with them throughout the world, is a "hard saying" today. This is no doubt the reason for the recent document issued by the Vatican, *Dominus Iesus*,[11] which we should remember was directed specifically to *Catholics*.

Without minimizing our ecumenical gains and sensitivities, the pope reminds us that the Church understands herself as the continuation of Christ in the world. On the most basic of levels, one must speak of our "being in Christ" through Baptism as intimately connected with our "being in the Church." The Church is the living continuation on earth of its divine Founder. The Catholic faith professes its belief that it is the visible Church in which and through which Christ acts and makes Himself present today. "In that body the life of Christ is communicated to those who believe and who, through the sacraments, are united in a hidden and real way to Christ."[12] As Saint Irenaeus so beautifully expressed it many centuries ago, "Where the Church is, there is the Spirit of God, and where the Spirit of God is, there is the Church and all grace, and the Spirit is truth."[13] Salvation is not an individual pursuit, achieved through personal efforts. We are saved only in and through the Church to which we must be connected.

Religious Illiteracy

Nothing more clearly and succinctly demonstrates the extent of the religious illiteracy among what is increasingly referred to as the lost generation, and perhaps their children, than the report issued by Archbishop Daniel Buechlein on behalf of the Committee to Oversee the Use of the *Catechism of the Catholic Church*.[14] This report highlighted the ten areas of doctrinal deficiency found in the catechetical materials published in our country and used rather widely in our religious educational efforts over the past several decades.

A careful examination of a large portion of catechetical texts that form and have formed for many years the reference points for religious instruction in our country reveals a number of defects. These deficiencies create a doctrinal or content vacuum in which a great part of the catechetical effort has taken place and in many ways led to this generation of people—many of whom are now parents—ending up highly illiterate in the things of faith. For some, any learning of faith matters ended early in life with little attention given to pursuit of spiritual knowledge.

This illiteracy is not an academic question. The Jesus who saves us is a historical Person who died, rose, and continues to be active in our lives in His risen glorified Body through the sacramental re-presentation of the Paschal Mystery. To claim to know another Jesus—other than the Lord of history alive in His Church—is to know precisely an *other* Jesus—other than the true, living Lord. "And there is salvation in no one else, for there is no other name under heaven given among men by which we must be saved," Saint Peter proclaims: no other name than the name of Jesus Christ (Acts 4:12).

The *General Directory for Catechesis* devotes an entire chapter to what is titled "catechesis and the process of evangelization."[15] As Bishop Donald Wuerl has pointed out, "We see presented in the document what most of us have experienced in our pastoral ministry, the mingling of both initial proclamation and ongoing catechesis and the blurring of lines that would clearly identify stages of development in the appropriation of the Faith. Too often the people we are dealing with catechetically, while perhaps sacramentally initiated into the Church, are entering for the first time any serious mystagogy."[16]

Bishop Wuerl further observes, "In our pastoral experience often we encounter young parents, those who are called to be the first teachers of their children in the ways of the Faith, who face their first serious personal catechesis when they themselves are invited to share in the catechetical programs for their children. As lamentable as this situation may be, it is also an extraordinary one. *This is a second chance both for them and for us.* How many of our pastors have said that for them the new evangelization is unfolding on two levels simultaneously: the introduction into the Faith of very young children, and the re-instruction of their parents. For so many catechists and catechized, this is a particularly enriching moment because this time around the young adults approach the Faith with a great deal more openness and out of their own felt need to know more.

I would submit that the intuition of the *General Directory for Catechesis* and the pastoral experience in our country are identical," concludes Bishop Wuerl. "On the one hand there is a recognition that our catechesis is in many instances experienced as a first time invitation to accept and live the Faith and on the other hand there is the realization that many, many young people are eagerly searching for some spiritual meaning and value in their lives and are thus open to an introduction to Christ, His Church and His teaching in a way that perhaps we have not seen in recent years."[17]

From within the Church, another powerful disrupting force is the intensifying polarization of the Catholic faithful. We all require skills necessary to deal with division and to do so in a way so that we continue to be a constant and clear voice for the authentic teaching and practice of the Church. While some people may wish to speculate on what the Church ought to be, Church leadership, and those in all positions of ministry within the Church, have the responsibility of leading the faithful to a full and clear understanding of the Church's teaching and the sacramental practice that forms a part of the received and treasured Tradition, handed down to us like a precious family heirloom for safekeeping.

Hunger for Meaning

On the brighter side, however, is a sense among some of our young people that the secular, material world does not provide sufficient answers for their lives. Over and over youth gatherings, as large as World Youth Day or as modest as small parish programs, speak of the searching for value and direction that characterizes a growing number of our youth and young adults. There is a hunger for God and the things of the Spirit, but it needs to be encouraged, informed, and directed.

I remember vividly a conversation I had with a young high school student returning from World Youth Day in Denver. In asking him what was the most significant thing about his experience, he didn't say "seeing the Pope," which I expected, but answered, "Father, I never knew there were so many other kids who thought like I do."

This search for meaning manifests itself in various ways, including interest in "Eastern religions" and various sects and cults. A notable feature of this spiritual searching is the amorphous new-age phenomenon. Its popularity is seen in the amount of literature and number of courses available. Just reflect on how angels and the "spirit" life have captivated the imaginations and hearts of so many today. Perhaps this quality of our culture—its search for meaning— provides a key for an approach to evangelization, at least to this particular group of people.

I was struck by a rather lengthy article in *The New York Times*, following the shooting spree at Columbine High School.[18] It devoted a full page to reporting on the "turn to religion" by many of the young people caught up in the tragedy in Littleton, Colorado. The author reported how so many of the young people found the school's counselors, using the secular reference as their model, unable to meet their needs. In case after case the young people spoke of their religious faith as the sustaining factor in their life—especially in this tragedy.

In reaching out to the young, many today have experienced their openness, sense of searching, and desire for a clear affirmation of the faith. The basic truths of the faith often evoke in them a positive and affirmative response to their deep-rooted questions.

Role of the Family

Of particular importance in the new evangelization is the family. The Second Vatican Council reminded us, as John Paul II repeated in the apostolic exhortation *Christifideles Laici*, that by virtue of our Baptism every member of the faithful is called to renew the temporal order and is charged with the "sanctification and evangelization" of the world.[19] First place in this effort falls to parents in relation to their children. As John Paul II pointed out repeatedly during the Year of the Family, parents are the first teachers of their children, and the initial responsibility to introduce them to the Faith falls to the mother and father, so that, just as they have engendered human life, they might nurture the life of faith that is the Church's first gift to their child.

In his *Letter to Families*, Pope John Paul II reminded us that the Church desires to stand at the side of all of us on the many paths on which we walk as we seek God. And among these many paths that lead, in the Church, to God, "The family is the first and most important. It is a path common to all, yet one which is particular, unique and unrepeatable, just as every individual is unrepeatable; it is a path from which we cannot withdraw."[20]

In the great struggle then to build the civilization of love and culture of life that is to mark this new springtime for Christianity, Pope John Paul II pointed to the family as the way through which both our human culture and our faith must pass.

Notes

[1]   Pope John Paul II, Address, "To the Bishops of Lithuania" (September 29, 1999), as reprinted in *L'Osservatore Romano*, English Edition no. 39, 8.

[2]   Pope John Paul II, *Ecclesia in America* (January 22, 1999), nos. 67-68.

[3]   Pope John Paul II, Address, "To the Bishops of Lithuania" (September 29, 1999), as reprinted in *L'Osservatore Romano*, English Edition no. 39, 8.

[4]   Ibid.

5   Pope John Paul II, Apostolic Exhortation on Catechesis in Our Time *Catechesi Tradendae* (October 16, 1979) no. 18.

6   Robert Wilken, "No Other Gods," *First Things* 37 (November 1993): 13-18.

7   Mary Ann Glendon, "Religion and the Court 1993," *First Things* 37 (November 1993): 28-30.

8   *Stenberg v. Carhart*, 530 U.S. 914, 952 (2000) (Rehnquist, C. J., dissenting).

9   Father Kris Stubna, "Freedom of Religion Does Not Mean Exclusion of Religion," *Pittsburgh Post-Gazette* (September 20, 2000).

10   Robert Bellah, *Habits of the Heart* (Berkeley, CA: University of California Press, 1985).

11   Vatican Congregation for the Doctrine of the Faith, On the Unicity and Salvific Universality of Jesus Christ and the Church *Dominus Iesus* (August 6, 2000).

12   Second Vatican Council, Dogmatic Constitution on the Church *Lumen Gentium* (November 21, 1964), no. 7.

13   St. Irenaeus, *Adversus Haereses*, 3.24.1.

14   See *Origins*, October 8, 1998, pp. 290-294.

15   Congregation for the Clergy, *General Directory for Catechesis* (August 11, 1997), nos. 55-68.

16   http://www.diopitt.org/wel_bishop_addresses_sacramentallife.php

17   *Ibid.*

18   *New York Times*, "Students Seek Answers in Their Faith" (June 6, 1999).

19   Pope John Paul II, On the Vocation and the Mission of the Lay Faithful in the Church and in the World *Christifideles Laici* (December 30, 1988), no. 30.

20   Pope John Paul II, *Letter to Families*.

Cardinal Wright, Father Lawler, and the Teaching of the Faith

PATRICK G. D. RILEY

W hen Bishop John J. Wright of Pittsburgh left for Rome as a freshly minted cardinal, he became responsible for the teaching of religion throughout the world. It is true that as Prefect of the Congregation for the Clergy he had to ensure that the Church met the spiritual, intellectual, and material needs of diocesan priests everywhere; but during his decade-long tenure in Rome he constantly emphasized that his chief responsibility was the teaching of religion to laypeople young and old.

The technical word for such teaching is *catechetics*, although Cardinal Wright often remarked that it could be off-putting, and insisted that it meant nothing more and nothing less than the teaching of religion. The pattern he proposed for catechetics was the conversation between the Risen Christ and two discouraged disciples on the road to Emmaus. Said Wright:

> He did not give a course in theology. He did not give them an essay in exegesis. He did not have a dialogue or a symposium on the "burning questions of the moment." He did not explain their depression of spirit in sociological or psychological terms. He gave them a lesson in catechetics.

But in hearing those "facts of doctrine, dogmas of faith," Wright continued, "their hearts burned with love and faith, and they ran back to Jerusalem with joy."

***Patrick G. D. Riley**, a professor of philosophy and veteran journalist, is author of many books including* Civilizing Sex: On Chastity and the Common Good *(Edinburgh: T&T Clark, 2000).*

Yet Wright often had occasion to complain that the catechisms published in his time as Prefect of the Clergy Congregation—tumultuous years in the wake of Vatican II—did not come up to that standard. Trendy theologians and minimalist Biblicists had made the truths of faith seem so shaky that Pope Paul VI had launched a "Year of Faith." When the Pope concluded it with his own "Credo of the People of God," even this straightforward restatement of basic Catholic beliefs drew fire.

One night in 1973, four years into his tenure at the Clergy Congregation, Wright was dining with several visitors to Rome, including his old friend Father Ronald Lawler, when the company fell to lamenting the state of religious instruction. Father Lawler recalled that Wright declared with emphasis, "The Church needs a catechism!"

Father Lawler and another dinner companion, Father Donald Wuerl, agreed on the spot to put a solid catechism together, while the Pittsburgh businessman Frank Schneider, also at the dinner, volunteered to put up the money. Thus was conceived *The Teaching of Christ: A Catholic Catechism for Adults.*

Father Lawler, a Capuchin whose experience ranged from seminary rector in Pittsburgh to teacher of ethics at Oxford, was for many years the only American member of the Pontifical Academy of Theology. He enlisted his brother Thomas, an expert in patristics, to join him and Father Wuerl and form an editorial threesome. Father Wuerl, who as Cardinal Wright's secretary in Rome had earned a doctorate in theology at the Angelicum, was a frequent contributor to *L'Osservatore Romano*, the Vatican City daily newspaper.

Eventually they assembled a team of more than a dozen writers. Among them were the moral theologian Germain Grisez, the spiritual theologian Father Jordan Aumann, O.P., Father John Hugo of the Pittsburgh diocesan theological commission—a pioneer of liturgical renewal who was Dorothy Day's spiritual guide—and Bishop David Maloney of Wichita, Cardinal Wright's classmate and lifelong friend.

The editors worked long hours both apart and together to produce their own individual contributions and to edit the contributions of the writers. The challenge, they later said, was to fit together so many contributions from different theologians. They had to make sure that the technical expertise of the theologians was rendered in "meat-and-potatoes" language, as it is put by Bishop Wuerl, now a successor of Wright as Ordinary of Pittsburgh.

To guide them they had the *General Catechetical Directory*, which Cardinal Wright had produced for the Holy See in 1971 "to provide the basic principles of pastoral theology," as its foreword states. But the *General Catechetical Directory* only summarizes "the more outstanding elements of the Christian message," it continues. Father Wuerl and the Lawlers had to make sure that *The Teaching of Christ* lived up to its name, whole and entire.

Cardinal Wright declared that they had succeeded in that endeavor. Introducing the first edition in 1976 he wrote, "It is difficult to imagine a book concerned with the content of the faith that would be more comprehensive in the ground covered, the result of more widespread consultation of those who should be the witnesses to the faith than the work of the present editors."

Officially, their catechism has been translated into thirteen different languages, but in fact there have been countless translations—literally countless, Father Lawler assured me, because Catholics in impoverished regions of the world had just gone ahead and translated it without seeking permission. How often that had been done is beyond computation. Publication figures of the English-language version alone have risen above the half-million mark.

Nor has the appearance of the highly successful *Catechism of the Catholic Church* rendered the Lawler-Wuerl catechism obsolete. Pope John Paul II, in publishing that standard document, even called for the writing of local catechisms "which take into account various situations and cultures." *The Teaching of Christ*, now in its fifth edition, has from its fourth edition appended an outline of the *Catechism of the Catholic Church* with detailed cross-references to pages in *The Teaching of Christ*.

Will *The Teaching of Christ* prove to be the classic that it seems destined to be? No one should be hardy enough to answer; yet I may be forgiven for venturing an answer anyway. I base it on several considerations, but here shall present only one. It is so striking, I think, as not only not to require comment but even to *defy* comment. Let the reader judge for himself. Let him read the concluding paragraphs of this superb work:

Our Native Land
Then only shall we cease to be pilgrims and strangers (cf. Heb. 11:13), and we shall know that we have come to the land where we are fully at home. Our period of exile (cf. 1 Pet. 1:17) will be ended when we have come to the Life to which our whole heart can give itself in gladness. Then shall we begin to know one another fully, in the light of God, and love one another entirely. We shall remember and understand all the experiences and trials of this life without regret, infinitely grateful that God has enabled us to serve Him freely and has crowned His first gifts with the second life that exceeds all our longing.

Nothing will be lost of all the precious things that were. In the resurrection the flesh of all whom we have loved will have been restored; the new heavens and new earth will guard all that has been holy and precious in time. God is our infinite treasure; but it is His glory to give superabundantly, and to enrich with added joys and human interpersonal love the deep central joy that is the life of each heart. . . .

To this life, which we now understand so poorly, Christ earnestly invites us. Now, in time, He calls out to us through the promptings of His Holy Spirit and the voice of His Bride, the Church. "The Spirit and the Bride say, 'Come.' And let him who hears say, 'Come.' And let him who is thirsty come, let him who desires take the water of life without price" (Rev. 22:17).

Catechesis by Example

WILLIAM SAUNDERS

Tacked to the bulletin board behind the desk in my office, situated between my phone and my computer, is a Mass card from Father Ronald Lawler's funeral. Since I spend too much time each day typing away on my computer or talking on my phone, Father Ronald's is the face that I probably see more than any other. It is a face that gives me great comfort. You see, I am convinced that Father Ronald is a saint and that his intercession helps me to carry on as best I can in the cause he loved most, that of the Church.

I met Father Ronald before I was a Catholic. Though I was on my way into the Church in 1996, I wasn't yet "in." To prevent any slipping and to keep me on track, Robert P. George invited me to come with him to the Fellowship of Catholic Scholars convention in Saint Louis. Needless to say, it was the first convention I attended. I'm sure Robby wanted me to meet, and to be surrounded by, unabashedly orthodox Catholics, no doubt hoping for "conversion by osmosis."

One purpose of the trip was to meet with Father Ronald, who had asked Robby and me to help in the great battle being waged over *Ex Corde Ecclesia*. As readers will recall, *Ex Corde Ecclesia* is the radiant vision for a truly *Catholic* higher education that John Paul II proclaimed in 1990. Not surprisingly, it met with unremitting opposition from those in the leadership of most Catholic colleges and universities in the United States. The Fellowship was engaged four-

William Saunders is the senior fellow and director of the Family Research Council's Center for Human Life and Bioethics.

square on the side of a true and vigorous implementation of the document. Father Ronald was a priest who loved the Church and who loyally served the Holy Father. He was not about to sit quietly by while the opponents of *Ex Corde Ecclesia* went about implanting it in a way that, ironically and intentionally, guaranteed that it would not be faithfully implemented. One of those from whom he desired assistance was Professor George, and I tagged along.

Since I had never met Father Ronald, Robby filled me in on who he was and what he wanted us to help with. In describing him, Robby said, quite simply, that Father Ronald was a holy priest. That stuck in my mind in days before we met Father Ronald. As one who, in a seemingly endless zigzag, was making his way toward the Church, I sought holiness—to witness it, to learn from it, to attain it—above all else. When we met with Father that morning over breakfast, I began to understand what Robby meant.

What impressed me from the first moment meeting Father Ronald was his humility. He did not, as we say in the South, "put on airs." He treated me with greater kindness than I, in some ways an interloper in his important meeting, had any right to expect. As many of you know, I work in Washington, and it is rarer than finding the Hope Diamond to find anyone who knows the name of one who is "lower" on the status-totem pole than he is. The old saying about Boston that "the Lowells speak only to Cabots, and the Cabots speak only to God" is true, in spades, in the world I inhabit. In that rather perverse world of public policy in DC, pride, not humility, is treated as a virtue. But, startlingly, Father Ronald was humble. He treated me as I'm sure Jesus treated each person He met.

The other thing that struck me about him was his love—deep abiding, passionate, and committed—for the bride of Christ, the Church. It was simple (assuredly not simple-minded) and straightforward; it sprang from his conviction, his inner knowledge, that the Church was who she said she was, and that her Magisterium was what Jesus had said it was to be (inspired and lead by the Holy Spirit). If Christianity is true, who would not die, or, what may be more difficult, who would not *live*, for her? It was clear Father Lawler would. I was inspired by Father Ronald's holiness, his humility, and his love for the Church.

I was also impressed by his steel. There was a famous book in the late 1960s in which the motto of the protagonist was "never give an inch." That could have been Father Ronald's motto. He would not yield one inch to those who, calling themselves "Catholic," would undermine the Church. He would not yield one inch to those who would feed poison to Christ's lambs. There is no place within the Church or within Catholic education for heresy or dissent. Father Lawler would not yield them a single inch.

And, of course, one might say that this is also the charism of the Fellowship of Catholic Scholars. When, echoing John Henry Newman's observation about the apparent triumph of Arianism in the fourth century, the Catholic world in the United States awoke to find itself in dissent, following *Humanae Vitae*, the Fellowship said, "no; we will not yield Christ's truth to a modernist heresy; we will stand and fight." And in so saying, it was born. Its great witness—a witness that inspired me and so many others—is its willingness, the willingness of its members, to suffer academic and professional martyrdom rather than betray the Redeemer. One is not surprised that one of the "parents," so to speak, of so heroic and orthodox an organization was Father Ronald Lawler.

As the years passed, I was received into the Church (to Father Lawler's great delight). I almost simultaneously began working on many of the issues of the "culture war." (Unlike some, I find this a fine and noble phrase. As John Paul II reminded us, the culture of life *is* engaged in a great war with the culture of death.) I worked on pro-family and pro-life issues, trying to reflect the Church's social teaching in public policy. Father Lawler was my biggest fan and supporter. He never failed to congratulate me over an article I published or a talk I gave. He encouraged me when I needed it. And he taught me (or perhaps I should say, "tried" to teach me, for I have still to learn it) a vital lesson—never to be cruel, never to attack my opponents personally, never to confuse "my" cause with Christ's, always to remember that Christ died for my opponents as much as He died for me, never to become the elder brother in the parable of the prodigal son.

Father Lawler taught me that Christianity is not a religion defined by what it is against. It is a religion of joy. Even if we must fight, as Lincoln put it, we fight with charity toward all, with malice toward none. I can recall many times, after I was undeservedly honored in being elected to the Fellowship board, when, as the board discussed one course of conduct or another, it was Father Lawler who reminded us (especially me) by his comments that charity was also a virtue. Charity, of course, did not mean being tolerant of dissent or heresy, but it did mean defending the faith in a way that did not obscure the radiant love of Christ for all of mankind.

The apostolic exhortation *Pastures Dabo Vobis* (I Will Give You Shepherds, 1992) notes the following "qualities and virtues" of a priest—"faithfulness, integrity, consistency, wisdom, a welcoming spirit, friendliness, goodness of heart, decisive firmness in essentials, freedom from overly subjective viewpoints, personal disinterestedness, patience, an enthusiasm for daily tasks, [and] confidence in the value of the hidden workings of grace as manifested in the simple and the poor" (no. 26). One might restate these as humility, charity, orthodoxy, and steel. One might shorten the list further simply to "holiness."

But whichever formulation you choose, it describes Father Ronald Lawler. He was a holy priest, whose life and example were of decisive importance in the lives of wayward souls like me. Of course, he was a great teacher (one of his students told me he was the greatest teacher he ever had), and he fought for truly Catholic institutions of learning. But perhaps one might be pardoned for thinking that it was the light of his personal holiness—his catechesis by example—that was his greatest gift of all.

Has Christ Only One Church?

FATHER RONALD LAWLER, O.F.M. CAP.

T he question we ask is no shallow one. Obviously it is not a
matter of glancing over the various churches labeled "belonging to Christ," and counting how many there are. One who
wishes to answer this question must probe the deep issues of faith:
who is Christ, what are His purposes, what would it mean for a
Church to be His? The question is a live one only for those who
have begun to know Christ and to have tasted the importance of
His saving work.

Let me begin with a light analogy drawn from a classic American
short story. Steven Vincent Benet, at the beginning of his story "The
Devil and Daniel Webster," shows us something of the nature of
Daniel Webster's understanding of this country, this Union, and of
the sense of Webster's love for it.

"Yes, Dan'l Webster's dead—or, at least, they buried him. But
every time there's a thunderstorm around Marshfield, they say you
can hear his rolling voice in the hollows of the sky. And they say
that if you go to his grave and speak loud and clear, 'Dan'l Webster—
Dan'l Webster!' the ground'll begin to shiver and the trees begin to
shake. And after a while you'll hear a deep voice saying, 'Neighbor,
how stands it with the Union?' Then you better answer the Union
stands as she stood, rock-bottomed and copper-sheathed, one and
indivisible, or he's liable to rear right out of the ground. At least,
that's what I was told when I was a youngster."

*Rev. Ronald Lawler, O.F.M. Cap., (1926-2003) was a distinguished
priest, theologian, philosopher, author, and longtime member of the
Pontifical Roman Theological Academy.*

Now, in Benet's story, Daniel Webster was giant of a man. He was a lawyer, but he did not love the Union as a legalist might. He did not love the Union simply because of some constitutional theory or some conceptual framework. He loved it because he loved liberty and life; because he loved to see free people, able to run their own lives, to be creative and full of joy, in a kind of right humanity that he felt this planet had never seen before. He loved the Union in the way that saints and scholars have loved the Church: not to worship structures, and certainly not to narrow lives. Chesterton spoke of his love of the Church in a charming treatment of the analogy of the "keys of the kingdom." We love the Church, and we are Catholics and Christians, "not because we worship a key, but because we have passed through a door; and felt the wind that is the trumpet of liberty blowing over the land of the living."[1]

The question, "How many churches belong to Christ?" is not a standard question—because the word "belong to" has not a single simple analysis. But asking the question this way can help to illumine many standard questions.

Today I will wish to insist (following Vatican II) that all the Christian churches and ecclesial communities that seek to serve Christ indeed belong to Him. I will want to say also, again following the Council, that, for the sake of all the human family, one Church is Christ's in a most special and dear way. One Church alone is Christ's, as being all that He willed His Church to be. Still the other churches are His too, and their members are to be reverently treated by us as brothers and sisters. Every church and ecclesial community is to be treated with reverence by us, for (as Vatican II insisted) the Lord uses each of them to bring people to salvation. But one Church is the sacrament of His presence so precious that everyone would be deeply hurt if we ceased to love it with all the energy His grace gives us power to love.

To speak of such questions often involves careful balancing of ideas; but it is not logic-chopping. To think about the Church should be, for believers, as much a matter of love and commitment as thinking of the Union was for Webster. The narrator in Benet's story knew one *had* to tell Webster that the Union remains strong; or Webster would come rearing out of the grave. And as I read Saint

Augustine, and Aquinas, and Catherine of Sienna, and Teresa of Avila, I sometimes feel I hear them ask, "How stands it with the Church?" And I think we had better be able to say to them, "The Church stands as she stood; one and holy, catholic and apostolic; still flawed, alas, in her humanity, but never abandoned at all by Christ, never without the fire of His Spirit." Within it we still rejoice in the sure word of truth in the midst of darkness; within it His grace still gives us power to become children of God, if we choose.

Vatican II: All the Churches Belong to Christ

Before the Second Vatican Council the stage was prepared for rich new developments in ecclesiology. Pope Pius XII's great encyclical *Mystici Corporis* drew upon rich new developments in theology and stimulated more. The Church was being understood more richly as the presence and the sacrament of Christ; legal categories were yielding to more personal categories, the existential and the essential were being brought nearer together. But it was far more than scholarship that affected new vision: the precious ecumenical activities initiated by Protestants were bringing to all Christians new experiences and new hopes.

Early in Vatican II's discussions of the Church, it became clear that the Fathers of the Council would not be content with old-fashioned ways of speaking of the Church. They were not about to construct a new Church, or a new faith; but they wished to speak the enduring faith in ways that served best the changed times and the new opportunities of grace. The first draft of the document on the Church (which was to become *Lumen Gentium*) was severely criticized. "It was considered too restrictive, too scholastic, and lacking in an ecumenical spirit."[2]

Even some of the most revered ways of speaking were to be affected by the new spirit. The first draft of the document spoke of the Church in traditional terms: "There is only one Church of Jesus Christ. . . . This Church . . . is the Catholic Church, governed by the Roman Pontiff and the bishops in communion with him."[3] The words faithfully echo what the Church had constantly said; but the bishops wished it changed, and approved new wording: "This is the only Church of Christ, . . . which our Savior, after His Resurrection, handed over to Peter to be shepherded. . . . This Church, established and ordained as a society in this world, subsists in [rather than *is*] the Catholic Church, governed by the successor of Peter and the bishops in communion with him" (LG 8).

Some bishops at the council protested: why say that the Church of Christ "subsists in" the Catholic Church? Why not make the identification more clear, and say that the Church of Christ is the Catholic Church, and the Catholic Church *is* the Church of Christ? The official *relatores*, whose task was to explain precisely what was meant by wording of the texts, so that all would be in agreement about what they were to vote on, explained precisely why the wording "subsists in" was used instead of "is." "In place of *is*, *subsists in* is used, so that the expression may be in better harmony with the affirmation about the ecclesial elements which are present *elsewhere*."[4]

These ecclesial elements are spoken of in paragraph eight of *Lumen Gentium* and in paragraph three of the Decree on Ecumenism *Unitatis Redintegratio* (UR). In the Decree on Ecumenism the Council taught, "Some, even very many, of the most significant elements and endowments which together go to build up and give life to the Church itself, can exist outside the visible boundaries of the Catholic Church: the written word of God; the life of grace; faith, hope and charity, with the other interior gifts of the Holy Spirit, as well as visible elements" (UR 3).

The Council goes farther. Not only are these gifts found in members of other churches, but the "separated churches and communities as such, though we believe they suffer from the defects already mentioned [we shall mention these defects later], are by no means deprived of significance and importance in the mystery of salvation. For the Spirit of Christ has not refrained from using them (i.e., the separated churches and communities) as means of salvation" (UR 3).

Do all these churches and communities belong to Christ then? It would seem clear that they do, in very significant ways. In them are given gifts that nourish authentic Christian life now, and the Lord uses them to lead people to salvation. It would not be just or true to say that these are entirely outside Christ's concern, or outside the full scope of the Catholic Church: they are not simply alien realities. They deserve our love and care.

In the final report of ARC-I—the final report given after the Anglican-Roman Catholic conversations of 1966-1983—there is a moving protest against any claim that would suggest that the churches of the Anglican communion are not churches belonging to Christ. That would require of Anglicans "a repudiation of their past history, life and experience—which in effect would be a betrayal of their own integrity."[5] But Catholic teaching requires no such thing. The Catholic Church does not hold other Christian communities and churches as simply alien to Christ and the Church; they too are instruments by which He saves. All the churches belong to the Lord.

But in the Catholic Church All is Found

While rightly insisting that Christ's gifts dwell in other churches too, and that Christ uses them as instruments of salvation, the Second Vatican Council taught that the Catholic Church is entirely distinctive. She alone possesses the fullness of all that the Lord wished His Church to have for the salvation of all. (In all the Council documents, the expression "Catholic Church" refers to that one visible Church which believers and unbelievers alike commonly call the Catholic Church; the one presided over by the pope and the bishops in communion with him.)

Not as history professors or as literary critics, but as witnesses to a faith they have tasted and lived, the bishops declared what they had received: that Christ "established and ever sustains here on earth His holy Church . . . as a visible organization, through which He communicates truth and grace to all men. . . . The visible society and the spiritual community, the earthly Church and the Church endowed with heavenly riches, are not to be thought of as two realities . . . but one complex reality. . . .

"This is the sole Church of Christ, which in the creed we profess to be one, holy, catholic, and apostolic. . . . This Church, constituted and organized as a society in this world, subsists in the Catholic Church, which is governed by the successor of Peter and by the bishops in communion with him" (LG 8).

And what precisely does "subsists in" mean? We have seen one reason that the Fathers chose to say the Church of Christ "subsists in" the Catholic Church rather than say that it "is" the Catholic Church. For, in the very paragraph in which they wanted to acknowledge that saving elements that are gifts of Christ can endure in the separated Churches, they did not want to use any language that would suggest that those Churches had no relation to the one Church of Christ. But the official *relator* explained to the bishops more fully what the text meant to signify, so that it would be clear to all what they would be approving if they approved the paragraph that said the Church of Christ subsists in the Catholic Church.

"The *intention* is to show that the Church, whose deep and hidden nature is described and which is perpetually united with Christ and His work, is concretely found here on earth in the Catholic Church. . . . The following points are successively treated: a) The mystery of the Church is present in and manifested in a concrete society. The visible reality and the spiritual element are *not two realities*, but one complex reality, embracing the divine and the human . . . . This is illustrated by an analogy with the Word incarnate. b) The Church is one only, and here on earth is present in the Catholic Church, although outside her there are found ecclesial elements."[6]

Two things then are said: we do not want to imply any denial of the great things Christ does through the ecclesial elements in other churches. But the visible Catholic Church is unique and most precious. She possesses all Christ wished His Church to be, while none of the separated Churches are fully what Christ's only Church is meant to be. (The Council more than once uses the word *unica*—only, sole—about the Church of Christ. She wants to say both: other churches possess treasures from Christ, and He uses them for salvation; but only one—in its fullness—is the Church of Christ.) These churches suffer from defects that tend to impoverish their members. They have defects in doctrine, in discipline, in church structure (UR 3); while the Catholic Church "has been endowed with all divinely revealed truth and with all the means of salvation" (UR 4). To have been given by God the grace of Catholic faith is to be brought to the fullness that all really seek. Indeed, the ecclesial elements in separated churches, precious and good realities, belong by right to the Catholic Church, derive their efficacy from the fullness of grace and truth God entrusts to the Catholic Church, and tend to lead those who are blessed by them back to the Catholic Church.

The Decree on Ecumenism continues: "It is through Christ's Catholic Church alone . . . that the fullness of the means of salvation can be obtained. It was to the apostolic college alone, of which Peter is the head, that we believe that our Lord entrusted all the blessings of the New Covenant" (UR 3).

What is the point of stressing that the Catholic Church—the Church we were baptized into—has the fullness of what Christ wishes His Church to have? Is it a matter of claiming for "us" more than "they" have? Really it is something much deeper, running throughout Vatican II, and all the inner mystical life of the Church and its saints.

There is a more richly developed personalism than Vatican I had known penetrating the Church's account of itself in Vatican II. To have Catholic faith is not merely to accept the teaching of the Church; it is to believe a person, Christ the Lord. Faith is a personal relationship with our Savior; and every adequate ecclesiology must describe a Church which serves a living faith like that Vatican II describes. "By faith man freely commits his entire self to God, making 'the full submission of his intellect and will to God who reveals,' and willing assenting to the revelation given by Him. Before the faith can be exercised, man must have the grace of God to move and assist him; he must have the interior helps of the Holy Spirit, who moves the heart and converts it to God, who opens the eyes of the mind and 'makes it easy for all to accept and believe the truth'" (DV 5). The Church is not so much an institution as a sacrament, a presence of the Lord. Where the Catholic Church is, there are gifts and experiences that are not found anywhere else, though grace reaches everywhere, and many good people are not united to her.

Many of the gifts of Christ found in the Catholic Church are shared also by our separated brothers and sisters. These include very great gifts: the presence of grace, the power of the Holy Spirit, the strength of sacraments, the gladness of the Gospels.

But in our splintered world, often through no fault of their own, separated Christians have been deprived of many of the gifts of the Lord. The Catholic Christian who has taken personal possession of the faith given him (many Catholics, regrettably, do not) has tasted gifts that are present only in one to whom the gifts of explicit Catholic faith have been given. When Cardinal Newman became a Catholic, it was not because Catholics were better people, more full of grace and love, or more scholarly, or more charming; but because Christ invited him to the rich banquet of Catholic certainty, the bracing strength of pastoral discipline, the powerful presence of all the gifts of Christ bound together in a happy unity in which each gift enriched the others—and more than merely a richer abundance of His gifts, but an intensified presence of the Lord in the sacrament of His Church. The heroes of my life when I was a young student in the university were converts to the faith: brilliant and good persons, like John Henry Newman, Gilbert Keith Chesterton, Jacques and Raissa Maritain. In every case their coming to the Catholic Church meant giving up much; but it seemed to them as nothing because of the blessed richness of the fullness of Christ they found there alone.

The Lord is present in diverse ways in churches separated from the Catholic Church. But there are some gifts, of deepest importance for the human mind and heart, that are adequately present only in that community of faith to which God has given the full range of Christ's gifts. When we have any gifts of Christ, they incline the heart to long for more: when we have tasted, we long for more. That is why Vatican II says that the "ecclesial elements," the gifts of Christ that we share with those outside the Catholic Church (grace, the Gospel, faith . . .), tend to lead those who rejoice in them toward the fullness of the Catholic Church. Christ's sacramental nearness as a Teacher who teaches in the teaching office of the Church, a Shepherd who guides us firmly and mercifully in ways of life—against all the tragically misleading ideologies of the time, is longed for by every person who seeks human and spiritual fulfillment. It is Christ, personally present and personally teaching in His Church, who is our freedom and our salvation.

The Radical Consequences of Flawed Ecclesiologies

Vatican II's teaching about the unity of Christ's Church was balanced and forward-looking. The Council Fathers willingly recognized the positive values in churches not united with her. Christ gives them precious gifts, "ecclesial elements," and uses them to bring salvation to people. Hence the Council is willing to speak in new ways, and to soften language that suggested that the uniqueness of the Catholic Church had to separate other churches radically from serving the saving plans of God. These churches deserve our reverent care and their members are our brothers and sisters in Christ.

But the Council Fathers never forgot that, while the Catholic Church is not the only church that serves salvation, Christ has given the human family unique gifts through her. There are radical differences between that Church in which all the gifts of Christ endure, and in which His saving presence is most rich, and the other communities which, while they have precious divine gifts, remain deprived of many of the gifts of Christ. The Church of Christ subsists in the Catholic Church; only in her is there concretely present in the world the fullness of Christ's saving gifts and presence.

But some theologians, misunderstanding the balanced position of the Second Vatican Council, have come to positions that tend to relativize and weaken the whole message of faith. Apparently small errors in ecclesiology lead into immense problems and incoherencies in faith, because the mystery of the Church is so central to our faith. Let us conclude our paper by tracing the path from a weakened treatment of the Church to a radical relativization of Catholic teaching in every area.

The Council taught that the Church of Christ *subsists in*, is present in, has concrete historical reality in the Catholic Church. We have noted what this saying meant to the Council Fathers. It did not at all suggest that the Catholic Church is essentially like every other Christian community. Rather, it meant quite the opposite. For the Council explicitly taught that the Catholic Church is a unique and complete realization of the Church of Christ: all His gifts, and the whole power of all His saving presence abides in her, while communities unhappily separated from the Church are flawed in serious ways.

Some theologians, such as Leonardo Boff, argue that the expression *subsists in* is far more radical than the documents of Vatican II suggest. He notes: as the Church of Christ is said to subsist, to have concrete existence, in the Catholic Church, "the Church [of Christ] may also be present in [subsist in] other churches."[7] That is to say that other churches have a claim to be the Church of Christ in precisely the same sense that the Catholic Church does. None is absolutely the Church of Christ; none has all the gifts God wished His whole people to have; each is only a cultural manifestation of something that cannot be adequately caught in a concrete form. The Church of blessed hope, in which the saving truth is decisively taught, in which God's people are securely brought from darkness to His own wonderful light, is not a concrete reality fully present anywhere in his world. Contrary to what Vatican II taught, the spiritual Church, the ideal vision, is not in any real sense the concrete Church.

And, like many religious educators today, Boff is willing to draw the radical conclusion that follows from his altered ecclesiology. The Catholic Church, Boff argues, is indeed a mediation, a concrete presence in time and history, of Christ's Church. But is not identical with the Church of Christ. He says this not only in the acceptable sense, that some elements proper to Catholicism, and promising salvation, have saving reality even outside the Church. But he says it in a far stronger sense, sharply opposed to Vatican II's teaching: meaning that the Catholic Church has not the full possession of all Christ's saving gifts, so that it is literally able to be for the people of God all that Scripture and the Councils have declared the Church of Christ able to be—an entirely secure teacher of faith. He thinks that we would risk a dangerous dogmatism if we held that the Church can be an entirely secure guide to life in Christ.

Other churches, of course, do not even claim what the Catholic Church claims. They do not insist that they have a teaching office, in which Christ personally is present, and which His Spirit guards in the truth. They typically do not claim that Christ made His Church a living reality in which His own voice would resound, in which He would be recognizable in the voices of visible leaders, calling into unity the people of God.

Boff captures the differences sharply by noting that the Catholic position has insisted on sacramental identity: that what is done in the Church, in the visible reality she is, is done by the Church that is fully God's Church, and so is decisively the work and teaching of Christ; while for Protestants there is non-identity.[8] Saint Paul did not hesitate to tell the Thessalonians that they were right to accept the words he had spoken, not as "the words of men, but as what they really are, the words of God" (1 Thess. 2:13). Paul spoke; but his speaking was so caught into the mystery of Christ and His Church that those who heard him could recognize decisively Christ's Word, and His saving truth, in the words of Paul. There is sacramental identity; what Paul spoke is precisely the Word of God; it is in human form, but it is the saving truth. Christ gives life to the communication; and a word of God and a power of God can be transmitted by the persons in whom Christ Himself works. We say this often when we speak in any sacramental way: Paul baptizes, but it is Christ who baptizes.

When the Catholic Church is saluted, as the Second Vatican Council saluted it, as the presence of the full mystery of Christ's living Church: that it is the presence of Christ Himself, and the fullness of His gifts guarding it in all the truth, then the visible reality of the Church takes on a certain transparency, and one who believes and heeds the Church can know that it is believing and heeding the Lord. But when the Church is treated as Boff and many today do, not as the full presence of the Church and its saving Head, but a limited presence of the Church, a cultural expression of the Church, on the same level as that of all other churches, then the entire logic changes. Then the many different churches of the time are trying, from different viewpoints and presuppositions, to speak the best they can the saving word of God. But that they fail to give a word of God that the heart can unqualifiedly accept is made clear, because they are all of one kind, and they contradict one another: there is not now for us an unequivocal voice of the Lord. The Church is no longer speaking God's word, and Christ Himself is not fully present and fully teaching and sanctifying in her. If the Church is not the fullness of His gifts and the richness of His teaching and shepherding presence, all teaching is relativized.

As Allan Bloom has pointed out in *The Closing of the American Mind*, relativism has many charms, though it is ultimately self-destructive. When people contradict one another, it seems more civilized to say that the opposed views are not really contradictions; but "different emphases and styles." It seems more hopeful for ecumenism and human accord to say that we have no interest in showing one person wrong, and the other right.

Ah, but the hunger of the human heart is not for the "truth as it appears to my culture and class," but for what is really true and really good. The heart's longing for a word of God to liberate us from the endless contradictions of the world is a hunger for a word that speaks truth as only God can, but speaks to us with the human gentleness of our human Savior, Christ our God. The longing of humanity is for a truth that really sets us free; that breaks through to state truly what is.

Throughout the Second Vatican Council there is a faithfulness to the Catholic vision, that human words can mediate with enduring truth the saving words of God Himself; and the visible sacrament of the Church can literally serve to make present God's saving work; that God is able to reveal the truth to us, and we are able to understand His message, by His grace.

Some, of course, say that it is dangerous to say that the Church can speak God's word faithfully, that Christ acts in her Sacraments, and that His Spirit guards her in the truth. And that is true; it is dangerous. But, as Chesterton remarked, "the Church went in specifically for dangerous ideas. . . . The idea of a birth through a Holy Spirit, of the death of a divine Being, of the forgiveness of sins, or the fulfillment of prophecies, are ideas which, anyone can see, need but a touch to turn them into something blasphemous or ferocious."[9] But the most dangerous of the Church's ideas is this: that what she teaches is God's truth, not a culturally conditioned utterance that will be explained away next Tuesday by some great scholar.

These ideas are dangerous, because they are so powerful. But powerful and dangerous do not mean bad; only powerful and dangerous ideas are strong enough to do the saving work that the whole human family longs to have accomplished.

Notes

1   G.K. Chesterton, *The Everlasting Man* in *Collected Works*, vol. II (San Francisco: Ignatius Press, 1986), 381.

2   James O'Connor, "The Church of Christ and the Catholic Church" in *Faith and the Sources of Faith: Proceedings Of the Sixth Convention of the Fellowship of Catholic Scholars* (Scranton, PA: Northeast Books, 1985), 45.

3   *Acta Synodalia Sacrosancti Concillii Oecumenica Vaticani II*, vol. 2 (Roma: Typis Polyglotis Vaticanis), pt. 1, pp. 167-168.

4   *Idema*, vol. 3, pt. 1, p. 177.

5   "Final Report" in *Called to Full Unity: Documents on Anglican-Roman Catholic Relations 1966-1983* (Washington, DC: USCC, 1986), 275.

6   *Acta Synodalia Sacrosancti Concillii Oecumenica Vaticani II*, vol. 3, pt. 1, p. 176.

7   Leonardo Boff, *Church Charism, and Power* (New York: Crossroad, 1985), 75.

8   Ibid., p. 80.

9   G.K. Chesterton, *Orthodoxy* in *Collected Works*, vol. I (San Francisco: Ignatius Press, 1986), 304-305.

Lessons from a Great Man

ROBERT LOCKWOOD

The first time I actually met Father Ronald Lawler, O.F.M. Cap., personally, he was about an hour late. I discovered that this was not an uncommon experience with that good Franciscan priest. When he finally arrived at the airport to pick me up, he explained without guile that he forgot about me. He apologized, then insisted on buying lunch to make up for his tardiness.

So there we sat, wolfing down cheeseburgers ("My doctor says that I should avoid red meat—he's a great man, though he needs to give more reasonable advice"). We discussed the two subjects that always dominated his thoughts: God's love, and how each is called to lead the great life, even doctors with bad advice.

Over his beer and my Diet Coke, we dawdled a bit with Scripture. "I think mankind's greatest fear," he mused, "is that Jesus meant everything He said."

One never left a conversation with Father Lawler without a thought to revisit as the day went on.

Father Lawler was a theologian, a scholar, and a teacher. His former students include Archbishop Seán O'Malley of Boston and Archbishop Charles Chaput of Denver. He was co-author along with his brother Thomas and Bishop Donald Wuerl of Our Sunday Visitor's best-selling catechism, *The Teaching of Christ*.

His friends—of whom the contributors to this book are just a small part—are legion.

Father Lawler taught at Catholic University, Saint John's University, and Saint Thomas University, among other institutions. He

Robert Lockwood *is director for communications in the Diocese of Pittsburgh.*

was the founding president of the Fellowship of Catholic Scholars and was for many years the only American on the Pontifical Roman Theological Academy.

I knew of that Father Lawler, of course. But the Father Lawler I came to know personally in his last years was a priest as comfortable talking with three-year-olds as with theology students and assorted dignitaries of Church and academic life.

When dropping by the office for a visit, he always had a tale to tell of one of the children from the legion of families that he worked with, like a grandfather who goes on and on.

"I give them candy and ice cream," he explained, "and I have become great in their eyes." But it was more than that, of course. He evangelized at every moment to every audience, small children or adult theologians.

The word "great" was always on his lips. He reminded people that they could be great, even if they were not so sure they could live up to the task. I asked him exactly what he meant by the "great life." He answered simply that "the Catholic life is the great life."

Helping people to attain—and to want—that great life was all that mattered to him. By great, of course, he meant holy. Will Rogers might have never met a man he didn't like; Father Lawler never met a person who couldn't be holy. He saw that potential in everyone, and was not at all embarrassed to remind you of that regularly, though it might embarrass you.

When he cited Scripture he would often have difficulty holding back the tears. The Good News of Jesus Christ was so good that it made him cry with happiness.

Some people battle cancer; some people surrender to it. Father Lawler was simply not interested enough to make it the focus of his efforts. He never really thought that he would beat cancer. Rather, he assumed it would lose interest in him. As the symptoms grew worse and worse he seemed to think of it more as the Great Annoyance than anything else.

He died from that cancer in early November 2003 at age seventy-seven.

Father Lawler believed. In every fiber of his being, he believed. It is what made him a great man.

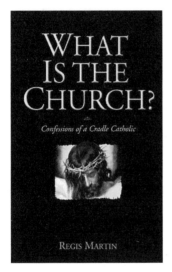

Catholic for a Reason

About the Series

This benchmark series brings together the expert knowledge and personal insight of top Catholic apologists on topics at the heart of the Faith. A must-have for any Catholic's bookshelf.

Catholic for a Reason edited by Scott Hahn and Leon J. Suprenant, will help you develop a better understanding of the Church as the Family of God. Catholic teachings on the Eucharist, Baptism, and Purgatory are explained in light of the relationship of God the Father to us.

$15.95 plus shipping and handling

Catholic for a Reason II will introduce you more deeply to your mother, Mary, the Mother of God. Writers like Scott and Kimberly Hahn, Jeff Cavins, Curtis Martin, and Tim Gray open the pages of Sacred Scripture to demonstrate the biblical basis of Catholic teaching on Mary.
$14.95 plus shipping and handling

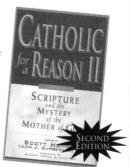

Catholic for a Reason III
Scott and Kimberly Hahn, Leon Suprenant, and nine other outstanding Catholic authors examine the Mass in the context of the Old Testament, the early Church, the Apocalypse, evangelization, and Christian living. This dynamic and very readable book will increase your understanding and deepen your praying of the Mass.
$15.95 plus shipping and handling